NATURE OF A SISTUH

NATURE OF A SISTUH

BLACK WOMEN'S LIVED EXPERIENCES IN CONTEMPORARY CULTURE

Edited by

Trevy McDonald and T. Ford-Ahmed

To: David
Thank you so much
for always stepping
forward and lending
genuine support
Tee Ford-Ahmed

Carolina Academic Press

Durham, North Carolina

ISBN 0-89089-859-6
LCCN 98-88954

Carolina Academic Press
700 Kent Street
Durham, North Carolina 27701
Telephone (919) 489-7486
Fax (919) 493-5668
www.cap-press.com

Printed in the United States of America

In Loving Memory of

Florence Elizabeth Jackson Ford
and our other foremothers who paved the way

CONTENTS

IV
SISTUHS WATCHING AND READING: REPRESENTATIONS IN MASS MEDIA

SECTION 1
SISTUHS ON TELEVISION AND IN ANIMATED FILM

SECTION 2
SISTUHS READING: QUIET STRUGGLES THROUGH LITERATURE

FOREWORD

Kim Marie Vaz

It is with great pleasure that I recommend to the readers of this anthology the scholarship contained within. How black women literally and figuratively carve out space for themselves in a multiplicity of settings that seek to limit, constrain, and impose notions of their correct "place" is amply addressed in these well-researched writings. Grounding their scholarship in the lived experiences of black women, the challenges faced by black women and the contradictions that must be negotiated around issues of home, school, work, culture, and individual aspiration, these contributors present clear and lucid explorations of black women's subjectivities. A major plus of *Nature of a Sistuh* rests in its accessibility and relevance to the real lives of women. While reading this work, I could not help but recall my own recent experiences returning to the classroom as a student after having been a professor for several years. I enrolled in a number of graduate level counseling courses at the southern university where I teach. In the group therapy course I took, our instructor required that as part of our class we enact group therapy sessions for the balance of the semester. A quarter of the class was male and the rest were female and a quarter of the class was black. The majority of the class was white and the professor was white and male. During one session as many were announcing that they had no race prejudice, a young white student said that, in fact, her family's maid was like "part of their family!" I chose not to let the remark go because I was tired of the way race seemed to be so absent from the consciousness of this set of students and so I challenged her on her assertion and she became visibly upset. The instructor came to her rescue and sought to dismiss my central concern with the student whom I shall call Kate. In attempting to get a handle on what was going on, the instructor first explored the possibility that I might not be "hearing" what Kate was saying and perhaps through misunderstanding of her point or possibly through some ghost from my past, I was responding to her in ways that promoted her spiral into anger. I experienced this response as benevolent, yet condescending. When the instructor discovered that I did "hear" Kate he then explored the possibility that I was being didactic and philosophical (which is a no-no in group therapy as "feelings" are privileged over intellect). He also suggested that since others had shared personal information about race, I was not appropriately participating because I was not personally invested in the issue at hand and not responding in ways that matched the others.

The issue of relevance for me and the one that I contested was the notion that an African American woman who is employed by a family *is* more of a member of the family than she is an employee. First, this is such an "old south" way of thinking that among African Americans and those white Americans who have the courage to look at race critically there is no explanation needed. For many white students in the south, the uncritical, accepting reasoning that they can do away with real life power imbalances by calling it something else (i.e., family) is very, very typical. When I say that "proximity to power" is not "power," I mean that any employee can not take the checkbook of the employer and sign checks as the employee sees fit without the permission of the employer. Ultimately, the actions of the employee are always under the control of the employer. The job and perks of the employee, *always* depend on the largesse of the employer. Certainly, bonds of affection exist among workers and employers, but it is clearly disadvantageous for any employee to believe that bonds of affection automatically erase real power imbalances. While I know many African Americans who would never contradict a white employer's statement that the African American is like family; I don't know a single African American so unsophisticated as to believe this illusion. As the Rastifarians might say they are merely "rendering unto Babylon what is Babylon's" African Americans, because of segregation, etc. use a mask (Paul Lawrence Dunbar, the famous African American poet wrote a poem entitled "We Wear the Masks") and dissemblance to function in white work settings. These ideas are so basic. How was it that this instructor who purported to examine "sexism in men's lives" did not extend the analysis to the interconnection with race?

In my defense of myself I told him that the way he *is* a white man is very different from being a black man. I was disappointed, but hardly surprised by his response. I wondered aloud "How he "treated" his African American clients—*did* he treat African American clients?"

If I appeared didactic, perhaps it is because he seemed so *oblivious*. Perhaps my didacticism was brought on by a fairly typical response of whites who do not think critically about race. The typical response is "the more I explain, the more *they* seem not to understand." The reason he did not understand is that it does require another way of looking at life. It meant realizing that other ways of looking at life exist and that as a white-skinned person he had privileges that *allowed him not to understand*. A few years ago, I attended a conference in India. When I got off the plane and met my party, polite as they were, they said that they were expecting "an American." American is a euphemism for white. Toni Morrison, the African-American Nobel Prize winner for literature, has pointed out that immigrants to the U.S. very quickly learn to increase their status and become "American" by absorbing the practice of looking down on African Americans. The point to be made here is that before they leave home, they have the idea that America means whiteness even as it means wealth.

In the journals we had to keep in this class, I wrote there is never a time when whites say that their white maids "are like family." And if they do, the meaning would be completely different. The idea that blacks are "part of the family" stems from slave owners' justifications to Northern abolitionists that the Africans they enslaved were their "children." What made Kate's statement so naive and the implications for her continuing this naivete so problematic is that she was perpetuating racism. Warm loving bonds between the races are all fine and well, but notice, Kate said that the maid was part of *her* family. There is no indication of reciprocity. I have never heard white people say, that they are part of the *maid's* family! The imperialism implicit in the statement that the maid is part of the family, should be "critiqued" as sustaining white privilege. A delicious quote by Elizabeth Spelman, a white woman who does think critically about race, conveys the flavor in my point. In speaking of the one-way direction of integration, that is of whites inviting blacks to join "their" institutions, she says, "How lovely: the many turn out to be one, and the one that they are is me." The narcissistic condition that characterizes white supremacy is that blacks are part of whites—not recognized as separate people with their own responses, desires, and concerns.

What was particularly appalling to me, was not the lack of awareness about white privilege—ignorance was not the problem. The problem was the class's *dis*interest in even examining how racism shapes their lives as whites—what being raced makes them think or not think about, and feel or not feel, but even the way one reacts is shaped in part by race. That those students were going to become guidance counselors in schools, where they will invariably come across African-American students, was alarming to me, because of this disinterest.

When the professor suggested that the issue was not "personal," for me, he overlooked the way I began the whole thread, on a personal note—relaying that I had been an employee at that institution and others and had personally witnessed institutionalized discrimination and further on, I disclosed that my grandmother had been a maid. It was from the position of the "family" of the maid that I spoke. While I did not believe that my position represented the whole of AfraAmerica, yet, it was a perspective not unique to myself. I was usually on my own in raising issues of race in these classes, but in this case, the one black male student supported me by saying to the class that he knew exactly what I was talking about—he needed no explanation—he *understood* implicitly. It is racism *and* sexism *and* classism that forces blacks to have this understanding. After my personal disclosures, I wondered why the professor had no questions for me, such as "what has it been like for me to be one of three African-American women in a predominately white group." "How did I feel after disclosing my experiences and asking people to look at things differently only to be met with defenses such as theirs?" Finally, there was the issue for me of "why" the professor asked me if *I* "heard" Kate and not vice versa. "Why" was he not just as concerned about whether Kate was "hearing" me? "Why" was he concerned about her feelings—how she was feeling right then and not how *I was* feeling. I concluded that if he could define me as being pedantic, then he can *assume* that I had no feelings, which he did. In his assuming such a thing, he could side-step the issue of race and "open" it up to the group to see how they were feeling (certainly a legitimate direction for a leader to take, but then it also allows for hiking on more familiar paths). There is a metadiscourse about white womanhood in relationship to black womanhood—that one is valued more, that one is to be *protected* more, but that would be an issue for another discussion we would never have.

I missed one class session, hence group therapy practice and was informed (by a black student) later that one of the young white female group members discussed how comfortable they were without me there. When I returned the following week, the other group members felt I should be informed but they did not reveal who said it. It just so happened that I had to bring my ten-year-old daughter to class who then witnessed what became a session wherein I was to be "called" upon by a "confrontational" approach to dealing with racial issues.

Prior to that semester, I had taken classes with this cohort of young women and in each class, I did address the way race, gender, and class would inform the issues the professors raised. During one class break, one woman from this group whom I'll call Rose, approached me and said: "In my family we call everybody the police of this, the police of that; you then are the multicultural police. Tell me, do black babies have the same kind of belly buttons as do white babies?" I was not retiring (I was not outrageous either) in my response and she and her cohort left "red-faced." This same student was the one who decided I made the group unsafe for her.

When the group raised this issue, I told them I was not unfamiliar with the discomfort of young white women whose racism I had exposed and so it did not bother me that they felt that I was not approachable. The instructor and the white students thought I could "improve" my approachability by listening to what they had to say. One young woman said that she could learn a lot from me about race, but she had learned not to ask me any questions because of my response to Rose. She felt comfortable with the other black women in the class, but not me. I told her that I was perfectly okay with that and encouraged her to look where she was comfortable. Well my lack of concern with modifying my own behavior to accommodate white racism was unacceptable to them and then a scenario re-inscribing racial scripts unfolded.

The instructor suggested that I did *violence* to the question asker by my self-protective response and that my choice to protect myself was none other than a rigid defense mechanism, hence pathological and in need of change. The instructor's handling of that group left me feeling re-victimized and violated by his characterization of my conscious decision to not engage with individuals who first clearly disrespect not only the work that I do, but second who raise a question that is tantamount to asking whether black people are human. I was appalled by the instructor's minimization of the significance of the belly-button question and his conscious inattention to the confrontational thus inherently violent manner in which the question was poised—"Kim, you are the multicultural police." He was clearly more comfortable and more practiced seeing me as being violent than to see and explore the attack itself and the racist institutions that allowed a young white woman to think it is perfectly okay to proceed in the way she did. That my reaction is a viable, and understandable one was recast by the professor as doing violence to a flippant person. How he decided that our encounter was "violent," I do not know, we did not physically touch each other, nor were voices raised.

I pointed out to the group that when there was slavery, the medical community described the enslaved people who ran away from their masters as suffering from a psychopathology called drapetomania. Drapetomania was defined by S. A. Cartwright, a southern physician in the mid-1800s as "the insane desire to run away—because sane Negroes were like children whose biology compelled them to love those in authority over them." The legacy of drapetomania could be seen in the group therapy interaction. That I did not feel compelled to interact with people who disrespect me was seen as problematic—the message was that "I" must change, not society. I maintained that such so-called rigid defenses are necessary coping devices that African Americans use because we live in a racist society. It is those in power (such as teachers and psychologists) who define our learned reactions to racism as pathology.

The whole evening, upon reflection, felt like a severe violation that had no real meaning for me in terms of learning—it felt purely gratuitous. The only redeeming value in the evening was that it provided an opportunity for my daughter to witness and learn a lesson that she would never gain simply by my telling her about racism. Her observations and conclusions about the entire evening went like this:

> You know that lady who kept telling you you were closing the door to communication, well she is the only one who controls her door. She has the key. While we were coming home, I thought about this song: "Can't nobody take my pride. Can't nobody hold me back." That lady locked the door to communication and she is the only one who can open it. They were trying to blame you but sometimes people blame others because they feel weak. Today at school there was a boy who stole candy and then tried to blame another boy. He was blaming that other boy because he was too weak to take responsibility for what he did. I don't want to be mean, mom, but your teacher missed the point.

Perhaps I seemed overly strident to those who would have liked me to appear or act "approachable" and to be *really concerned* about why I am seen as intimidating and making group trust difficult for them. But real communication for me can not proceed on the basis of my being seen as engaging in mutual violence and where I am characterized as in need of change and the system and those acting out the system's mind set are allowed to get off the hook. What I learned in that class is that in multi-racial group settings, group therapists ideally should have some knowledge about issues of race and gender. Without such an awareness these future therapists merely reinforce and re-enact society's racial scripts and actually harm the very individuals they are charged with assisting.

If one does not know what the racial and gender scripts are that shape and mold how multi-racial groups work, the real issue underlying the whole issue of my absence could be missed. What happened when I was out that week had little to do with whether I personally "attacked" Kate (they brought this up again), that was the symptom, it was not the cause. The real issue was Rose's inability to deal with and face her own racist attitudes. (She never uttered a word during that whole evening.) That the matter was brought up in my absence was significant, because the issue really was not about me. There is a parallel of what happened in class around this issue and how history has dictated the race relationships in this country. The incident in Rosewood, Florida began when a married white woman who had affairs with white men while her husband was at work, cried rape and that it was a black man who did it. Now, all the white men knew that this woman was unfaithful to her husband, but the white men formed themselves into a lynch mob and proceeded to find the black man who supposedly raped her. The white husband knew on some level that his wife was unfaithful, but could never bring himself to accept this until many black people had been lynched, shot, or run out of town. Rosewood literally ceased to be listed on the map for over 50 years. The student, Rose had re-enacted this type of psychodynamic by her assertion and then retreat into silence, for she let the lynch mob loose.

I told them that I felt like there was a public lynching afoot and I was to be the one hung because certain people could not deal with their own issues and it seemed easier to try and silence me and bring my behavior in line with what made them comfortable than to "own" the real issue of white racism. I told them that they had a great challenge ahead of them and the potential to do much damage. I e-mailed my colleague[1] who had already discussed some of these issues. I told her I had just completed my final for this course and asked her what grade was lower than an "F." She responded that "I'm not sure. Perhaps being arrested for belligerent student attitude in the face of a hostile climate? How would one indicate that on a transcript?"

Nature of a Sistuh explores the manner in which black women widen the imposed interstices not only in the academy but also in the spheres of the media, religion, and corporations. The editors and contributors have used their scholarly voices to, in Priya Kapoor's words, "question the whole kit and caboodle." I am certain that any reader will be able to add her or his own story to their tapestry and gain some new tools for continuing the much needed womanist activism in his or her own personal and political arena.

---

1. Many thanks to my colleague, Carolyn DiPalma for processing this class experience with me and for the Elizabeth Spelman reference.

ACKNOWLEDGMENTS

We are extremely pleased that after much careful thought and planning *Nature of a Sistuh* is finally a completed project which can now be shared with many. We would first like to congratulate each contributor and thank her for her patience, dedication, commitment and passion to this anthology. We would also like to thank Kathy Kay at Carolina Academic Press for her continued patience and support.

Trevy A. McDonald would like to thank her colleagues at North Carolina Central University for their support and encouragement as well as Erik Turner for proofreading. She would additionally like to thank her mentors Dr. Anne M. Johnston at UNC-Chapel Hill and Dr. Wendell Beane at UW Oshkosh for their guidance in her development as a scholar.

T. Ford-Ahmed wishes to acknowledge, with grateful thanks, the support and continuing guidance provided by Barbara J. Oden, and her graduate school mentor Dr. Jenny L. Nelson.

Most of all, the editors wish to thank those women who shared their lived experiences with each of the contributors. For it is through the sharing of these lived experiences that other Black women in academia, corporate America, religious institutions, mass media and other walks of life may be uplifted, inspired, and empowered.

Trevy A. McDonald and T. Ford-Ahmed
Spring 1998

NATURE OF A SISTUH

INTRODUCTION

Trevy A. McDonald
T. Ford-Ahmed

This project, in its infancy, began as panel designed by five African American women who explored definitions by and about Black women for a Graduate Student Women's Studies conference at Duke University in November, 1992. As it began to mature, *Nature of a Sistuh* was redeveloped and presented with a focus on communication studies at the Speech Communication Association (now National Communication Association) Conference in Miami Beach, Florida November, 1993. With the continued presentation of scholarly qualitative research by and about the lived experiences of Black women in contemporary culture, *Nature of a Sistuh* moved into its adulthood in the form of this book.

The twentieth century has been an era of perpetual growth and development for Black women in American society. From the popular culture advertising and film at the turn of the century where the image of "mammy" was pervasive; to the 1960s where the image of "welfare queen" was on the rise; to the present where Black women's stories, both true and fiction, rise to the top of bestsellers' lists, Black women are continuing to move from that predefined object to self-defining subject and toward center. Books by cultural critics bell hooks, Patricia Hill Collins and Paula Giddings have been the order of discussion in academic settings across the U.S. At the same time, Black women's fiction by authors including Alice Walker, Toni Morrison and Terry McMillan have been the focus of paper presentations, articles, and feature films which explore self-definition.

Nature of a Sistuh, a book by and about Black women, speaks to the objectification and the definitions made of them by what Althusser called "ideological state apparatuses." These devices include educational institutions, corporations, organized religion, and television and other mass media. In this book women utilize a variety of qualitative methodologies to redefine themselves within these contexts. Through narrative analysis, oral history, hermeneutics, phenomenology, critical pedagogy, cultural analysis, and ethnography, the contributors to this book examine their constructions as "others" and chronicle their struggle to become subjects who chart their success and future.

From the hallowed halls of the "ivory tower" to the cement ceilings of corporate America, *Nature of a Sistuh* explores, in some instances, the self-reflexive experiences of Black women rising on the ladder of success. Their climb is made more achievable through their excursions to the "well" where they quench their spiritual thirsts. And it is the quenching of their spiritual thirsts which empowers Black women to resist the oppression of limited and one-dimensional media representations.

Nature of a Sistuh begins by exploring the lived experiences of Black women on the rise as they begin their journey. In Parts I and II the authors examine the arenas of academia and corporate America respectively.

There is not a more isolated subgroup in academe than African-American women faculty. Having neither sex nor race in common with white males who dominate higher education and receiving minimal support from white women and African-American men, Black female academicians' experience has been that of presenting a "twenty-four hour position paper." In "Giving the Sistuhs their Due," Janice D. Hamlet reveals stories of struggle, resistance, empowerment and triumph through a collection of personal and group narratives. Similarly, Karen Strother-Jordan, in "Defining Essence in the Public Image of a Black Woman" analyzes the written rhetoric of Patricia Williams' *The Alchemy of Race and Rights* to discover the often overlooked experiences of a successful Black woman. Despite the obstacles of being the "other" in a place not quite ready to accept the difference that diversity brings, Patricia J. Williams graduated from Harvard law school and uses her rhetorical style as a form of resistance in the classes that she teaches at a major research university.

It is the experiences shared by Hamlet, Strother-Jordan, Williams and others that aid scholars like Sonya Ramsey in finding "her own voice." Ramsey's "Discovery and Reclamations" examines the opinions and experiences of African-American women teachers in Nashville, Tennessee during the transition from segregated to desegregated schools from the 1940s to the 1980s. These oral stories provide a historical voice for thousands of Black women in the urban South and aid the author in shaping her attitudes toward other women and her scholarship.

A discussion of the lived experiences of Black women in Academia would not be complete without the voices of those in graduate school. Priya Kapoor's "A Chance of Double Lives" reveals the dominant structures in higher education through in-depth interviewing and conversations with African-American female graduate students at a majority white institution. While a continually unveiling phenomenon of inequality and discontent in academia is disclosed, recommendations are made to assist administration, staff, and faculty with systematically abolishing prejudice and bias against this community of students.

During the week announcing the verdict that acquitted L.A. police officers of beating Rodney King, three Ph.D. graduate women explicate their experiences in a predominantly white institution located in the Appalachian Southeast. In "Corporeal Explosions," T. Ford-Ahmed uses in-depth interviews to uncover the essence of their experience and demonstrates how the students overcome their fears in a system they feel is violent and alienating.

Many describe the experience of women in corporate America as one of constantly attempting to shatter the glass ceiling. For Black women the ceiling is even more difficult to break as it is often constructed of concrete rather than breakable glass. Part II begins by examining the importance and role of mentoring in the corporate success of Black women with Pamela Y. Dykes' "She Works Hard for Her Money." For women with families another set of issues arises. Audrey Curtis Hane's "Metaphors for Negotiating Work and Family" aims to reveal, through the use of metaphoric analysis, how Black professional women with children define themselves as workers and mothers, and also how they experience their attempt to combine work inside and outside of the home.

Black women, both in academia and corporate America, can relate to lived experience shared with Jeanne L. Porter, "There's Always a

Line of Separation." Porter gains insight into the ways that African-American women adapt, survive, and succeed as leaders in predominantly white male organizations. Through the use of the Symbolic Interactionist perspective, "There's Always a Line of Separation" explores self-definition and self-reflexivity among Black women in corporate settings.

The spiritual and mediated reality of Black women's lives must be considered in any meaningful examination of their lived experiences in contemporary culture. In Parts III and IV the authors regard the crucial issues of their spirituality in religious and cultural practices as well as their positioning in the secular world of mass media.

A focus on women is rare in research on African-American spirituality, it is rarer still in reports of American experiences adapting traditional African cultures in the USA. Brigitte Rouson's ethnographic journey into the world of two priestesses of the African Yoruba and Akan tradition is an excursion into spirituality, and more broadly in culture, that leads to a womanist principle of loving the whole and cultivating an understanding of extended community. Their road "most traveled" runs counter to most notions of subordination based on gender. These women instead give priority to the concepts of being community-centered and maternal, affirming the important roles of men while in no way viewing themselves as subservient.

Upon surveying the "written" history and contemporary literature of the Black church in America however, the relative scarcity of women's voices would lead one to believe spirituality is inherently male. Michael Bradley contributes this view, which has been interpreted by many as "heresy" to what he describes as some religions of the world evolving from the psychology of their ancestors. At a 1992 Yale Divinity School symposium, Bradley proclaimed that "Western man is basically more violent than other human groups because of significant Neanderthal ancestry; that racism, sexism, ethnocentrism and inordinate technological 'progress' are all symptoms of this Neanderthal mindset" (p. 218). He pointed out that religions in the African tradition and other world religions do not "incorporate or embrace 'exclusively/chauvinism' and 'violence' to a comparable degree" (p. 218).

In "Aunt Hagar's Daughters" for example, Deborah A. Austin reveals that although 70% of the 30 million Black church members are women, 96% of the pastors are male. This almost exclusively male leadership characterizes the Black church as a place where the "pulpit" is the sole domain of men while women are to remain in the "pews." Through analysis of narratives Austin seeks to identify the "grit" of women who aspire to leadership roles in the Black church.

Quainoo's "Of Grace and Glory" examines patterns of phraseology, idiom, and topics of sermons *delivered* by African-American women clergy. Her work clearly indicates that while most women still struggle with subordination, some are giving identity to and are re-shaping the focus of the Black church. These authors indicate that in spite of environmental challenges women can preach, that both women and men must ask new questions about their faith and their families, and that stress factors as racism and sexism must be confronted and destroyed. These two essays further expose Black women as explorers of history and challengers of the constant: *men exercise the authority*, and suggest that ministry as a male cast in the Black church is being dismantled.

In Part IV, *Sistuhs Watching and Reading*, representations of Black women in television, film and literature are explored. For several decades mass media images of Sistuhs have been the subject of much debate. Scholars continually highlight the fact that historically we have been portrayed in ways that reaffirm cultural biases about us. No other mass media has been more guilty than television. Bell's "The More They Change, The More They Remain the Same" explores these representations through the popular hit show *Living Single*. Using Labov's and Waletzky's six narrative elements she identifies the cultural codes and concepts of acceptance or rejection to identify how African American women negotiate meaning and why they remain fans of the show. McDonald on the other hand, focuses her essay on the production and technical framing by 'others' of Sistuhs in popular music videos. Her audience study explicates the signification of the technology used to interpret women to a young adult market.

Adwoa X. Muwzea in her search for a theoretical basis for cinematic discourse appropriates Toni Morrison's literary discussion of Blackness and symbols of Blackness as narrative presumptuous shortcuts. Disney's *The Lion King* is the main source for Muwzea's deconstruction although as Muwzea points out, Disney Pictures never made reference to the African emperor Sundiata, the lion king, nor the role of women in his life. Similar to McDonald's explication of a technically objectified femininity, Muwzea's essay addresses how icons of Blackness, including aural cues are used as shortcuts to support a legacy of white supremacy in the Disney version.

The collection concludes with *Quiet Struggles Through Literature.* Jeanne L. Porter, Doris Dartey, and R. Goldman Vander reflect on womanist versions of leadership culled from literature. Ernest J. Gaines novel *A Lesson Before Dying* provides a backdrop for Dartey's discussion on the significance of critical pedagogy to Black feminism as an oppositional approach to teaching disadvantaged minority groups. Porter's phenomenological analysis of Mama Day's leadership in Gloria Naylor's novel presents us with an image of Black womanhood rooted in the community. She supplies us with a deeper understanding and appreciation for the leadership experience of African-American women who operate in a realm ignored by dominant forms of inquiry, and who operate in an manner silenced by traditional leadership discourse. Similarly, Dartey argues that documenting lived experiences of 'ordinary,' 'illiterate' women such as those characterized in Gaines' novel can be appropriated by the academy and can contribute to the development of theories. And it is because of the insider position they possess within their communities they are able to enhance the pedagogical significance for uplifting their people.

R. Goldman Vander concludes this literary section by reflecting on yet two other women as presented through the eyes of playwright August Wilson. She fittingly concludes this section by showing that as sistuhs enter a new millennium of changing American culture, their lived experiences address their conditions in society, offer redefinitions of themselves, and their silence is eradicated.

References

Bradley, M. (1993). The lesson of Rodney King. In H.R. Madhubuti (Ed.), *Why LA happened: Implications of the '92 LA rebellion* (pp. 212–220). Chicago: Third World Press.

I

SISTUHS IN THE IVORY TOWER: EXPERIENCES IN THE ACADEMY

1

GIVING THE SISTUHS THEIR DUE

THE LIVED EXPERIENCES OF AFRICAN-AMERICAN WOMEN IN ACADEMIA

Janice D. Hamlet

> Each morning as I turned into the long winding driveway of this quaint little conservative college, I would take a deep penetrating breath. It had become a ritual, helping me to relieve the tension that immediately developed in the pit of my stomach whenever I approached the campus. As I continued to drive, my mind would wonder in anticipation of what subtle act of bigotry would be done on my behalf today. Maybe someone would tell a racist joke in my presence. Or maybe I would be omitted from a faculty meeting, a common, yet what I considered to be a conscious, oversight. Better yet, maybe I would receive another subtle invitation to leave this private college and seek employment elsewhere, where there were more of "my kind." Who knew what each day would bring? I had always been taught to believe that God sends trials to teach us valuable lessons, but as I turned into a parking space, turned off the ignition, I whispered in earnest sincerity, "Lord, please don't teach me anything new today."

This is an excerpt from my journal. I am an African-American female professor who has been teaching at predominately white colleges and universities for a little over a decade. When I first recorded this experience in 1987, I thought I was alone in my experiences. But after reading a study entitled *Black Women in Academe* (Moses,

1989) and talking with other African-American female professors at various academic conferences, I quickly came to realize that my experiences were not unique but rather typical of the lived experiences of African-American women in academia.

There is not a more isolated subgroup in academe than African-American women. Constance Carroll (1982) writes that there is no one with whom to share experiences and gain support, no one with whom to identify, no one on whom an African-American woman can model herself. African-American women have neither race nor sex in common with white men who dominate the decision-making stratus of academe. Equally significant, they have very little in common with or get support from white women or African-American men. To this end, it is not unusual to hear African-American female professors define their experiences as "twenty-four hour position papers" (Sutherland, 1990, p. 17) in which they are continually challenged to defend their right to exist in the academy.

From the personal narratives of African-American female professors in various disciplines and academic levels, this essay responds to the question: what does it mean to be an African-American female professor on a predominately white campus? Narrative research methods were used to gather the professors' stories as a means of developing a greater insight into the challenges they confront daily.

Narratives have received a great deal of attention in recent years. What used to be regarded as a literary tool has now spread throughout various disciplines of the human sciences, ranging from anthropology to jurisprudence. The impetus for this surge of interest has been, in large measure, the growing belief that narratives represent a universal medium of human consciousness.

Women's personal narratives are oral stories told by women about their own experiences. Langellier (1986) has identified six characteristics that distinguish women's narratives from the dominant models of storytelling. First, women's narratives may not be tellable according to the dominant expectations of personal narratives structured by a remarkable event or action. Instead, women's stories tend to focus on commonplace events, typical or usual, or stories of emotions rather than dramatic interest. Second, women may tell non-linear, open ended stories of descriptive detail that are not marked off from the surrounding conversation. Third, women often collaborate as storytellers, telling stories as a group rather than as individuals.

Fourth, women may tell stories for the purpose of self-sharing rather than self-enhancement. Women's personal narratives bond women as women in their similar experiences and shared meaning. Fifth, women's personal narratives may not make a point but have an evaluative function. The narratives may search for and discover culturally interesting materials for women's experiences. Finally, women's stories may be sex-specific and context-specific. That is, some of these stories may be told only to other women in private rather than in public settings. Dominant narratives can be told in private and public settings (p. 2–6).

Telling personal narratives does something in the social world. The narratives are a part of the ongoing rhythm of people's lives as a reflection of their social organization and cultural values. In the language of the personal narrative is an act of self-presentation (Goffman, 1974). Narratives by African-American women play an important part in this ongoing social process by allowing us to hear their voices as they have had to face insurmountable odds.

Some years ago, three African-American feminist scholars edited an anthology entitled *All the Women are White, All the Blacks are Men, But Some of Us Are Brave* (1982) suggesting in the title the unique dilemma of African-American women. The narratives from the African-American women included in this essay illustrate experiences in view of this unique dilemma.

The lived experiences of these academicians fell into five categories: (1) affirmative action; (2) relationships with colleagues; (3) service to the university; (4) classroom experiences; (5) professional growth and achievement.

Many conflicts arise for African-American women when they publicly communicate their experiences. As a result, the authors of the narratives offered are identified only by status and discipline. In cases where the narratives were published in magazines and academic journals, the authors are identified.

Affirmative Action

What underlies subtle race and gender bias is an irrational, culturally induced belief that African-American women and other people of color are fundamentally less capable of rising to a high level in academia than white women or men, and that they were swept into their institutions by the pressure of affirmative action (Swoboda, 1990).

Once African-American faculty have gained entry, mutually reinforcing structural arrangements and social and psychological factors provide cues which alert these scholars to the manifestations of white racism in academia. In other words, conditions and treatment warrant beliefs that they are not welcomed.

Inclusive in these negative affirmative action tactics is the act of "tokenism" and being labeled a "role model." Tokenism, the practice of fulfilling legal and/or moral obligations by a nominal conformity, masks racism and sexism by admitting a small number of previously excluded individuals to institutions (Greene, 1990, p. 81). Tokenism is implicated in academia whereby starting in the hiring process, African-American scholars are rarely offered specific details about their relationships with a traditional department in particular, and the institution in general. The following anecdotes taken from the narrative of three African-American female professors affirm this belief.

> I was one of two new faculty hired in 1988. The other person was a white female. She was considered the new hire and I was considered the "token" needed for affirmative action purposes. My colleagues, including the other new hire, never let me forget it. I was suppose to be forever grateful and be seen all day with an "Aunt Jemima" smile on my face to show my gratitude. While the other new hire was orientated to the department and given responsibilities, I was not. My chair, however, told me to "become advisor to the Black Student Union because they needed a black role model." (Assistant Professor, Speech Communication, July 1992).

> My appointment was seen as an affirmative action hire. People did not expect me to be successful. It was very difficult for me to get important information from colleagues or my chair so I eventually found a mentor in another department who very willingly provided me with necessary information about tenure and promotion guidelines and about funding for research. When it came time for me to come up for review, my chair and the department personnel committee were shocked at seeing my portfolio. They didn't expect me to have anything because they had made certain not to tell me. They did not expect me to be suc-

> cessful. Some were actually rude enough to tell me so, thinking they were giving me a compliment. (Assistant Professor, Journalism, June 1992).

> I was treated most graciously when I first came to the campus. My chair and many of my colleagues were relieved that they had finally "gotten one." So the pressure was off. But as time moved on, I have been insulted, ignored when I offered suggestions in faculty meetings, treated with arrogance and a sense of superiority, especially by white males. There is a feeling that I was only hired for display purposes. The men seem shocked that I actually expected to be treated like a "regular" faculty member and would settle for nothing less. Slowly but surely they are beginning to come around. (Assistant Professor, History, June 1993).

According to Reyes and Halcon (1988) this "one minority per pot syndrome" is associated with the unspoken fear that too many faculty of color will curtail the department's rise to a superior academic reputation. Concurring with Reyes and Halcon's conclusion, Sutherland (1990) notes that the academy fears that an increase in minority faculty would undercut an important component of white supremacy, namely the European male intellectual hegemony. African-American female professors wrestle with their emotional responses to these situations.

In addition to the experiences identified in the above narratives, tokenism is also put into practice when African Americans and other people of color are put on display for various reasons, i.e. accreditation teams on the campus, visiting African-American dignitaries, and search committees.

Equally problematic is the use of the label, 'role model.' In academic circles, the label 'role model' has primarily served to pigeonhole African-American female professors. One professor noted:

> We are expected to be stereotypically ethnic and must be willing and able to relate with special warmth and compassion to all others who share our cultural background. This willingness and ability to function as a role model is a qualification that professors of color must possess in addition to their academic credentials. As a result, the term has taken on somewhat sinister overtones for some professors of color—it is an enormous responsibility to be drafted as a spokesperson for one's race and gender. (Morgan, 1990, p. 123).

The role model label even when willingly embraced can be a psychological burden. It makes those who take it seriously worry that they have to be perfect (Allen, 1990). Since we are told that our reason for being is that we are role models, we attach undue weight to everything we do, not only how and when we choose to teach but even how we wear our hair takes on special importance (p. 40).

The role model label seems to imply that African-American women are intellectually inferior, unqualified for anything but serving as role models for African Americans. Although serving as role models for African Americans is a valuable and much needed service, the role model label downplays the teaching, scholarly and community contributions African-American women make. Equally significant, it ignores the fact that African-American females can also be role models to white students.

Relationship with Colleagues

Many African-American female professors have pointed out that the lack of collegiality in their departments isolates them from professional networks, research grants, and other opportunities. Without this support, many African-American females are forced to develop alternative avenues of support such as finding mentors in other departments or at other institutions. Stereotypes, too, often contribute to the reality of their experiences. For example, African-American females are perceived as being sex objects, unintelligent, angry, aggressive, lacking authority, independent, nurturing, frivolous, more concerned with 'stylin' than political, educational and social issues, sharp-tongued, tough and bitter. Many times these stereotypes are used as weapons by department chairs and assigned mentors as an excuse to avoid interacting with the African-American female professor. They assume that she can make it on her own, consequently setting her up for failure. Note the following experiences of African-American females regarding collegiality in their departments.

> Because I could not find a mentor in my department I have had to create a network across the nation through the internet. These colleagues have been very instrumental in helping me to raise the right questions to my chair concerning promotion and tenure. However, when I raise these questions to my chair, they are an-

> swered with redneck stares. He usually acknowledges my questions, he just doesn't answer them. So I spend more time discussing matters with the dean (a woman) than with my chair, making it clear to her why I am not discussing these matters with my department chair. She has been very supportive and indicated to me that she was hesitant to say anything to him about my going over his head to see her, for fear that he would attempt to write negative evaluations about me in my tenure and promotion file. To my knowledge, he doesn't have any idea that the dean is serving as my university mentor. (Assistant Professor, Speech Communication, August 1993).

> The atmosphere is very isolated and very alienated. In my department, the academic staff is all-white and I am the only female. The entire support staff is white females and these people have been taught, 'I am better, I am best, I am superior and I am worthy.' And they believe that people with brown skin are not as good as they are. It's not only a major hindrance in your work and in your performance, but it is an emotional and psychological detriment. (Associate Professor, Sociology, July 1992).

Concerning interaction with colleagues, African-American female professors often hear the brunt of jokes, subtle and overt racial and gender insensitivities from their white colleagues, both male and female. Because many of these African-American professors are junior faculty members, they feel they have little power to change things (Moses, 1989).

Also, because of comments like "all you people ever do is complain," or "you people are too sensitive and defensive about being black," many African-American professors, both female and male, feel compelled to keep quiet for fear of being labeled a troublemaker, or merely adopting the philosophy that you "get along by going along."

Note the following anecdote:

> Yes, I keep quiet when white men and women say inappropriate things to me. I have to work with these people and only God knows what my chair and members of the personnel committee would write in my file if I told them to go to hell. So I bite my tongue, hide my feelings and turn the other cheek. Remember the poem *We Wear the Mask* by Paul Laurence Dunbar? "We wear the mask that grins and lies. It hides our cheeks and shades

> our eyes..." That's me. And I go home everyday and release the frustration through working out on my exercise bike, or listening to music or calling a friend to talk it out. (Assistant Professor, Journalism, July 1992).

It is important to note that conflicts concerning collegiality are not all centered around African-American females and their white counterparts. Equally problematic are conflicts between African-American females and African-American males as noted in this personal experience.

> It was my first day in my new office on my new campus. As I approached my door I smiled as I saw that my nameplate had been attached to it. I had moved to this new environment a month before the beginning of the fall semester so I would have ample time to get settled in on campus as well as in my new apartment. Today I needed to unpack. As I stood in my office unpacking and shelving books, my African-American male colleague heard my movements and walked over to my door to talk. This was the first time I had ever been in a department that had more than one African American at one time. Usually departments hire one to replace the one that got away. I was looking forward to having an African-American colleague. It was one of the reasons I had accepted the position. But that feeling didn't last very long. As we talked, a white woman, a secretary in another department, approached my doorway and ignoring my presence and our conversation, immediately started a conversation with my male colleague. He, too, ignored my presence and started talking to the white woman. He never bothered to introduce me. They talked for about four to five minutes. After realizing that I had faded into invisibility, I proceeded to continue my chore of unpacking and shelving books. At the end of their conversation, the white woman looked into my office and asked my colleague, "who's that, you got a new maid?" It took every fiber of my being to hold my tongue but I did simply because I was new and didn't want to start off on the wrong foot. He said, "Oh, that's Dr. ____. She's a new professor in our department." The white woman turned up her wrinkled nose and responded in a rather snotty tone of voice, "Ohhhhh." She then turned to my colleague and said, "Well I'll see you." She walked away. My colleague then turned to me and proceeded to continue the conversation we had been engaged in, before the white woman

approached him, without any thought to what had just occurred. As he talked, I just stared at him and he wondered what was wrong. The possibility of any real collegiality between us was destroyed on that day. (Assistant Professor, Speech Communication, August 1992).

Service: Performing Multiple Roles

Increased political awareness of the need for gender and ethnic diversity in faculty committee work and university service has created a disproportionate demand for service from African-American women. This increased demand interacts with the demographic scarcity of both groups to impose tremendous burdens that usually are given only token credit at renewal and tenure time (Swoboda, 1990).

There is also a tendency for the majority to see these women as caretakers for the race and they are frequently asked to solve problems or handle situations having to do with racial difficulties that should be dealt with by others. The following three anecdotes illustrate this concern.

> I am frequently seen as the person who can solve all of the problems (the mammy) concerning African-American students and all kinds of things get dumped on me. When my white colleagues have misunderstandings with African-American students, instead of talking it out with the students, these professors will instruct the students to come see me. I am expected to smooth things out. I don't. I have repeatedly reminded those who need to be reminded what the position was that I applied for and was hired. Being a mammy was not a part of the job description. Sometimes you have to remind white people that you are worthy of respect because they forget. I don't mind reminding them. (Assistant Professor, Sociology, July 1994).

> Overall, my treatment has been fairly positive although stressful at times due to competing demands and multiple roles and expectations. The accountability and time demands that the black female professor encounters are especially pressing given the fact that black women occupy even fewer academic and administrative positions than black men. Nobody recognizes the burden. White professors contribute to this problem of overwork for me because they refer black students to me in hopes that I will help

> them find resources when they choose to do papers on black issues. I am also on a number of committees for no other reason than the fact that the committee needed a minority. (Assistant Professor, Education, July 1993).

> Service contributions are not weighed heavily in merit and promotion decisions at my university since it is regarded as a research institution. As a consequence, the multiple roles that African-American female professors like myself are forced to maintain and the university/ethnic/gender service obligations that we are required to fulfill erode sacred research time. (Assistant Professor, History, 1993).

Students, too, can be possessive and demanding. Student demands often range from requests for time-consuming personal counseling on non-academic matters to assistance with research papers on African-American issues to be submitted to courses outside of that particular African-American female professor's department. Students also seek counseling about problems that they may be having with white professors. One professor shared this experience.

> I have had black students come to my office and just sit. I'd ask them if they wanted to talk about something, anything, and they would say no. They just wanted to sit. Then I have had other black students who come to my office to tell me about racist remarks their white professors make in their lectures and ask me, now what are you going to do about it? (Assistant Professor, Speech Communication, July 1992).

There is never any reward for work outside of teaching and research; in fact African-American females are often at a disadvantage when they become eligible for promotion or tenure because so much of their time is taken up with these types of responsibilities.

Classroom Experiences

African-American women are not only ushering in new research but are also championing new pedagogical practices. Unfortunately, these approaches are often viewed as a product of incompetence or dismissed as lacking rigor. Students' feelings about African-American women in the classroom are often extraordinarily complex. While students often approach women (in general) for guidance more frequently than men because they are seen to be more receptive and nurturing, students may interpret the very warmth and openness they seek as a form of weakness. On the other hand, cooler, more overtly challenging female professors may be evaluated as rigid and controlling (Swoboda, 1990).

The subjects that many African-American women, especially those in the humanities, social and behavioral sciences teach (subjects related to race, gender, and social change) are often threatening to white students, especially men, who then direct their fear and anger at the professor.

One African-American female professor sized up this aspect of the student discrimination experience like so:

> I find that white students, mostly males, seem to resist the intellectual and pedagogical authority I bring to the classroom. They openly challenge my credentials, argue over grades and comments I write on their papers, and generally don't expect me to be as academically demanding as their white professors. I have had white male students say to me in a threatening tone of voice that they need an A from me because they know that they are not going to get one from Dr. So and So (name of a white male professor). (Assistant Professor, Journalism, 1992).

Another African-American female professor recalled this incident.

> I showed my students four speeches videotaped from the televised 1984 Democratic and Republican conventions. I showed them the speeches of Mario Cuomo, Jean Kilpatrick, Ronald Reagan and Jesse Jackson. We talked about the content of their messages and discussed the diversity in delivery as it related to gender, race and ethnicity. Generally, the entire class got involved in the discussions and I thought everyone not only enjoyed the activity but also learned something about it. But after the semester ended and I got back my student evaluations, I read over and over that in this activity, I had forced my ethnicity on them. I was shocked. (Assistant Professor, Speech Communication, 1993).

Other resistance tactics used by white students include nonverbal hostility, such as hateful stares, muffled snickers or merely carrying on conversations among themselves while the professor is lecturing, to communicate their disdain for the African-American female professor. Some African-American students, too, can be disrespectful to African-American female professors. Many think that the common race factor entitles them to an A grade whether they do the work or not.

Still another resistance approach emanates from the Eurocentric consciousness which forms white students as well as many African-American students' attitudes and behaviors. Many African-American students find themselves expending maximum effort to explain the cultural limitations of Eurocentric scholarship and obtaining minimal effects. Also, students' exposure to cultural imperialism in education prompts them to seek white faculty validation of the information presented to them by African-American professors (Sutherland, 1990).

Professional Growth

Many departments assume that African-American women can only do race or gender related research with authority, and that such research is second rate. This problem is compounded by the fact that many African-American women and other faculty of color are breaking new ground, challenging established theory and academic practice and publishing in emerging field or subfields that are only recognized by new journals and that they may be seen as radical or advocacy-oriented rather than scholarly. They run the risk of arriving at renewal or tenure decision time without a community of scholarly understanding and support (Swoboda, 1990).

The following anecdotes illustrate the extent of this problem.

> I was hired because of my alternative research perspective and now it seems that the same perspective that got me hired could get me fired. Colleagues seem unwilling to attempt to grasp an understanding of anything that is different from the traditional way of viewing things. Now, as tenure time is approaching, I find myself needing to seek endorsements for my research from scholars that I have met at conferences and who are familiar with my research approach. This may be the only recourse I have available. (Assistant Professor, Speech Communication, 1992).

> I am surviving because I do two sets of research: one on African-American women's issues, and one that is main-

> streamed within my discipline. It is the only way I believe that I will have legitimacy when tenure comes. (Assistant Professor, History, 1993).

African-American women are well aware that white colleagues and students harbor deep-seated convictions that they are somehow intellectually inferior and that their endeavors will lower the white standards of rigorous academic life. However, one professor notes:

> We know that the fear of our scholarship is directly linked to the potential of our ideas to alter the very structure of the academy. Our ideas will influence the intellectual growth of generations of students. Our ideas will become books that help to reshape social, political and cultural images of black people. This is why the research of black women scholars is so critical. It records our true history and affirms our commitment to social change. (De Veaux, 1995).

It is important to note that there are some African-American women who work in very comfortable environments where collegiality is welcomed, academic opportunities are available and professional growth is nurtured. According to one professor:

> My colleagues seem to respect me as a person and as a professional. I know there are some who resent my being here but I have finally come to terms with the reality that this is their problem, not mine. I had a wonderful mentor when I started and have served as a mentor for several women who have come into my department after I did. I'm proud of what I have accomplished. (Associate Professor, Sociology, 1993).

Another professor noted:

> I have a great job and, as a whole, good colleagues. I also have some racist, vicious colleagues, but the good outweighs the bad most of the time. I plan to stay here because the university is located in a major city that is comfortable for African Americans. I have good friends here and my family is here. I have finally realized that racism and sexism are everywhere. I have no illusion of finding a place where they do not exist. (Assistant Professor, Journalism, 1992).

Conclusion

As any group interacts, it develops a history, which is usually passed on to new members as narratives. These narratives establish a sense of social reality for the group. The anecdotes presented in this paper reflect African-American females' recognition that they share a common denominator of experiences in their lives. African-American women bring to the forefront a critical self-consciousness about their positionality defined as it is by race, gender, class and ideology. The positionality or place they are assigned in the margins of the academy informs, however, it does not determine the positions these women take.

The study of African-American women in academia has suffered from scholarly disrespect and neglect. It is also apparent that little has improved for African-American women in terms of race relations as mainstream society continues to hold on to the stereotypes and perpetuate the myths that exist concerning them. African-American women in the professions are pressed into performing these symbolic stereotypical roles that conflict with the tasks they are hired to perform. There is little research or theory that presents a balanced picture of African-American women. This deficiency, however, affords African-American women in academia (as well as in other professions) an opportunity to correct the false perceptions as they continue to network and share their stories. As noted by Howard-Vital in her article "African-American Women In Higher Education: Struggling to Gain Identity" (1989) unless African-American females take an aggressive, unrelenting lead in identifying who we are, we will continue to react to distortions and perceptions created by others.

What does it mean to be an African-American female professor on a predominately white campus? The experience means that these women are likely to be isolated from their colleagues, treated disrespectfully by colleagues and students, challenged daily by colleagues and students, and relegated to performing a variety of symbolic roles. However, it is important to note that the majority of African-American women in the academy are survivors. The experiences offered in this paper represent African-American women who see themselves as winners in ways their white colleagues can not imagine. Their stories are ones of struggle, frustration, and at times, even rage, but none are of defeat.

References

Allen, A. (1990). On being a role model. *Berkeley Law Journal, vol. 6*, part I, 22–42.

Carroll, C.M. (1982). Three's a crowd: the dilemma of black woman in higher education, in P. Bell-Scott, et.al. (eds). *All the women are white, all the men are black, but some of us are brave.* Old Westbury, N.Y.: The Feminist Press, 120.

De Veaux, A. (1995). The third degree: black women scholars storming the ivory tower, *Essence,* (April).

Greene, L.S. (1990). Tokens, role models, and pedagogical politics: lamentations of an african american female law professor, *Berkeley Law Journal, vol. 6*, part 1, 81–92.

Goffman, I. (1974). *Frame analysis: an essay on the organization of experience.* Cambridge: Harvard University Press.

Howard-Vital, M. (1989). African american in higher education: struggling to gain identity. *Journal of Black Studies, vol. 20,* no.2, 180–191.

Langellier, K.M. (1989). Personal narratives: perspectives on theory and research. *Text and Performance Quarterly, vol. 9,* no.4, 243–276.

Morgan, D. (1990). Role models: who needs them anyway? *Berkeley Women's Law Journal, vol. 6*, part 1, 122–127.

Moses, Y.T. (1989). *Black women in academe.* Washington, D.C.: Project on the status and education of women, Association of American Colleges (August).

Reyes, M. and Halcon, J. (1988). Racism in academia: the old wolf revisited. *Harvard Educational Review, 38* (3), 299–313.

Sutherland, M.E. (1990). Black faculty in white academia: the fit is an uneasy one. *The Western Journal of Black Studies*, vol. 14, no.1, 17–23.

Swoboda, M.J. (1990). *Retaining and promoting women and minority faculty members: problems and possibilities.* Madison, WI: The University of Wisconsin System.

2

DEFINING ESSENCE IN THE PUBLIC IMAGE OF A BLACK WOMAN

THE LIVED EXPERIENCES OF A LAW PROFESSOR

Karen Strother-Jordan

> I write the way I write because I am the kind of person that I am. My styles and my content stem from my experience. I am a woman and I write from that experience. I am a Black woman and I write from that experience. I do not feel inhibited or bound by what I am. That does not mean that I have never had bad scenes relating to being Black and/or a woman, it means that other people's craziness has not managed to make me crazy (Clifton, 1974).

Black sisters, African-American women, women of color are consumed by the struggle for maintaining a strong self-concept. Clifton articulates her self-concept as a stand against the struggle. This struggle is illustrated in many situations as a closeness to what is most often called the human condition. Toni Cade Bambara (1972) calls this human condition the truth about human nature, the truth about the human potential. Wrenched in our work, are the experiences of significant importance which guide our struggles and make sense out of who we are. The human condition is revealed in its complexity or in its true sense of experienced worth. The human condition makes us profoundly conscious of what harms, degrades, denies and destroys one's essence of the oppressed victim, but disregards the differences which we all experience as a result of ignorance (Bambara, 1972).

As a Black woman, I am reminded everyday of my presence as the "other" whether in the form of students who are surprised by my accomplishments or from a society who continues to do double takes when they become aware of my academic stature. Whether it's the simple "Oh really," when you explain what you do or the condescending "You've done well for yourself" the human condition that Bambara explores becomes a living phenomenon of difference for the "other."

This chapter will explore the critical consciousness between two often neglected dialectics of race and gender through the written text of Patricia J. Williams' *The Alchemy of Race and Rights*. The modes of inscribing the discourses of race and gender develop through a series of disclosures that allow Williams to illustrate common understanding with her audience. Thus, the concern with the politics of race and gender, as defined by Williams, is central to the narrative of the text. The text also exhibits a therapeutic quality as Williams writes in a style similar to that of a diary.

Ms. Williams writes at length of who she is as a person. As an Associate Professor of Law at the University of Wisconsin, she graduated from Harvard Law despite the harassing obstacles of being the "other" in a place not quite ready to accept what her difference presents. Her credentials should suffice as meeting, at the very least, the minimum criteria of her colleagues or the hundreds of law students who are astonished to find out that their contracts law professor is a Black woman. Twentieth century "double consciousness" is the term that best describes the process that Williams weaves throughout her personal and professional life. As a Black feminist, Williams places herself in the center of what it means to say "the personal is the political." Williams is aware at all levels of a society that attempts to define who she is based on the hegemonic stereotypical nature of oppression. Specifically, how society continues to define and thus, degrade Black women.

This chapter will furthermore critique Williams' written rhetoric in order to provide some perspectives for interpreting Williams' world view and the nature of her rhetoric. This world view can be best understood through the rhetorical strategies she uses. Studying Williams' rhetoric is valuable and intriguing, not only because her discourse is eloquent, but because the style in which she writes draws in the reader to discover the pain which she experiences as a successful, yet not quite accepted Black woman.

Finally, through the discussions of selected rhetorical theories this chapter will also attempt to provide arguments for how rhetorical analysis can explain language as a significant means of creation, delivery, justification, and legitimation of the rhetor's principles or ideologies; and how through rhetorical analysis the motivations of the rhetor can be revealed.

Justification

The voices of women and people of color, although strong and dignified, are many times ignored and not integrated into the course requirements of university curricula. In fact, unless the course is either a specific women's studies or ethnic studies requirement, the written work of the "other" is seldom highlighted and recognized as valuable pedagogical material. Students should not have to ask themselves why are there not more African-American, Latino, Native-American or Asian-American women and men writing valuable texts. Unfortunately, this is the case in many universities across the United States and abroad. *The Alchemy of Race and Rights* cleverly addresses these concerns through the examples Williams draws from in her lectures. She strategically presents case studies in her lectures that expose her students to issues and concerns of the "other."

Williams' discourse has been staked out as the exclusive interdisciplinary property of constitutional law, contract law, African-American history, feminist jurisprudence, political science, and rhetoric. It is the very use of her voice within her discourse that has placed her in the center of the snarl of social tensions and crossed boundaries. Williams states, "to speak as Black, female, and commercial lawyer has rendered me simultaneously universal, trendy, and marginal" (p. 6). Williams is aware of her position that can best be understood as a precarious phenomenon.

The Text

The Alchemy of Race and Rights is a clever synopsis of the daily lived experiences of Patricia Williams. The text differs from the traditional scholarship in the area of law distancing the approach from the static, stable, formal rationalism. Williams states, "I use a model of inductive empiricism, borrowed from—and parodying—systems analysis, in order to enliven thought about complex social problems" (p. 7). Williams examines the legal issues within the framework of disciplines such as psychology, sociology, history, criticism and philosophy.

Identifying the competing dialectics between being a commercial lawyer as well as a professor of contract and property law is one example of how she negotiates her presence. Although she has stated that colleagues have identified an important competing dialectic as how she articulates herself as Black and female, Williams herself does not believe that who she is represents being 'at oxymoronic odds' with that of commercial lawyer. As Black women we realize that we are not able to separate our Blackness from our womanhood. Therefore, the question of whether one sees herself as Black or woman first is irrelevant. We are Black women period.

Divided into sections which are grouped by legal jargon, Williams uses "legalese" in developing the meaning of what discrimination actually looks like. This is illustrated in her experience of being denied admittance into a Benetton boutique. Williams states,

> The installation of these buzzers happened swiftly in New York; stores that had always had their doors wide open suddenly became exclusive or received people by appointment only. I discovered them and their meaning one Saturday in 1986. I was shopping in Soho and saw in a store window a sweater that I wanted to buy for my mother. I pressed my round brown face to the window and my finger to the buzzer, seeking admittance. A narrow-eyed, white teenager wearing running shoes and feasting on bubble gum glared out, evaluating me for signs that would pit me against the limits of his social understanding. After about five seconds, he mouthed "We're closed," and blew pink rubber at me (p. 45).

Institutional racism here is represented in a company whose very advertising campaigns center on the premise of wrapping every one of the world's peoples, Black or white, in its cottons and woolens.

The use of the law categorically supports the claims she makes yet simultaneously presents a contradiction in terms by illustrating the points that she makes, but showing how the law does not serve all individuals equally. Williams states "I am interested in the way in which legal language flattens and confines in absolutes the complexity of meaning inherent in any given problem; I am trying to challenge the usual limits of commercial discourse by using an intentionally double-voiced and relational, rather than a traditionally legal black-letter, vocabulary" (p. 6).

The approach Williams takes throughout the text mirrors deconstruction of what law represents for some and what it actually means for the "other." As an educated woman, Williams illustrates quite vividly why she as a professional Black woman actually means absolutely nothing since hegemonic society views her Blackness as negative and not worthy of recognition. To be Black and to be a woman, is to be a Black woman, a woman whose identity is constituted differently from that of what is safely situated in white society. Williams states,

> Black individuality is subsumed in a social circumstance—an idea, a stereotype—that pins us to the underside of this society and keeps us there, out of sight/out of mind, out of the knowledge of mind which is law. Blacks and women are the objects of a constitutional omission that has been incorporated into a theory of neutrality. It is thus that omission becomes a form of oppression, as oxymoronic as that sounds: racial omission is a literal part of original intent; it is fixed, reiterated prophesy of the Founding Fathers (p. 121).

Williams articulates the difference of Blackness as it intersects with the law and how Affirmative Action should seek to replace an ideology supported by a society that does not value difference. She is also clear in her analysis to point out racial omission of Blackness which dates back to historical hegemony. Williams' ideological frame of reference can be best understood as it intersects with feminism.

Black Feminist Ideology

Even a cursory glance at the literature available on Black women writers reveals that there exists a more than adequate supply of material for research into the distinguishing features of discourse. Therefore, the purpose of this section is to sketch a broad outline of literature that best summarizes the issues that Williams analyzes in her text. For the purpose of this chapter the themes covered can be best categorized into several areas, which are: (1) Black feminist theory, (2) a brief review of Black women writers, (3) double consciousness, and (4) difference between feminism in general and Black feminism.

What has happened in the critical feminist movement in the past thirty years can be called a "revolution within a revolution," one that was initiated by and has been sustained chiefly by Black women (Collins, 1991). The impact can be felt in virtually all aspects of contemporary life through literature, art, music, dance and culture. Although Williams does not self-identify as a feminist, she does include herself in the critical feminist movement. This positioning has provided an opportunity for her to support what her Black colleagues are doing to raise awareness between white feminism and Black feminist theory.

Sampson (1993) articulates the feminist critique as anything but a monolithic body of work. In fact, assertions have been made to conceptualize feminism in the plural which would stress the multiplicity of liberal and radical formulations recognizing the diversity of how race, class and culture are viewed (MacKinnon, 1989; Gatens, 1991).

Thus, to undertake a project that focuses on a Black woman writer is to enter the many-voiced discourse in which issues of race, class, and gender are being explored in multiple combinations. The field is diverse and complex in the representation of Black women's voices. Central to the dialogue is Black feminist criticism. Collins (1991) defines Black feminist thought as encompassing diverse and contradictory meanings. Highlighting the question of who can actually be a Black feminist, Collins illustrates through the process of Black women's experiences that all African-American women, regardless of the content of our ideas, are Black feminists. Thus, Black feminism has much to do with a consciousness that centers specifically around the lived experiences of Black women. This is a challenge sure to gain momentum as Black women begin to articulate their experience and an audience rises to receive and appreciate the discourse.

Piper (1990) challenges what she identifies as the "triple negation of Colored Women" in Eurocentric discourses, a problem that she describes as discrimination against women because of our race, gender and class. Delineating specific strategies that Euro-patriarchs and Euro-feminist/women employ to dismiss the work of Black women,

Piper further observes that such critics objectify Black feminism by the use of gender and race stereotypes. Although Black women's lived experience is unique and diverse, it employs the similar theme of gender identification that Euro-feminism espouses.

Carby (1987) stresses the distinctions between how Black women have been represented and how we will continue to change in *Reconstructing Womanhood: The Emergence of the Afro-American Woman Writer.* While presenting the major features of Black women writers' positions and pointing out what she considers fallacies in each, Carby warns against a transhistorical, essentialist epistemology that she finds prevalent in much feminist writing of Black women. Carby encourages a responsible, historical theory and methodology. This would stress the concern with historically verifiable conditions in which twentieth-century Black women writers constructed their texts.

Christian (1985) disagrees with Carby as she indicates that Carby's view of history is different from her own, which she considers to be less rationalistic, more intuitive and creative.

Smith (1987) says Black feminist theory "refers not only to theory written (or practiced) by Black feminists, but also to a way of reading inscriptions of race, gender and class in modes of cultural expression" (p. 39). Her assertion that it is not her intention to reclaim the Black feminist agenda from those who are not Black; to do so would be to define the field too narrowly, emphasizing unduly the implications of a shared experience between Black women as critics and Black women as creators who represent Black women's reality.

Williams' position of Black feminism is in alignment with bell hooks. hooks (1989) creates an understanding of feminism among white women by stating that "many Black women reject white feminism because it stands for the attempt of white women to dominate, exploit and oppress Black women." It is oral narrative that is ideally suited to revealing the "multilayered texture" of Black women's lives.

In constructing and asserting indirectly a "Black feminist" ideology in the text, Williams' discourse is at the center of epistemological and narrative bipolarities, confronting and challenging both Black and White, male and female readings of the world. The position I assert as a result is that Williams ideological position directly determines the form and content of the narratives she uses as examples. Her narratives present a reading of the world that is greatly influenced by her recognition of her difference as a Black woman and how she negotiates that difference she experiences through society. Williams states,

> I think: my raciality is socially constructed, and I experience it as such. I feel my black-self as an eddy of conflicting meanings—and meaninglessness—in which my self can get lost, in which agency and consent are tumbled in constant motion. This sense of motion, the constant windy sound of manipulation whistling in my ears, is a reminder of society's constant construction of my blackness (p. 168).

These feelings Williams articulates are feelings of racial ambiguity that are negotiating meaning between accommodation and condescension. These feelings are nothing new to many Black women who are forced to recognize how society constantly constructs who we are and what that represents. These feelings are usually detrimental to our psyches because they materialize when our guards are down ultimately becoming lethal to our self-concept. Personally, I am constantly aware of how I see myself and how my peers see me. Whether it's presuming to know where I stand on a particular issue, or the condescension revealed when describing research that involves recognition of Blackness.

Williams speaks ever so candidly of the "difference." This assertion of difference is concomitant with her distancing herself from a largely white, middle-class feminist movement that she views as irrelevant to the special historical conditions of Black women. She elaborately positions herself as the "other" in her own historical construct and then she critically critiques the problematic situations as a symptom of how race and class are negotiated. Throughout her critique, Williams' use of the law represents clearly center to margin discourse.

Center to Margin Discourse

hooks (1990) argues that her space of radical openness is a margin, in a sense, a profound edge. Marginality as hooks states is "to be in the margin is to be part of the whole but outside the main body"

(p. 149). Margin to center discourse emulates that which is similar to the center, but which can actually never fully integrate to the center. As a person of color in academe, I am constantly moving between margin to center, not quite reaching the center, but knowing that the center is where my colleagues are. As a Black woman, Williams' discourse mirrors this type of marginality. Although she is quite capable of teaching using unique and creative personal experiences, her students cannot identify with the examples because they are caught between knowing what the center is and consciously placing Williams outside of that center to her own radical margin.

This conscious placement is not uniquely Williams'. In fact, many of us Black women and men can relate to this phenomenon by our students. The one example that vividly comes to mind is teaching European-American/middle-class students about race and class. No matter how hard one tries to explain a concept, many students cannot move their thinking from the center to the margin. That is, they can only interpret experience based on their own understanding of reality. Their reality has never been a part of the margin since their experience is the center.

Feminine Voice

Williams writing style is saturated in what can be classified as a feminine voice. Her style integrates the logical academic prose with personal stories to illustrate a truth about her being. In her truth, there is no fear of revealing the innermost personal sanctum of who she is and what makes her the Black woman she is. de Beauvoir (1989) would argue that how women see themselves is through the "representation of the world." However, this representation of the world is defined by the work of men and they describe it from their own perspective which often is confused with the absolute "truth." Thus, the writing style that Williams uses, although unique from a woman's perspective, is quite common as it is defined by men. Williams would argue that how she writes is indeed defined by men, but that has nothing to do with truth. It has all to do with her lived experiences.

Many theorists, both feminist and nonfeminist, have identified negativity with the feminine. Each has done so in their own way to locate in womanhood that which eludes representation and other forms which unconsciously confine meaning in the feminine. Kristeva (1982) through her interpretations has made connections between womanhood and the elusiveness that has occurred throughout history. Lacan (1977) accepts the proposition that the speaking subject is not the subject of but the subject to the conventions of linguistic discourse. This analysis applies with equal force to the sexual differentiation of subjects. Girls and boys receive the gender identities by virtue of the social linguistic conventions of their social context. Lacan (1977) posits that the very entry of the subject into the realm of language, the conventional system of meaning he calls symbolic is associated with the feminine.

Derrida challenges the idea that the author of a work is in charge of its meaning. He argues that concealed within any positive statement of meaning is an absent, other meaning, suggesting that difference rather than identity is necessary to our understanding.

Alienation and Reality

People of color, specifically Black women, often experience alienation in the academy. McGary (1992) argues that alienation exists when the self is deeply divided because the hostility of the dominant groups in society forces the self to see itself as defective, insignificant, and lacking the possibility of ever seeing itself in positive terms. Although Williams does not personally exhibit these characteristics, the fact that her students question her ability to teach speaks to this alienated state. Many of our students have never been taught by Black men or women, therefore the credibility factor is stacked against us when we are faced with a situation of teaching European-American students for the first time.

Alienation is not new, in fact it is the result of privilege, but the legacy of resistance. Black women understand alienation as a live facet of feminism. Feminism did not embrace Black women. Black women faced alienation as a result of not conforming to a tradition that denied our voices. This resistance resulted as feminism in general refused to hear the struggle of women of color as different than Euro-American struggle. Feminism spoke to the center which was inhabited by white women. Women of color spoke from the margin and were alienated for not reaching the center.

Williams discourse is the same type of resistance to the tradition of hegemony. Her lived experiences are valid, but her approach is challenged simply because its marginal discourse. It is not shared by her students or her colleagues, therefore they cannot accept the style in which her discourse resonates.

Rhetorical Criticism of the Artifact

Rhetorical criticism as we know it today has traditionally grown out of the presupposition that rhetorical theory consists of the rules and canons by which we can artfully persuade our fellow men and women to come around to our way of thinking and act accordingly to our wishes and desires vis-à-vis the issues under discussion (Hart, 1994). If one is to assume this traditional understanding of criticism, the application of using rhetorical theory as a vehicle for explicating the desired intent of Williams discourse can best be realized as a reality between the text and the reader. As Williams writes, her purpose is two-fold. She attempts to convey the following: first that the essence of her experiences as a Black woman is essential in her understanding of the world, and second the unintentional understanding that the law does account for differences. Williams accomplishes her purpose through an examination of her lived experiences.

Rhetorical criticism is best understood as the examination of the interrelationship of language and social action. Criticism allows the critic to create meaning as a result of interpretation of a phenomenon. Thus, criticism is used to reinterpret social meaning as it also serves to create understanding. The strength of criticism in relation to Williams' discourse provides an interpretation of her discourse with a socially meaningful context. As the critic, I used interpretation based on my understanding of society, and how Williams' experience overlaps with my experience. As Black women in academe, our lived experience is guided, in part, by the type of students we tend to interact with. Thus, our lived experiences will inherently resemble each other's in so far as we both understand the workings of a hegemonic society.

As the critic, I was influenced by the discourse of Williams because I could relate to the issues that she raised. Therefore, my interpretation became an interpretation of Williams' discourse that reinterpreted the social meaning of my own lived experience.

Conclusion

In the *Rhetoric of Motives*, Kenneth Burke (1950) proposes 'identification' as an alternative to persuasion as the key term of the rhetorical process. Burke's purpose was a revision of rhetorical theory to consider rhetoric and motives in formal terms, as consequences of the nature of language and its enactment. Burke recognized the power of persuasion as the key purpose of rhetoric which implies the existence of an agent who is free to be persuaded.

Williams' discourse in many respects lacks identification for her students not because she is ineffective in what she says, but because her students cannot identify with her lived experiences. As Black women we are faced with the dilemma of appealing to the students who in many cases have absolutely no understanding of the cultural or ethnic differences. The bigger question becomes how do we identify with students who are not exposed to the multiple realities that exist in a diverse society? Are we to assume that there should be some level of awareness that we should come to expect from students, or are we to simply identify with their experiences?

I believe that it is not enough to simply presume that students who are operating from the center can never understand the complexities of marginal discourse. It is truly a gift to effectively identify with the experiences of our students to find their comfort in moving away from their center to the margin that will allow them to understand the lived experiences of the "other."

References

Bambara, T. C. (1972). *Gorilla my love*. New York: Random House.

Burke, K. (1950). *A rhetoric of motives*. Berkeley: University of California Press. Reprinted 1969.

Carby. H. (1987). *Reconstructing womanhood: The emergence of the Afro-American woman novelists*. New York: Oxford.

Christian, B. (1985). *Black feminist criticism: Perspectives on Black women writers*. New York: Pergamon Press.

Clifton, L. (1974). *An ordinary woman*. New York: Random House.

Collins, P. H. (1991). *Black feminist thought*. New York: Routledge.

de Beauvoir, S. (1989). *The second sex*. New York: Vintage.

Foucault, M. (1972). *The archeology of knowledge*. Translated by A. M. Sheridan Smith. New York: Pantheon.

Gatens, M. (1991). *Feminism and philosophy: Perspectives on difference and equality*. Cambridge, MA: Polity Press.

Hart, R. P. (1994). Wandering with rhetorical criticism. *In Critical Questions: Inventions, Creativity, and the Criticism of Discourse and Media.* (Eds.) W. L. Nothstine, C. Blair, & G. A. Copeland. New York: St. Martin's Press.

hooks, b. (1989). *Talking back: Thinking feminist thinking Black*. Boston: South End Press.

Kristeva, J. (1982). *Desire in language: A semiotic approach to literature and art*. trans. T. Gara, A. Jardin & L. S. Roudiez. New York: Columbia University Press.

Lacan, J. (1977). *Ecrits: A selection*, trans. A. Sheridan. New York: Norton.

MacKinnon, C. A. (1989). *Toward a feminist theory of the state*. Cambridge, MA: Harvard University Press.

McGary, H. (1992–93). *Alienation and the African-American experience*. The Philosophical Forum, XXIV(1–3) 282–298.

Piper, A. (1990). *The triple negation of colored women*. Art Papers, 14, 12–20.

Sampson, E. E. (1993). *Celebrating the other: A dialogic account of human nature*. San Francisco: Westview Press.

Smith, D. (1987). *The everyday world as problematic*. Boston: Northeastern University Press.

Williams, P. J. (1991). *The alchemy of race and rights*. Cambridge, MA: Harvard University Press.

3

RECLAMATION AND DISCOVERIES

AN AFRICAN-AMERICAN WOMEN'S HISTORIAN'S EFFORTS TO CHRONICLE THE EXPERIENCES OF AFRICAN-AMERICAN WOMEN TEACHERS IN NASHVILLE, TENNESSEE, 1942–1983

Sonya Ramsey

The sun shone brightly across the well-manicured lawn. Waves of nervousness engulfed me as I maneuvered my car down the winding driveway belonging to the ranch-style home of Mrs. Dorothy W. Baines. Unlike most of my other research subjects, she had taken an active interest in my selection of candidates by suggesting other women I should interview and asking me questions about my family. I felt as if I was one of her former middle-school pupils instead of an adult graduate student. However, as I entered her home, my feelings of anxiousness dissipated. Displayed in front of me was a lovely setting of cake and red fruit punch all carefully placed on white lace doilies, coordinated to match the crimson and cream colors of my sorority. This was indeed a gesture of kindness, since Mrs. Baines belonged to another, sometimes rival, sorority. Whereas oral historical research serves as the evidential base of my dissertation on black women teachers in Nashville, Tennessee, the interactions that occurred among my subjects and myself also contributed to my scholarly research. In addition, they provided insights into my self-perception as a graduate student and practitioner of African-American Women's History. I learned that although I was studying a subject in a familiar city, there were still discoveries to be found and new analyses to be performed.

In this chapter, I wish to revisit the summer of 1995, where I conducted more than thirty interviews with African-American female teachers in Nashville, Tennessee, who taught during segregation or the early years of public school desegregation from the 1940s to the 1980s. As I reflect upon my experiences, I want to examine my own personal journey as a student and educator. Another goal of this chapter is to discuss how obtaining these interviews enabled me to write my dissertation while also reinvigorating my desire to contribute to the historical knowledge of African-American women's lives.

If there is such a concept as fate, then I think that it is my destiny to write a history of black women teachers. Several members of my family have been involved in the educational arena, including my mother, father and late paternal grandmother. As I grew to adulthood, I realized that they implanted a desire in me to choose a career that positively affected the lives of others. Yet it took participation in a 1993 summer oral history project to fully consider the important impact black women educators had on their students and in their communities. As a researcher in the "Behind the Veil: Documenting the Jim Crow South Project," sponsored by the Duke University Center for Documentary Studies, I interviewed more than one hundred African-American North Carolinians who remembered segregation. Although community leaders shared with us lists of people with different occupations to randomly choose, I always seemed to get the opportunity to converse with teachers. I became known as "the teacher interview lady." However, as I listened to their stories, I realized that the larger saga of how desegregation affected teachers should be told.

During segregation, African-American teachers had the responsibility of educating children in a system designed to hinder their educational progress. The role of African-American teachers went far beyond teaching academic skills, since segregation relegated a majority of their pupils to jobs as domestics or manual laborers. Often dressed as the consummate professional in business attire, hats, and white gloves, urban women teachers took responsibility for instilling self-confidence and pride in children who faced the tragedies and hypocrisy of racism in their daily lives. These teachers, together with the children's parents, attempted to show students how to adapt and live in a discriminatory nation. At the same time, they prepared them psychologically to participate in an integrated society of the future.

After a fruitful summer interviewing North Carolinians, I knew that I wished to expand and continue my research. I then decided to use the skills I acquired as a "Behind the Veil" participant to examine the experiences of African-American teachers in Nashville, Tennessee, as they made the transition from segregated to desegregated schools. I based my study in Nashville because of its familiarity as my childhood home, and its role as a "New South" city with a strong educational focus. I also wished to examine the Southern urban teacher's experience from the 1930s to the 1980s.

African-Americans consistently comprised approximately one-third of the city's residents during the years after World War II, as Nashville's black community offered strong religious and community institutions to the urban educator (see Lamon, 1980). A plethora of churches opened their doors for worship and growing black businesses offered goods and services to Nashville's African-American residents. For example, R.H. Boyd's National Publishing Board was a powerful influence from its founding in 1896. This publisher of religious materials for all of the Missionary Baptist Churches in the United States offered employment and sponsored social activities and community services to Nashville's black community. Nashville's black citizens also took pride in their own colleges and universities. By the 1940s, the city boasted several institutions of higher learning for blacks including Fisk University, Meharry Medical College, Tennessee Agricultural and Industrial State College (now Tennessee State University) and American Baptist Theological Seminary, a training school for ministers (Doyle, 1985).

Tourist guides promoted Nashville as the "Athens of the South" because of its myriad of higher educational institutions. Nevertheless, during the era of racial segregation, the state capital held tenaciously to a social and economic order that revolved around racial discrimination. The city's African-American children attended poorly funded schools and made due with used textbooks deemed unfit for white children. Yet, in spite of these poor conditions, Nashville's segregated schools served as cultural centers in their communities, attracting some of the best-qualified teachers in the state.

Nashville served as a mecca for women interested in the teaching profession, and they held the majority of teaching positions in the public school system from the 1940s to the 1980s (U.S. Bureau of Census, 1950–1960). Although new opportunities in the nursing, clerical, sales and manufacturing fields opened to some African-American women in urban areas, teaching still provided the best opportunity to obtain professional status. Because African-American women also faced gender discrimination, few entered fields open to African-American men, such as railroad work. As professionals, African-American teachers interacted socially with the nurses and the elite wives of Meharry Hospital doctors and other university faculty. I selected participants by using methods I learned previously as a researcher, and I used a sampling concept described by scholar Michele Foster as community nomination. In this process, community members suggested whom they wanted to represent them, conveying their information through direct contact with the interviewer (Foster, 1994). In today's violent society, senior citizens and women are sometimes warned not to open their home to anyone. Fortunately, through my involvement in the community nominating process, I had familiar names to use as I asked my subjects to share their memories and experiences. I also advised them that the interview could discontinue at any time. While the researcher still controls the information gathering, by involving the community, the interviewees consider themselves as important components of the research process. This is pertinent in order to dismantle the legacy of distrust felt toward outside researchers. This wariness possibly emanates from the tendency of researchers to come into a community with an objective to gather information without fully informing or involving their subjects. The uneasiness also reflects a fear of negative portrayal due to the profusion of stereotypical or misrepresented images of African Americans. The community nominating selection process also captured the African-American community's conception of what it means to be a good teacher (Foster, 1993).

That sorority involved the "nicer ladies" in our community. Nicer meaning those who had a high scholastic standing, whose reputation as a lady was honored by the community. "A lady in my lifetime and still when I use the term lady I don't use it often, is a person who stands out, who is different from all of the others, who has something about her that tells you that she likes herself and she wants you to like her but she isn't trying to be like everyone in the crowd but stand above the crowd" (Virginia Westbrooks, tape recording, July 1995).

I have always had a persistent and consistent interest in the ways African-American middle-class women defined themselves as women and as a class in Southern cities during the twentieth century. Consequently, I aspire to analyze how these segregated urban environments helped to create and shape their self-perceptions and class identity. My master's thesis and other graduate work examine black women in education. A broader goal of my study is to contribute to the historical canon by offering a larger history of middle-class black women in a Southern urban environment; therefore, I sought to study teachers who described themselves as professional or middle-class. As a narrowing measure, I proceeded to select women who participated in exclusive clubs and sororities in college and in later years. During segregation, the ability to attend a university was indeed a privilege. In some cases, sororities and exclusive social clubs used middle-class ideological standards of dress and social behavior in addition to grade averages and campus participation to select members during this era. After receiving a list of names of teachers from several sororities, I found that some of these women originated from economically deprived backgrounds. Nevertheless, as they attended college and began careers as educators, they assumed a middle-class identity. I was interested in examining how their college experiences and teaching helped to shape their self-identity as women.

Growing up in Nashville during the 1970s and 80s, I also hoped my dissertation would address some of my own personal concerns. As a student, I attended more than seven different schools during my twelve years. A child of integration, friendships crossed racial lines, as desegregation seemed to dismantle barriers. However, once I reached high school, I had to maneuver between racial groups to maintain friendships. Although I achieved academically as one of few black students in most of my classes, I felt ignored and isolated. I attended a predominately black university to regain a sense of self.

As a product of a desegregated school system, I am thankful for my interracial friendships and my educational opportunities. Yet, I am deeply interested in the educational experiences of blacks during segregation. I also marvel at how older African Americans worshiped their schools. Most of them can remember special teachers in their lives. This teacher-student relationship during segregation propelled students not only to achieve academically, but also to develop the self-confidence and life skills needed to ensure success.

Now equipped with a state-of-the-art tape-recorder and lists of possible subjects, I embarked on a journey that would both prepare me for the future as an African-American female professor and form a bridge to the past as I attempted to analyze the past experiences of earlier generations of black women. As previously mentioned, one of the goals of my dissertation is to offer an examination of professional African-American women's lives in a Southern urban setting. While I dressed conservatively and conducted interviews in a formal, but respectful manner, I often pondered how their preconceived thoughts about my class status affected the interview. Raised by a non-profit educator, I grew up in a working-class area that was sandwiched between an older middle-class neighborhood and a housing project complex. While I saw myself standing on the outside peering in through the rose-colored glass that encased the private world of the black elite, my acquired educational status and value system now seemed to connect me to these ladies and other members of the African-American middle-class. My new found ease at interacting with these women, some of who were leading members of the most exclusive black organizations in the city, forced me to reevaluate my self-perceived class status.

While I gathered important primary historical information, I also had the rare opportunity to observe how these women evaluated me. They simply concluded by my appearance and educational level that I belonged to the black middle class and established strong connections with me based upon sometimes incorrectly assumed shared experiences. Actually based on historical criteria, I did belong to the black middle class. During segregation, educational status and behavior were strong descriptors of black middle-class status. Although I did not have the financial foundation, as a Ph.D. candidate, I had the potential to one-day assume a position in the professional middle-class world. In some ways this realization was disarming. It is not popular in the academic community to aspire to upper or middle-class status. Progressive scholars are supposed to use their work to enlighten the masses, not barricade themselves in an academic ivory tower. This realization also reinforced my dismay as I continue to experience a widening gulf of misunderstanding growing among myself and the familiar places and faces of my old neighborhood. As a child who grew up one block from low-income housing, I had always held a research interest in middle-class black women because I felt that they were a fascinating, yet different entity. These ladies faced segregation and discriminatory treatment as African-American women whenever they entered the larger society. Yet, behind the doors of their comfortable homes they attempted to create an exclusive world of bridge parties and socials elevating themselves from the debilitating pressures of race and poverty. How would my realization that I was perceived as a full-fledged member alter my research focus? While I continue to struggle with my own definition of class in my dissertation, I learned that summer that the lines defining class continue to be fluid and overlapping. While financial worth is now probably the largest indicator of class status in the black community, educational attainment and social behavior still figure prominently as definers of status. Ironically, those same indicators have fueled growing class divisions among African Americans as certain types of dress, speech and behavior are habitually used by popular culture to negatively define class level.

"I didn't ask to come here. I was sent here. But since I am here and I see what you are doing to my poor little black students I am going to stay here as long as I can" (Anne Talley Lenox, tape recording, August 1995).

A sizable segment of my teachers taught only African-American students for the majority of their educational careers. While the majority of my interview subjects taught in both black and predominately white institutions, in both situations, these teachers often undertook a maternalistic role toward their charges. Whether they provided clothes for needy pupils during segregation or served as racial protectors as black children boarded buses to faraway schools, these teachers felt a responsibility to implant confidence in their children in addition to their academic courses. While my subjects treated me as an adult, their willingness to assist regardless of whether or not I requested their aid, in some ways mirrored their maternalistic role in the classroom. While my oral history project's aim was to support my dissertation, in some cases the subjects' considered it their purpose not only to share their experiences, but also to promote my progress as a student. In addition to the use of references, the most significant factor contributing to my ability to proceed involved the enthusiasm of these women to assist me in my endeavor as a scholar. For example, while some of my subjects quickly granted their permission, others were hesitant. In several instances, the willing participants persuaded their counterparts to grant me an interview because I was a young black woman scholar, a future teacher. Other women I spoke with suggested other educators and guided me to important primary research sources. They also shared names of prominent black businesswomen and scientists outside the scope of my dissertation. As some of my subjects took an active interest in my success, I also developed a sense of responsibility to contribute to the historical knowledge of and about African-American women and to make sure that I told their stories with accuracy and completeness. For the complex role educators played in the black community's quest for racial equality while sometimes facing the disillusioning effects of desegregation illuminates the black educators' experience.

The modern-day sense of uplift displayed by these teachers was only one of the factors that helped me to have a successful research project. Another important component that contributed to my work involved the desire of my subjects to share their own experiences. Works that describe and analyze the role of the African-American teacher in American society, such as those by scholars Michael Fultz (1995), Stephanie Shaw (1996), and Michele Foster (1997), have only emerged in the last few years. Previous scholarship on black teachers often conveyed a theme of incompetence due to the lack of educational access and economic deprivation (see, for example, Bachman, (1931); Lamon, (1980); Tushnet (1987)). While some of the statements regarding a lack of access and materials are accurate, the complete and comprehensive historical analysis of urban black women teachers during segregation and as they made the transition to desegregated schools has yet to emerge. While correcting misinformation, this study would also dispel negative stereotypes regarding black educators. For instance, for several decades in Nashville the African-American teachers possessed higher educational attainment levels than their white counterparts, yet they received lower salaries until the late 1930s (Bachman, Lamon, and Tushnet). These Black women considered themselves master teachers. I wanted to examine why they felt so confident.

To a scholar, the role teachers held during the school integration process offers several issues to discuss and study. During the Civil Rights era, African-American community leaders fought for an end to segregated education and black teachers supported their community's quest. This position cost a high price as negative descriptions of segregated schools often described their teaching staffs as incompetent and inferior. Some African-American teachers also suffered employment losses or in Nashville's case, received massive transfers as a result of desegregation. Yet, these women realized the possible opportunities that integration could bring. They tried through cooperation, compromise and sometimes confrontation to make the process work for their students and themselves. I sensed that my interviewees wished to convey their ambivalence towards integration and the effects it had on their careers, their personal lives and their communities. I planned to be a conduit to communicate their ideas and opinions.

Methodologically, as these women shared their thoughts, I concluded that although my research relied on their statements as evidence, the ways in which they expressed themselves were also significant. I decided to share their voices with an audience by playing recordings of their interviews in several conferences and workshops. While prevailing thought perceives the African-American community as monolithic, the actual sounds of their voices conveyed the distinctiveness of these women. While my work draws upon the similar experiences and opinions of my subjects, I never want to lose sight of their individuality. The recordings of their life histories will be held in a permanent archival collection, so that other scholars can listen and learn. As a scholar, I held their request to tell their true story of tragedies and triumphs with the utmost importance.

I also concluded as a scholar of African-American, Women's and Educational history that I might not tell a story of glory and celebration. It is my responsibility to tell the most precise account possible. While I established strong connections with the teachers whom I interviewed, it will not hinder my ability to provide an accurate description of the effects of desegregation or the particulars of middle-class life. As Nashville still grapples with school desegregation and plans to achieve racial balance are being discontinued throughout the nation, my dissertation remains relevant to today's issues. On a personal level, I consider my research experience as a first step on a journey towards greater self-realization.

As the largest group of professional African-American women in Nashville and throughout the South for decades, the account of their transition into a desegregated or lesser-segregated society as workers and as women mirrored the complexities of the African-American struggle to achieve economic parity and social freedom during the twentieth century. Consequently, in analyzing these women's lives, I plan to make important contributions to the historical and educational fields by providing a multi-dimensional view of the intersections of race, gender and class through the lens of African-American teachers. The use of oral history allowed me the opportunity to examine the effects of desegregation on their professional careers, and how the dismantling of segregated education affected their personal lives and communities.

While I expected to gather pertinent information about my topic, I also gained insight as these women led me to examine my own personal ideology and self-perception as a scholar and as a woman. I realized that although some of these women had to "represent the race" as they entered unfamiliar and uncomfortable school requirements, I face a lesser burden. I feel fortunate that I am not a "first," I don't have to prove the academic excellence of black women to those who would think I am inferior just because of my skin or gender. Well, I haven't had to so far, and if I do, I will be prepared because others have gone before me. As affirmative action and other remedies to racial injustice are being attacked, I feel future scholars such as myself may one day have to fight for their very existence on the university campus. As exemplified by several of the women educators in my study, who struggled against negative stereotypes, racism, economic inequalities in salaries, and school funding, it is my responsibility to prepare for challenges I might face with a solid foundation of scholarship, professionalism and perseverance.

References

Anderson, J.D. (1988). *The education of blacks in the south, 1860–1935.* Chapel Hill: University of North Carolina Press.

Bachman, F. P.(Director). (1931). Public schools of Nashville, Tennessee: A survey report, Nashville, TN: Division of Surveys and Field Studies George Peabody College for Teachers.

Doyle, D.H. (1985). *Nashville: in the new south: 1880–1930.* Knoxville: University of Tennessee Press.

Foster, M. (1993, Jan). Educating for competence in community and culture: Exploring the views of exemplary African American teachers. *Urban Education* 27, 370–394.

Foster, M. (1994, Spring). The role of community and culture in school reform efforts: Examining the views of African-American teachers. *Educational Foundations*, 5–26.

Foster, M. (1997). *Black teachers on teaching*, New York: The New Press.

Fultz, M. (1995). African American teachers in the south, 1890–1940: Powerlessness and the ironies of expectations and protest. *History of Educational Quarterly*, *35*, 401–422.

Lamon, L. (1980). *Blacks in Tennessee, 1791–1970*. Knoxville: University of Tennessee Press.

Shaw, S. (1996). *What a woman ought to be and to do: Black professional women workers during the Jim Crow era*. Chicago: University of Chicago Press.

Tushnet, M.V. (1987). *The NAACP's legal strategy against segregated education, 1925–1950*. Chapel Hill, NC: University of North Carolina Press.

United States Bureau of the Census. (1950–1960). *Census of the population, 1940, Nashville, Tennessee and characteristics of non-white population for standard metropolitan areas, urban areas and urban places, 1950, 1960*. Washington, DC.: US. Government Printing Office.

United States Bureau of the Census. (1950–1960). Race and age of employed persons except on public emergency work and of experienced workers seeking work by occupation and sex for the state and for cities of 100,000, Nashville, Tennessee. Washington, D.C.: U.S. Government Printing Office.

4

"A CHANCE OF DOUBLE LIVES"

PHENOMENOLOGICAL STUDY OF BLACK FEMALE GRADUATE EXPERIENCE

Priya Kapoor

Introduction

The purpose of this chapter is to reveal the dominant structures in higher education through a rigorous process of in-depth interviewing and conversations with African-American female graduate students at a majority white institution. The women's words expose the inherent tensions in the overarching discourse of multiculturalism that pervades American campuses and offices of affirmative action situated there, but these same campuses fail to retain most minority graduate students who enroll in various graduate and undergraduate programs. Previous research identifies two vital factors that influence and therefore hinder minority retention (Latino and African-American)—the lack of mentoring and low availability of financial aid (Kapoor, 1992).

More specifically, I am trying to understand how African-American women studying at a majority institution experience graduate life. By defining the problem in the broadest manner possible I was able to open the forum for women respondents (narrators) in a way that they were able to foreground what they found most pertinent in their lived experience as graduate students.

Even though the extant literature and research on minority participation in higher education aids in dichotomizing between blacks and whites and seems to pass the final word on the issue, it cannot be ignored. The lacunae in this vast body of positivistic research has helped me decide that it is the stories of women that I seek rather than objective analyses of their situation. Black women have long been barred from the production of knowledge. They have a history of "silence" (hooks, 1984; Wallace, 1990; hooks, 1994). Their voices have been disregarded "like pictures without words or music without lyrics" (Wallace, 1990). Others have freely spoken for them in the past and continue to.

In writing about African-American women I feel compelled to present an unlaundered version of their history—in their own words. I refer to the women as *narrators* for this reason. My main sources of information are the fellow graduate students whose words provide the theme and the analysis for this paper. Black women have been shy participants in knowledge production because of innumerable social problems that have continued to dog them, namely illiteracy, high school dropout rate, homicide rate, violence within the community—the targets being mainly women and children. Other social problems include homelessness, inadequate housing, poverty, drug addiction, alcoholism, teenage pregnancy, and unemployment (Wallace, 1990). In Wallace's words "financial ruin, ignorance and despair seemed to follow us around like badly trained pets wanting food and water" (1990, p. 117). The existential plight of the Afro-American has been termed post-colonial—"no longer colonial but not yet free" (Wallace, 1990). These are just a few of the existential problems faced by disadvantaged members of the African-American community. These instances do not typify all of the struggle of women of color but present a basis on which most issues concerning them could be raised.

Michele Wallace has faith in the power of feminism as a movement that can bring about social upheaval and "change society in a way beneficial to all" (p. 215). She uses the metaphor of the black w/hole—something that gives an illusion of nothingness but is intensely full—to symbolize black female creativity contained by a "complex structure of American (US) inequality" (p. 219). Whereas bell hooks summons, through her writings, women who have remained at the margins and "at the edge" to adopt a more active role at the center. She stresses in her writings that "feminism must become a mass based political movement if it is to have a revolutionary, transformative impact on society" (p. 161).

bell hooks (1984) criticizes the fact that attempts by white feminists to silence black women are seldom written about even when such instances occur both in and out of the classroom. Even though liberal reforms have been instituted for the benefit of African-American women, it should not be assumed that the "systems of domination" have been abolished (hooks, 1984). African Americans do enjoy increased visibility in mass media and other places of employment however upliftment is slow to come. The true effect of affirmative action will be felt when there is an emphasis on doing away with this "politic of domination" which makes change impossible.

Minority Retention and Multiculturalism: A Review of Literature

One of the chief aims of affirmative action is to make higher education more accessible to minorities. Since the late seventies, minority enrollment in colleges began declining despite the adoption of affirmative action by most institutions of higher learning (St. John, 1991). Minority graduate degree holders are grossly under-represented among the pool of degree holders in the United States. This downward trend in graduate enrollment has concerned policy makers and researchers and thus has stimulated investigations of the reasons for this decline (Robbs, 1988). One reason is that at the policy level, minority recruitment and retention has still not been recognized by universities as a fundamental purpose of higher education (Garcia & Seligsohn, 1978). Affirmative action merely pressured universities to admit more black students and faculty (Rodriguez, 1992). What was needed perhaps, apart from more aggressive recruitment policies, were educational and campus environments that are truly accepting of racial and cultural differences and similarities (Carter, 1990).

These concerns assume importance because there is an increasing proportion of minorities in the U.S. and their educational, social and economic status is sure to have a significant impact on the future of the country (Adams, 1990). Another concern is that the majority population is aging and suffering a slow growth rate. "Therefore, the successful enrollment and retention of minorities in higher education must become a national priority in order for the nation to accomplish a fully participative multicultural society" (Adams, 1990, p. 449).

My purpose, then, is to interview African-American women friends to explore and unravel structures of domination that they might experience in their daily lives. What makes their particular experiences different, and what synthesizes these experiences to common themes? African-American women are bludgeoned by two ism(s) in their lifetime—racism and sexism. I have used the above review of literature to show that very few stories have been written about women marginalized on the basis of color. I have framed the experience of African-American women as problematic. What partly makes their situation problematic is that the perpetrators/instigators of sexism and racism deny their involvement in it. We need to know how racism and sexism are framed in the American society to understand the context in which it is experienced. The interviews I have conducted follow the methodology outlined in the following section.

Methodology

Phenomenology is both a philosophy and a methodology (Nelson, 1989). The purpose of phenomenological research is to understand the life world or the *lebenswelt* (Polkinghorne, 1983). A phrase repeated in Husserl's writings is "to things themselves" which reemphasizes the focus of phenomenological research on that which happens in lived experience. Therefore, the embodied experience is held supreme during analysis (Nelson, 1989). Phenomenological research is intersubjective and strives for equal partnership among researcher and researched.

The major concern of phenomenological research is with meaning and how it is constructed. Meaning is intentional in that it is about some*thing*, therefore, it cannot be constructed outside of the lived world, in a vacuum. A phenomenon has no meaning except in relation to another phenomenon. Every phenomenon overlaps and becomes coextensive with other phenomena. Meaning arises through their inter-signification.

A phenomenon is that which allows the presence of something or that which reveals itself (Merleau-Ponty, 1962). And so, phenomenological research data (capta) is gathered through in-depth interviews on what is experienced by persons as they describe it, in concrete terms. The emphasis is on rich, detailed descriptions of situations or experience just as it is presented to the interviewer by the narrator (Nelson, 1989).

No one perspective has primacy over the other because together, these perspectives constitute a phenomenon. In other words research is always influenced by the presence of the researcher (Hale, 1991) and in their interactions with the researched (intersubjectivity). Therefore, in phenomenological research, there is a commitment to intersubjectivity and horizontalization (Nelson, 1989).

The three women I have interviewed are graduate students in the School of Telecommunications, pursuing a Master's degree. The women knew me prior to my approaching them for an interview. Therefore, I did not have to worry about building a rapport with my narrators who seemed more than willing to speak to me about their experiences at the University. All the women are in their twenties and unmarried. Two of the women have lived abroad for an extended period of time—one spent part of her childhood in Japan, and the other lived in Africa as a Peace Corps volunteer. The third narrator is a native of Ohio and has lived in America all her life. They hail from different regions within America and their experiences though not entirely unique, are diverse and vary from each other greatly. However, similarities emerge amidst their eclectic range of experiences.

To capture the differences (amid the similarities) in their experiences, I decided on separate interviews. Were I to undertake further research I would encourage discussion in groups of two or three to collect capta and get a fuller description of the narrators experience. Also, I would make a suggestion to future researchers to include more women who have children or those that are married. This method worked well for my purpose in trying to record in the women's own words their experience of life at the University.

Phenomenology "brackets" the experience of a phenomenon so as to reveal the essential structure of the experience (Crow, 1981). Thus, I began the discussions with my narrators, by bracketing my knowledge of racism, sexism, and my awareness of the other problems African-American graduate students experience on the University campus (based primarily on findings in the quantitative methods class and review of relevant literature). I bracketed the knowledge of my position vis-à-vis the research problematic, too.

The informal atmosphere of the discussion enabled the narrators to describe their lived experience freely. Intersubjectivities between the narrators and the researcher were recognized, and they used their own perspectives to access their particular experiences. As persons talked about their experience of graduate life, what was perceived is a discursive process of consciousness that illustrates and explicates their experience of personal, social, and cultural reality (Nelson, 1986). Hale (1991) emphasizes that research outcome is always influenced by the presence of the researcher and her interactions with the researched (intersubjectivity), and so, to set aside bias to be objective is not possible.

The phenomenological interview approach allowed me to be more attentive to each of the person's responses (Patton, 1983). I changed the protocol of the interview depending on the flow of the conversation. I cannot say if I became a better researcher as time went by, but I definitely tried to learn from my previous mistakes. For instance, in one interview, I kept my tape recorder distant from the narrator, which detracted from the quality of the sound. I had been anxious to make the recorder seem as unobtrusive as possible. Later, I was able to judge better the approximate distance I should maintain between the narrator and recorder.

None of my narrators had experienced such an interview procedure where they were not subjected to a fixed question-answer format. In one instance the narrator kept asking if she was "giving me what I wanted." The fact that the interviews were not structured, but followed the narrators response, did not detract from the process of learning of their particular experiences.

The interviews spanned between forty-five minutes and two hours. I designed a topical protocol with some open-ended questions focusing on their experiences at school, both in and outside of classroom situations. I included an open-ended question asking the women to recount a typical day at the University and converse about all the persons they meet, talk to, or ask for advice. The women usually began answering in chronological order—what they did in the morning etc.—but the very process of thinking about who they trust as friends led to descriptions of specific incidents and stories, unpleasant and pleasant, that were important to them, in retrospect.

I began all my interviews by asking the women about how they decided to come to that particular university. This happened to be, to my surprise, an effective way to begin a conversation. The conversations later led to descriptions of more concrete and specific experiences. This question was not originally part of my topical protocol. I devised this question to start a discussion with my first respondent when I realized that I had forgotten to keep a copy of my topical protocol. I finally adopted this strategy for subsequent interviews.

The interviews were conducted in numerous locations, determined by convenience. I usually suggested the settings but my narrators verified if they were comfortable with my choice. After each interview I recorded my response on the progress of the interview, in a journal. I also spent time thinking about how I could improve my skills for the next interview. I now, understand more clearly, my task as researcher, where I need to listen "in stereo" to the "muted channels" of women (Anderson & Jack, 1991) who are trying to define their position and experiences in a dominantly male and apart from that, dominantly white society. The interview experience not only improved my listening skills but also made me sensitive to issues of race and color that my limited experience had shielded me from. I became increasingly engrossed and involved in the experiences of my narrators. I feel a commitment and responsibility to present their voices to appropriate authorities. In taking on the responsibility of interpreting their lives in the arena of public discourse, I will be challenging many of the conventions of "normal academic practice" (Olsen & Shopes, 1991).

After listening to tapes of our conversations and reading through the transcripts several times, I began my initial thematization. Some common themes emerged from the three interviews that I conducted. I highlighted excerpts of the conversations that when put together and viewed holistically, revealed the structures and essences of their experience. I used the method of free variation to group the statements (Polkinghorne, 1983). Horizontalization of experiences (accepting equality of descriptions) helped me arrange capta into meaningful themes. Horizontalization also made me see the similar aspects of the experiences.

This abductive, analytical process allowed me to categorize and clarify the structure of what was said, first, into five themes and then finally into one theme—"double lives." This final thematization, in drawing on the earlier five themes, reveals how the narrators' lives are structured (also how a dominant structure/system forces them to lead a certain lifestyle) in a white majority institution and a white majority society. I came upon these themes through an intuitive process of going through the transcripts numerous times. Even though I kept an open mind to unravel the structures of experience, I realize that it is almost impossible to reach a complete reduction (Nelson, 1989).

Initial Thematization

I found five initial themes when doing my first reduction. While the themes are strongly related they also stand on their own as part of the experience of graduate life as a minority student. The themes are: "the yellow brick road," "peers but not peers," "just at the border: gonna seep out," "the whole kit and caboodle" and lastly, "*question* the whole kit and caboodle." My choice of grouping the themes is intentional as I feel they are related, and I explain what constitutes these themes as I go along.

The Yellow Brick Road

The first theme that emerges is that of mentoring—of who a mentor is in the words of the narrators and how they have experienced mentoring in their academic and personal lives. There seems to be unanimous agreement that mentoring is an integral part of being at this large midwestern University, which currently embodies their whole life. They use their own terms to define a mentor.

> Someone who was very much concerned about ME and what would happen with MY life. Kind of like acted as a guide, a sounding board. Someone who can show me the way to get to your objective...keeping me abreast of what I needed to do...I think it is a process that happens pretty naturally. And it's a process that takes a lot of time...A person who's kind of like special and always there. (3)

> Someone who's looking out for my best interest...That's a mentor—someone who would take you by the hand and show you the way. (1)

> The best advice you get is from someone who knows you, not someone that you pay or someone that you see periodically.... What does matter is knowledge and intellectual and interpersonal communication...I can always find someone of race and gender,

> somewhere in the field but if that person has interest in me and I have interest in that person and we have the same interests... (2)

> I want someone who's been through what I'm going through. Who's been through *the yellow brick road*, and I can follow them. (2)

> Friends have the experience of personal—you know things that *we all* go through. (2)

Both friends and professors have been involved in the mentoring process. The narrators consider the advice of their professors valuable when it concerns their academic lives. They rely more on friends when it comes to personal matters as well as certain academic concerns such as advise about what classes to take or which books to buy, because "they have been through the yellow brick road." Some mentors are more special than others because they take extra effort and time to guide their students.

> ... You know offered me, offered to personally help pay for conferences... and J. R.... just get in the car and I'll pay for gas.... He'll drive and he'll include me... I knew that was gonna happen and you know they said they'd do it and when I got here they did it.... They made me feel so special... He really took a personal interest in me.... The Dean of the college actually sat down with me. (1)

> We can talk about anything from politics to weight to nutrition to men... She makes things personal, she is very personable. And it's all the person's personality and what makes a relationship work. (2)

> I get most of my advice from peers.... And I try to get different perspectives... and I try and synthesize things and try and put my own thoughts to it. I always go to my advisor for advice.... He knows the ins and outs and that's important but then I ask students advice. (2)

> As far as the other side of mentoring—getting close to the person, I don't feel that with the person... Not really really tight like I've felt with some people (mentors) from the past. Because mentoring takes a lot of time. (3)

Peers But Not Peers

Even though the term "peers" suggests fellow students, some students are "peers but not their peers." This then becomes the next theme that emerges from my narrators descriptions. The narrators seem to distinguish friends from peers. Friends who they spend time with or go to for advice are very different from other fellow students who the narrators do not consider as peers. These "peers who are not peers" become the "they" from whom my narrators perceive themselves different, and have been made to feel "different." It becomes quite clear that these "peers" and "they" stand for the majority white population. Some excerpts from our conversations follow.

> The audience (for B.E.'s lecture) is pretty much the *same*...the thing that strikes me is that many people last night see themselves to be socialist or to be on the left. I think they are very exclusive...(3)

> You don't feel as if you're amongst people who are on the same level. You don't feel as if you're amongst peers. (3)

> They (narrator's parents) wanted me to know what I was up against...And at home they told me *my real values.* (1)

> In the night I said it's just another thing where we got all the hippest people in town and *they* just don't get it. (3)

> My mind doesn't flow from A to B...My friends don't follow my mode of thinking and I'll just go here and come around and I'll synthesize things altogether and if I talk to some of my friends—they'll think from A to B. (2)

> We really need to start making the connections (between L.A., Tianamen Square and Thailand incidents) because what's current to them is the pressure....We can't count on the media to do that...*they're* separating them from us, *they're* not making the connections that people can see. (3)

> I see myself different. I see myself willing to take a risk. I'm not so stuck in one thing that because it is one way it always has to be that way. (3)

> *They* have all these privileges and they're supposed to be representing *me*? No way! No way. (3)

> I don't think people got the real political overtones of what she was trying to say. Because I don't think *they* are really capable of really trying to get it. *They* were thinking—this is wrong but at the same time *they* were laughing at the humor and everything got left by the wayside...To get *them* to realize that no you would never be identified in an airport as a courier no matter what you do because you don't have the basic skin color. (3)

> Even the people who are cool or who think they are "with it" sometimes they don't—sometimes there's no real connection.... *They* don't understand how they are not understanding implicates *them* in it. (3)

> *You've* got to realize that people are different by nature and *you* shouldn't put the same people in the same category. (2)

> If you go to one of the African-American parties you say these are not the people I went to class with today. It's more laid back. It's different. (1)

> If I went to a white person I don't think they would understand. It's lack of empathy. I mean you can't be empathetic to something you haven't experienced. (1)

Just at the Border: Gonna Seep Out

The narrators have gone through particular experiences where they have been made to feel "different." Very often these incidents are not overtly racist or sexist and leave the narrators in wonder and a little unsure about this "feeling." These experiences reveal the structure of racism where the majority population treats the minority population somewhat differently from their own and in this way, makes its bias known. Some of these experiences include:

> And many times you go into the classroom and you hear these borderline racist remarks, borderline sexist remarks, it's just at the border and you know its gonna seep out. (3)

> There's this one bartender [at a local bar] and he just has this negative attitude. I'm beginning to *wonder if he's racist....* He'll give you a hard time..."Sweetheart move your butt baby." (2)

> When I was a freshman, it was just awful. Whenever there was a fight (among Black students) it was on the front page (of the college newspaper)...(1)

> *It's a feeling* in the every day or every other day or every other week incidents. But in a sense it can happen anywhere you are in the States. It's just a feeling and you just—I don't know. (3)

> Only the other night a Black student had a party and in 15 mins. the Police were in and everybody had to go...This was Friday. Saturday, the house opposite mine, white student—had a party. The police never came and the music was blaring....Everything was fine and *nobody ever said anything*...But I want my people to have the same. (1)

> I had gone home. I left on a Thursday and got back Sunday...I went to my mailbox and saw another notice saying that I'd been playing loud music and had been disruptive and that several tenants had complained....And I said *I wasn't home.* (1)

> There was this professor who said,... "just because you've good grades in other classes doesn't mean you're going to get good grades in here..." And that same quarter I came down with measles...And she said "you know *you people* always have an excuse." (1)

> No matter how multicultural a professor thinks he is, you still have stereotypes of international, or African-American, or minority students, or those who are not in the mainstream. They have their own ideas about it and I look back and smile at them when they say we're open minded and say oh yaa and I just shake my head and in the back of my mind I know what I'm dealing with. (1)

The Whole Kit and Caboodle

Having been through differential treatment on campus and out of it makes my narrators aware of *a system* (referred to as "the whole kit and caboodle" by one narrator)—one that they are forced to learn about and operate in. The awareness of a system comes with a full awareness of their own role in it and of how theirs is a separate culture. In one instance, the narrators comment on the country's health care system (which she says is not a system) reveals precisely the system that she is forced to follow.

> The health care system—there really isn't a system—its based on greed.... It's the doctors, it's the lawyers, it's the government, it's the whole kit and caboodle. Everybody is getting a little bit of people's sicknesses, illnesses and *that's sick*. (3)

> I don't believe in this picking the worst of three evils (voting for the 3 presidential candidates). I'm tired of that and I think that it plays too much *into the system*. (3)

> There's always a chance that you live double lives kind of. There's the life you live that's White American and the life that's your own culture. And you have to lead both. (1)

> You have to live two different lives and you have to learn *how to live with the system*. And it's like AAAh!... My parents stuck me in schools with white people... and they worked hard to pay for it so that I could learn to live that other life... Because *they're* not going to adjust to your lifestyle, or who you are, or what you enjoy... (1)

These recurring incidents where they are not being "understood" lead to a lot of frustration among the narrators. This exasperation has evoked reactions like:

> it's *really frightening*... they were some of the politically "open people" on campus. (3)

> So last night when I went to see this woman "B. E." it was *very very distressing*. (3)

> It's a lot of biases or let us say that, a lack of knowledge or ignorance, ignorance is the word. (2)

> There's gonna be people who don't get along, but if that happened in the Black community—my god, they'll get out their metal detectors... *you want to scream*. (1)

> ... *It made me so angry*. But I want my people to have the same. (1)

> I went to the ombudsman, he's a white male and he said she's a real good friend of mine and I really can't see her doing that. And I said *AAAAAh*! (1)

The narrators have their own way of dealing with the "kit and caboodle" (the system) which gives them a certain amount of power. This power to "escape" sustains them in this imposed system. One means of escape from the system is going home and another is to tutor students who present different perspectives, or seek friendships with international students.

> I go home because they're people I can talk to and I don't have to pay for it.... I just go home because I have friends who are a social outlet... When I'm home I'm relaxed... (1)

> I knew that they had a lot of international students here, pretty well... multi-racial atmosphere here. (2)

> I'm close to Min (Chinese), okay so related to personality and nationality—I go to Jose (Latin American) if I want to talk about a Hispanic guy, what will Yolanda say, we'll talk in Spanish.... If it's just personal advice like being African-American female, I'll call Robin... (2)

> I learn a lot about the community and how different people think. It's more than just tutoring. I gain much more from tutoring than I do from studying... To me, interaction, visual and vocal, is more important to me. (2)

Question the Whole Kit and Caboodle

The narrators feel that self-organization, collective effort, and mass mobilization may change their situation. Unless they collectively question the system (kit and caboodle) not much change can follow.

> My question is question the whole kit and caboodle... what's wrong is the way you can gain power. We've got these people in DC making decisions for us. (3)

> We need to start thinking a little bit differently... (3)

> I'm going to get people together to do something because there's no reason to be treated like that. (2)
>
> I think anything is possible. If in South Africa you can organize a national strike, in Germany a national strike, then why can't we do it here. I think that's the only way we're gonna get anything to change is if people say I'm tired of this shit and *take some power.* (3)
>
> People feel they are not participating because they are *not* participating. (3)

All themes merge and arrange themselves around one major theme—kit and caboodle—that exposes the structure of the dominant system that all the participants of the study are operating in—be it the experience of mentoring, friendships, learning to deal with the system, identifying peers that are part of the "whole kit and caboodle," or questioning that very system.

Final Thematization and Reflections

For my final thematization, I recontextualized the previous themes and focused on how the experience of their (African-American narrators) lives is structured. From this reduction, the theme that emerges is closely linked to the initial themes. A quote that best describes the final theme is: "*There's always a chance that you live double lives.*" This is a revelatory phrase that unravels the essence of the existential dilemma of my African-American female narrators. The structure of their (dual) lives is revealed and so is the dominant overarching system that forces them to lead such a life. They are being constantly told or made to feel that they are *different*, by the majority population, and they too perceive themselves *different.* But they are caught in a situation where they have to behave like "them." The *need* to lead that other life is conveyed in the following quotes:

> You have to live two different lives and you have to, *have to* learn *how to work with the system.* And it's like Ahhh...My parents stuck me in schools with white people. And I mean stuck me in there...so that I could learn to live that other life. (1)

> My mind doesn't flow from A to B... My friends don't follow my mode of thinking.... (2)
>
> There's always a chance that you live double lives kind of. There's the life you live that's White American and the life that's your own culture. And you have to lead both. (1)
>
> I think I'm different and I felt that way for a long time.... But how I'm different, I don't know. (3)

Often, the difference between the dual lives that the narrators lead, blurs and becomes indistinguishable until they do not know how different they really are from the life that they are forced to lead. Because the narrators are forced to lead a double life, they resent *and* accept their situation at the same time. Those who do not accept the authority of the dominant system, those "who say I want to be *me* across the board," usually "fall through the cracks," explicates one narrator. This duality/split between how they feel and how they are constrained to be, makes their situation in a majority institution and in the American society extremely problematic.

Therefore the oppression (in the form of racism and sexism) that induces them to "lead a double life" is perpetrated by the dominant structures of both the institution and the society. bell hooks identifies two ways in which such forms of institutional and social oppression are perpetrated: by the individuals who dominate, and "by the victims themselves who are socialized to behave in ways that make them act in complicity with the status quo" (1984, p. 37).

In Conclusion: Implications for Action

This project has opened my ears to the muted voices of black female graduate students at a majority white University in the US. A continually unveiling phenomenon of inequality and discontent in academia reveals itself. The findings of this research should also serve as an imperative to the University administration and the staff/faculty of the different departments of majority Universities to work out a plan to systematically abolish prejudice and bias against this community of students. A budget should be kept aside to work at providing adequate mentoring and financial aid to minority graduate students.

This piece of research establishes the importance of mentoring and guidance for each minority graduate student.

An appropriate strategy needs to be devised in order to meaningfully implement the recommendations and help retain minority graduate students at most institutions of higher learning in the US and ease their shock in entering a majority University. The strategy must ensure that mentoring and financial aid issues are handled by a decentralized system, probably by the separate colleges so as to prevent dealing with the needs of minorities as a homogeneous mass of people. This recommendation seeks to include other subordinated groups of students (Asian American, Hispanic American, native American etc.).

This strategy also calls for full, dedicated, faculty participation from within a department, to aid retention services. These suggestions do not ensure minority retention neither do these suggestions attempt to heal the scars of previous experiences of racism and sexism. However, if implemented, these measures would provide the incoming minority students a tolerant environment, more conducive to academic pursuit. An inability to follow this recommendation is to be guilty of, as hooks (1984) puts it, tuning out, dismissing, and silencing the voices of the minorities, to be heard only if their statements echo the "sentiments of the dominant discourse."

References

Adams, E. (1990). Benjamin Banneker honors college: Gateway to scientific and technical doctorates. *Journal of Negro Education, 59(3)*, 449–462.

Anderson, K. & Jack, D.C. (1991). Learning to listen: Interview techniques and analysis. In (Eds.) Gluck, S.B. & Patai, D. *Women's Words: The feminist practice of oral history.* (pp. 11–27). NY: Routledge.

Carter, R.T. (1990). Culture and black student success. *Educational Considerations. 18 (1).* –11.

Crow, B.K. (1981). Talking about films: A phenomenological study of film signification. In (Ed.) Deetz, S. *Phenomenology in rhetoric and communication.* (pp. 1–22). Washington D.C.: Univ. Press of America.

Garcia, S.A. & Seligsohn, H.C. (1978). Undergraduate black student retention revisited. *Educational Record. 59 (2),* 156–165.

Hale, S. (1991). Feminist method, process and criticism: Interviewing Sudanese women. In (Eds.) Gluck, S.B. & Patai, D. *Women's Words: The feminist practice of oral history.* (pp. 121–137). NY: Routledge.

hooks, b. (1984). *Feminist theory: From margin to center*. Boston: South End Press.

hooks, b. (1994) *Teaching to transgress: Education as the practice of freedom*. New York: Routledge.

Kapoor, P. (1992)Minority participation in institutions of higher learning. (unpublished).

Merleau-Ponty, M. (1962). *Phenomenology of perception*. London: Routledge & Kegan Paul.

Nelson, J. (1986). *The other side of signification: A semiotic phenomenology of televisual experience*. (dissertation).

Nelson, J. (1989). Phenomenology as feminist methodology: Explicating interviews. In (Eds.) K. Carter & C. Spitzack. *Doing research on womens communication: Perspectives on theory and method*. (pp. 221–241). Norwood: Ablex.

Nelson, J. (1989). Eyes out of your head: On televisual experience. *Critical Studies in Mass Communication. 6*. 38–403.

Olson, K. & Shopes, L. (1991). Crossing boundaries, building bridges: Doing oral history among working class women and men. In (Eds.) Gluck, S.B. & Patai, D. *Women's Words: The feminist practice of oral history*. (pp 189–204). NY: Routledge.

Patton, M.Q. (1980). *Qualitative evaluation methods*. London: Sage Publications.

Polkinghorne, D. (1983). *Methodology for the human sciences*. Albany: State University of New York Press.

Rodriguez, R. (1992). Retention programs seen moving to academic departments. *Black Issues in Higher Education*. 28–29.

St. John,. E.P. (1991). What really influences minority attendance? Sequential analysis of the high school and beyond cohort. *Research in Higher Education. 32 (2)*. 141–158.

Wallace, M. (1990). *Invisibility blues: From pop to theory*. NY: Alpine press.

5

CORPOREAL EXPLOSIONS

THE LIVED EXPERIENCES OF AFRICAN-AMERICAN GRADUATE WOMEN DURING AN EXPLOSIVE WEEK

T. Ford-Ahmed

The discourse that has been constructed in academe over the last two decades has been that of multiculturalism. Predicated on the basic assumption that people of color must be trained, educated and graduated if the U.S. is to maintain a presence in the New World Order, a culturally diverse perspective has become a discursive priority in the offices of counselors, university presidents, state boards and in a classroom in which I was a participant.

The discourse that evolved in Louisiana was the result of a controversial gubernatorial race. Following the hotly debated contest that occurred between former KKK leader David Duke and Democrat Edwin Edwards, the Louisiana Board of Regent members discussed the possibility of a required course in their institutions on race relations (Moore, 1992). Moore reports that while some scholars viewed this as solid proof that liberals had gone mad others felt that such a course would be no different from any other core requirement (p. 48). Such a course in race relations need not produce racial harmony, but it could position higher education as a major player in leading the way. Moore believes that old standards of course content, scholarship and academic quality will not be effective in leading us into the 21st century global village. He further postulates that what got us here will not take us there with the changing demographics, technology and social systems.

Background Leading to Research

Although changing the curriculum was not on the minds of the students assembled in the communication research class I attended, multiculturalism and our university's "lead" in the discourse arose as a topic of interest. Further class discussion led to agreement that our own institution's involvement in recruitment, retention and graduating minority graduate students would be a valuable study to implement. Using a scientific approach, the twenty member class launched an extensive literature review.

The literature revealed that predominantly white institutional (pwi) attempts at maximizing cultural pluralism was problematic; especially in the area of retention and graduating minority students (Elam, 1989, McCombs, 1989, Adams, 1990; Wyche & Frierson, 1990; Rodriguez 1992).

The conclusions drawn from the studies usually recommended some type of assistance in the form of monetary support or early intervention of counselors in high school and at the undergraduate level. These were implied as determinants of retention that led to successful completion of terminal degrees offered by majority institutions (Carter, 1990; St. John, 1991; July, 1989).

The class subsequently distributed a questionnaire to nearly 100 Black and Hispanic graduate students enrolled in the university. It revealed the following: Some students had faculty and academic advisors. Others did not. Some were satisfied and others were dissatisfied with their life in the institution, but everyone continued their graduate education. Some were members of campus organizations, while others had no involvement at all. What did it all mean in relation to the students' lived experiences, those where thoughts, emotion and values remain intact (Langellier & Hall, 1989)? A different framing of the issues, one that truly inquired about the daily routine and interactions of minority graduate student life, had to be explored.

When six members from the class found themselves together in another course the following semester, a qualitative study was undertaken in an attempt to understand the range and specificity of human experiences. Collectively 'meaning' not 'measure' would be sought (Giorgi, 1966 in Crow, 1981) from the phenomenon of minority graduate experiences at the institution in which we were enrolled. (A predominantly white university of nearly 20,000 students situated in the midwest.)

Toward this end, members of the newly formed group chose partners to interview a variety of ethnic and racially diverse students found in the margins of a majority culture institution.

Another woman of color and I, chose to talk to African-American female graduate students enrolled in the University's College of Communications. My associate talked to women working toward a masters degree and I spoke with doctoral students. Through a series of in-depth interviews and the personal narratives of these women we hoped to gain insight regarding an institutionalized discourse predicated on a white male/white female experience.

This report draws on the experiences of three African-American women Ph.D. students. Its purpose is to explore how their experiences in a majority institution are expressed and how the major themes of temporality, corporeality, spatiality, and relationality are organized and defined. The interviews took place during the week of the announcement of the verdict that acquitted police officers in Los Angeles of the brutal beating of Rodney King, a black male motorist who was stopped by the officers following a high-speed chase on a Los Angeles freeway.

The verdict and its aftermath were prevalent discursive structures within which the participants and myself were situated. In the small town in which our college was located, a crowd of between three and five hundred gathered at the center of campus to express their outrage over the "not" guilty verdict the day prior to the interviews. A photograph of Black students and faculty clinging to one another and crying appeared in the school newspaper. A sense of confusion, anger and helplessness permeated the crowd when it was decided that a request be made that the college president and the mayor send a letter of support to the mayor of Los Angeles.

This conscious and conflicted positioning in the larger public discourse reveals the political significance of the three Ph.D. students' personal everyday experiences and provides the contextual backdrop against which this research may be viewed.

Methodology

Phenomenology as a research method takes each experience in its own right as it shows itself and as one is conscious of it. This consciousness of experience occurs in the body; the basic mode of being in the world. Without a situational context for conscious experience neither origin or organ exist (Stewart & Mickunas, 1990).

Phenomenolgy holds that to exist is to be in the world with others, to be influenced by others, to be constitutively involved with the phenomenon as a participant and an observer. It encompasses intuitive reasoning which involves an abductive situational logic bringing attention to once invisible issues (Nelson, 1989). This additional insight can compliment traditionally positivist research. This intersubjectivity, as it is called in existential phenomenology, is a do-able and an appropriate method for women researching women's experiences (Langellier & Hall, 1989). It is especially appropriate for black women doing research with other black women, for it is their voice—their narrative—that gives rise to their empowerment (Bell-Scott in Wiley, 1993). By bracketing or setting aside presuppositions and assumptions of my participants (the narrators) the essence of their experiences emerge.

The first two narrators were easy to locate within the College of Communications. The first volunteered when she learned of the study and a second was referred by a classmate. Both women were midway through their doctoral programs. One was married with one child while the other was single without children. In order to find a third African-American female Ph.D. student I had to move outside of the Communication College into the College of Education. There a divorcee with one child (who was completing her dissertation) was located. She added another dimension of experience to the study.

The night following the gathering on campus, the two tools necessary for in-depth interviews were checked and re-checked: the tape recorder and the topical protocol. However, the next morning I rushed to meet my first narrator without the protocol of questions. I was panic stricken. I needn't have worried however, for my interviewee had a variety of issues she wished to discuss, particularly the verdict relating to the Rodney King beating. This case required a more informal conversational approach (Patton, 1990). As

I listened to my narrator the panic subsided. I found that I was able to propose relevant questions that put us on a track that provided rich descriptions. The larger discourse predicated on the Simi Valley verdict opened a flood gate of graduate school experiences and specific situations that the graduate students willingly shared. All three interviews were completed and the texts transcribed within the next three days.

After transcribing the interviews the phenomenological steps of thematization, reduction and interpretation were followed (Nelson, 1989). Certain statements were grouped into initial themes and connected to other utterances within the participants' narratives. Once the themes were identified the second step in the methodology was performed.

Reduction occurs when important words and phrases reach out to you. It refers to reducing complex problems to their basic elements by narrowing one's attention to what is absolutely essential in the problems (Stewart & Mickunas, 1990). Once these have been identified, it is then possible to connect them to other utterances within the participant's narrative and correlate them to the phrases of others interviewed (Nelson, 1989). Husserl referred to this step as the "epoche," meaning to suspend judgement, or bracketing presuppositions about the world so that the phenomenon under investigation will not be laden by historically generated value norms (Lanigan, 1979).

The third and final step in the methodology is interpretation (hermeneutics). Through awareness of the actions and speech acts of the narrators, meaning can be derived. Through acute perception understanding (verstehen) can be gained (Polkinghorne, 1983). This is the time of careful reflection of the particpants' experiences. It is the most difficult process of the methodology because, at this point, the interviewer must be totally responsible to the interviewee (Borland, 1991). The validity of this step rests on the assumption that we can understand each other's meaning, since we all share a similar life-world (lebenswelt).

Initial Themes

Following the transcription of the three taped interviews into a format, I realized that the style I had chosen—adapted from Stevick

(1973)—placed my interviewees narration in the center of the page and the meanings that emerged to one side of the page. For example Moja's (Swahili for interviewee number one) narration was transcribed in the following manner:

Reflections (meaning)	Brief Transcript from 1st Interview
	(Sitting down to begin the interview with Moja [M].) Describe your graduate experience. What has it been like?
Relevance questioned. Self & "other" experiences a collapse (i.e., I & you). Desires to be in and w/o the structure.	**M. Sometimes I wonder 'why am I here?' I could be doing something else. Something more meaningful. Part of it probably has a whole lot to do with me...I know I I get into, you get out of it what you put in to it.**

Classical sociological theorists and some woman scholars might suggest that this format for transcribing the audiotapes was a natural thing for me to do; that it is indicative of the African-American experience and a 'developed' way of seeing reality. hooks (1984) for example, explains that black Americans have experienced living on the edges of towns, across the tracks and in the margins; as being "a part of the whole but outside the main body" (preface). Likewise, Collins (1991) describes this positioning as the woman outsider or the outsider within. This culturally determined way of looking from the outside in and from the inside out can also strengthen and provide solidarity among black women. hooks (1990) explains that women must distinguish between imposed marginality and marginality *chosen* as an act of resistance.

When the marginally noted reflections were clustered and co-related to the other two Ph.D. students' transcribed texts, the first step of the methodology was performed: that of thematizing. The themes that emerged from Moja, Mbili, and Tatu's texts were overwhelmingly corporeally based. They revealed:

a) the body as threatened (overworked-tired-helpless)
b) a body in conflict with negative/positive roles
c) a relief seeking body
d) an enabled body.

To further clarify the thematization process of the methodology, an excerpt from Mbili's narrative is explicated below. (The narrative has been translated into summary statements and checked to see that the sense has been maintained.) Mbili is the Swahili word for the number 2; it signifies the second narrator.

Reflections-1st reading	Transcription from 2nd Interview
	(Mbili [Mb] was writing when I sat down at the table to begin the interview)
	What are you doing?
	Mb. Writing an article.
	What about?
	Mb. Reflecting on my experience this week. It's been a weird, intense week.
	Tell me about it.
Rodney gets the face here (becomes the signifier) although he wasn't on trial. Police remain faceless. (Blameless?) *Experience as threatening*	**Mb. Since the Rodney King verdict, the day after and all that's transpired here, just conversations I had with people. Particularly one professor and a couple of students telling me about incidents of being followed by police down here. It probably happened to almost every Black man down here. If not [here] it's happened to them in their home town. Being followed just because they were, they were black. Out on these roads or on foot. One guy said he was followed on foot and circled by four cop cars going home from town. *It happens everywhere and all the time.***
	Now some students that I've talked to have indicated that they have done well here, some have said they've done poorly. What's been your experience?
(Metastatement) Self assessment based on some criteria, then edit & reassesses. Reassessment	**Mb. I haven't been a model student. I shouldn't say that. When I've had the opportunity to apply myself I've done really well. Every year. Every year except for this one, I've worked and I've always been burning the**

Conflict subject positioning	**candle at both ends. I've found it very difficult. [My child] is a lot more self-sufficient now but I found it very difficult my first two years. Being a mother, a wife, a student, and a worker. The job I had... made me just want to throw up my hands. And they have a lot of quotas you have to meet. I felt a lot of pressure from that part.... my main focus to tell you the truth was I didn't see, and I still don't see that [employer] reaches out to Blacks. And I really wanted to make it known to Blacks that this is an option for you.**

(The following discusses difficult times in Mbili's program)

Not willing to give up	**Mb. I weighed everything and I thought God, you've put this much time into it. Why drop out? Would you ever come back?**
	Describe an incident that even made you contemplate it. Dropping out of school, I mean.
Overwhelmed by tasks *Need for relief* *Evaluating price* *Note: part of "stuff on head"*	**Mb. Knowing I was going into the year in a deficit with all this stuff on my head. Like I said, starting the year knowing that by the 4th week I had to have papers done from the previous quarter or it would threaten by being here. I would think is it worth it? Is it worth me going crazy? I'll end up doing it again this quarter, 24–7 for like 2 weeks, being into my work. Which means letting my family go. And which is really hard. Just letting the house go. Which means letting food go.**

Following this procedure through eighty-two pages of transcribed text from the three students, clustering and correlating the marginal notes; the themes of the threatened, helpless, conflicted, and enabled body are revealed.

The *threatened body* emerges from Mbili's narration. This body is experienced through the sense of others, signified by the danger black men face on the streets everywhere. This same sense of connectedness to 'other' was often expressed. When direct questions were proposed to Mbili, she often answered in 'we' terms and sometimes in 'he' terms indicating her ability to totally transcend or leave her own body to become one with the community and/or her spouse.

Her *helpless body "throws up hands,"* and generally feels incapable when her other self, expressed through the black male, is encircled by four cops. She also expresses the time-lessness of the phenomenon. Merleau-Ponty (1968) points out that linear time does not exist. Time cannot be differentiated from the past, present, or future. This ideology is apparent in Mbili's life-world where she finds the black male dilemma happening *"...all the time."* It also exists in boundary-less space for it happens *'everywhere.'*

The *conflicted body* is expressed in revelatory phrases. For example it carries a lot of *"stuff on my head"* and is concretely expressed as being *"difficult...[to be] a mother, a wife, a student, and a worker."*

Experiences of the *relief seeking body* are revealed through gestures of unexpected crying when she thought talk would be enough. She states in one section of the narrative (not reported above) that during her first year of studies she went into one of her professors offices *"and I started talking and the next thing I know I'm just crying...letting it all out."*

The *enabled body* is at rest when *"doing something culturally specific"* as in the case of one of the jobs she performed coordinating activities for other students, or finishing three incompletes while carrying her regular courseload.

Reduction

The themes themselves are then connected and co-related in the second step of the methodology. Van Manen (1990) refers to this step as 'textual labor.' An appropriate metaphor for describing the 'job' one does when engaging the transcribed text once again. When the three narratives were compared again, the following theme emerged quickly: that of a fragmented phenomenal body.

"The Fragmented Phenomenal Body"

In the case of Moja, not only was the physical body torn from itself in revelatory phrases but, so was the mental body. This mutilation of the psycho-physical self rattled the spirit of these women resulting in burdens of self-doubt. Feminist scholar hooks (1984) argues that women have often been deprived of intellectual development and so they feel insecure about intellectual work and thus may question its relevance. Moja certainly reiterates this insecurity when she states that:

> *I've learned how to get through courses, but I don't know how much it's getting in here (points to her head). You know because I think you can, you can learn how to get through courses, you can learn how to make the grades and that becomes such a focal point sometimes. You just have to make the grades and I mean that I haven't internalized some of the things that I should have and I could have because I was concentrating more on just making the grades, and getting out of the class and so you know, that's why I say a lot of it is on me.*

Moja has a "lot on [her]" similar to Mbili who began her year "in a deficit with all this stuff on my head." Both appear to have overlooked some important things in favor of the mundane (i.e. making grades.) For Mbili too, graduate work is no comparison to important things as food, family, and home. Moja's political awareness during the week of "the verdict" has caused her to ponder the relevance of earning a degree. She asks herself:

> *Why am I here? (snicker) I could be doing something else. Something more meaningful. Part of it probably has whole lot to do with me, but I think a lot of my educational experience has not been that meaningful.*

However, she later reveals through a slip of the tongue that "I know I get in-to" and changes it to "You get out of it what you put into it." It's as though her 'self' and her 'other' (as in the case of Mbili) intersubjectively, experience a collapse. For while she wishes to get *in*- to the structure she also wishes to be with-*out*.

Mbili's meta-statement regarding education is similar. She admits that she has *"not been a model student"* and then admonishes herself with *"I shouldn't say that! When I've had the opportunity to apply myself, I've done really well."* She later admits that her overworked body has prevented her from applying herself the way the system would have her apply herself. For these two women the structure has collapsed leaving them with feelings that the self is capable but, perhaps the institutional requirements are not worth their considerable effort.

Evidence of the fragmented phenomenal body is expressed in graphic terms by Tatu (narrator number 3) whose involvement in her dissertation preparation once caused her to forget to pick up her child from school. Her guilt leads her to question her 'other' about self-mutilation as well as the relevancy of a degree.

> *My God what kind of mother am I? Should I blow my fucking brains out or what? How can I get so involved that I forget about my only child. It's not like at this age I'm going to have anymore... Sometimes I think this (graduate study) just isn't going to help me at all. May add a few more pennies to my pay check but (laugh). I suppose I could (laugh) join the brothers and sisters in the hood and help kick some boo-day. At this point in time it seems just about as important and probably a lot more satisfying (laughter).*

Mbili also seeks satisfaction for 'self' although she often "... *holds herself up to something that's not achievable... [and] sometimes [feels] very inadequate.*" This is especially evident in the admiration she holds for her mother who *"did it all"* (cooked, kept shiny floors and took the kids to cub scouts.) A type of self-mutilation also occurs for the very act of trying to live up to her mother's model of standards *"just blows [her] mind"* and creates inner conflict. The little things like washing-not washing dishes gets on her nerves. So do empty cupboards. She would like for those things to be taken care of and when she is unable, they still stay with her: *"I'm always thinking, I don't know, little things... coordinating stuff... it's the little things."* The little things manifest themselves in very big ways. They cause her to view the accomplishments of others as positive and her own as negative. However she knows, *I'm not rotten... I'm a very optimistic person... I'm capable... I can, I can, I can wash the dishes, I can cook, I can do all those things at the same time.*

Her preconscious argues with the conscious body and reasons that she *"simply holds [her]self up to something that's not achievable."* Mbili later states (in relation to a summer assistantship that went bad): *"Now my back's up against the wall."* She also describes an incident in which she contemplated leaving school.

> *The very beginning of this year I was going into the year in a deficit with all this stuff on my head. Knowing my fourth week of school I had to have papers done from the previous quarter or it would threaten, you know my being here. I would think is it worth it? Is it worth my going crazy?*

Earlier in Mbili narration she states that she just wants to throw up her hands; and at other times she has all this stuff on her head while burning candles at both ends. Tatu joins this corporeal dismemberment. She states in relationship to finding childcare assistance she could afford some twenty miles away from campus that:

> *After I pick up (child) and spend some quality time, it's time for me to go to the library. All my friends are at the library too so-o-o here I am shooting back across town at midnight sometimes.... You know I can't believe I put myself through the wringer like that.*

The fundamental existential theme of corporeality is heightened in some instances by the past/present of temporality, thus producing powerful images. For example the head—thought of as the seat of control—is often out of control. So much so that the body cannot handle all of the activity. As experienced by these women, it is on overload. No longer can task-performing hands function, for they are tossed into the air. Hands that are in the air cannot wash dishes, perform a job, prepare a paper, or turn pages of a book. The present body is immobilized by either being pinned to a wall, weighted down by 'stuff' or squeezed dry after being forced through a wringer. It is further snuffed out by the fissure of fire igniting both ends and burning until it is a mere illusion of its once capable self. For these students, relief is sought through a body bonded by a variety of intra- and interpersonal communication strategies.

"The Relief Seeking Body"

Nelson (1989) posits that because women experience and express a world differently that they may experience/express an entirely different world (p. 226). The difference is apparent in the expression of African-American women who experience a mental body imploded as well as exploded. For them the fundamental three R's of relief, release, and respite are a dire necessity. It is often found in talk, in crying, escapist adventures or simply in being home with family.

Tatu attempts to flee. She phones home to say "Mom...I just gotta get away from this for a while. I got to get away from here...." After a conversation revolving around metatalk she is eventually soothed by her mother's talk. "It *calms me down*," she states and further confides:

> *There were times this week when I couldn't focus on my studies or anything else and I'd grab the most off beat book off the shelf I could find and start reading with a vengeance. It's as though I'm looking for something false and sordid hidden in the text. Or I'll find myself staring at the TV and viciously criticizing some show that I ordinarily wouldn't watch. Anything, anything as long as no scholarship is involved. You know academic texts, buzz words. I mean it could have been anything....*

Moja explains that she shares an office with a classmate and "*when it gets to be too much I can turn around and dump on him... he listens.*" Moja also has a professor who talks to her when she asks questions. Although it is not personal talk it apparently soothes her. She expresses it this way:

> *(Smiling) I really like Dr. (———). He, um has two habits that (snicker). One, if you ask him a question, he can answer a question for an hour you know. And his other thing is, his motto seems to be never use a small word if a big one will do. He's funny, but I really like him.*

Mbili admits that she has found herself at night "just crying." She also recounts another incident with a black woman professor.

> *...I went into Dr. (———)'s office and I started to talk to her and the next thing you know I'm just like I said, I'm crying. And I definitely don't cry in front of other people....I don't think I'm a soft person....*

This is not the social model of self she wishes to project but yet, her preconscious body is given to fits of crying anyway.

The narrators are engaged in a search for some-one or some-thing to reintegrate themselves; to serve as insulators against their environment. While one peruses media for evidence that the system she wishes to join is value-less, meaning-less, the others seek support from anyone operating within the system.

Interpretation

In this final phase an attempt is made to make sense of the reduction and to make it intelligible to others. As a social endeavor it "is dependent on the accomplishment of sense-making within the realm of analysis, insofar as it may find its place within the social life of the very society it seeks to know" (Silvers, 1982, p. 232). With this in mind the fragmented cognitive and physical body of the narrators are the result of the pressure and demands imposed by a structure of a system outside. It is difficult to manage and negotiate a system from the outside. It is especially troublesome for African-American women who must also struggle with the oppressive forces of both racism and sexism while maintaining a household and a job (hooks & West, 1991).

Economic deprivation bears a special significance to African-American graduate women also, for they are most likely to be the last considered for research assistantships (Kahn & Robins, 1985). While research data shows that students who receive these type of grants are more likely to persist in completing their graduate programs, blacks often use the money to pay their tuition (DePalma, 1992). Michele Wallace has noted that "financial ruin, ignorance and despair" form the same attachment to African-American women as trained pets in need of food and water (Wallace, 1990).

The resulting combination of social-economic deprivation and the pressure/demands of the system produces self-doubt and stress among the lived bodies of these students that are difficult to balance. Only one narrator expressed satisfaction or pleasure in the structure, and that was when she was doing cultural specific things for students like herself. Otherwise, her body was as her sisters: caught in a type of frenetic energy that simply places so much on one's head a body cannot keep pace. A malfunctioning cybernation—without feedback—renders the spirit questioning its can do-ness.

The announcement of the verdict that freed the officers of beating Rodney King undoubtedly, informed this study. The narrators realized during this week how out of control the system tended to make them feel: beaten and disoriented, much like the vision of Rodney

King in the amateur videotape of his arrest. Perhaps they felt as did New York Representative Floyd Flake who uttered, "When Rodney King was on the ground getting beat, we were all on the ground getting beat" (Wall, 1992, p. 10). A spiritual loss of one's-self in a fragmented duality of the head and body was rendered a cultural version by Tatu when when she uttered in a folksy dialect: "If I evah had any doubt 'bout positionality befo' it was sho nuff made clear this week."

This statement bears testimony to marginality when one feels there is an absence of real choice. That week, I believe we questioned ours in the academy.

References

Adams, E. (1990). Benjamin Banneker Honors College: Gateway to scientific and technical doctorates. *Journal of Negro Education* 59(3), 449–462.

Atwood, G.E. & Stolorow, R. D. (1984). *Structures of subjectivity: Explorations in psychoanalytic phenomenology.* Hillsdale, NJ: Lawrence Erlbaum Associate.

Borland, K. (1991). Interpretive Conflict. In S.B. Gluck & D. Patai (Eds.) *Women's words: the feminist practice of oral history.* p 63–75. New York: Routledge.

Bradley, M. (1993). The lesson of Rodney King, In H.K. Madhubuti (Ed.). Why L.A. happened. Chicago, IL: Third World Press.

Carter, R. T. (1990). Culture & Black students success. *Education considerations.* 18(1), 7–11.

Collins, P. H. (1991). *Black feminist thought.* New York: Routledge.

Crow, B. (1981). Talking about films: A phenomenological study of film signification. In S. Deetz (Ed.). *Phenomenology in rhetoric & communication.* Wash., DC: University Press of America.

DePalma, A. (1992, April). "As Black PhD's taper off, aid for foreigner assailed." *New York Times* p. B26.

Elam, J.C. (1989). The Mentor-protege relationship: Its impact on blacks in predominantly white institutions. *Blacks in higher education: Overcoming the odds.* Athens: Ohio University.

hooks, b. (1984). *Feminist theory from margin to center.* Boston, MA: South End Press.

———. (1990). *Yearning: Race, gender, and cultural politics.* Boston: South End.

———. & West C. (1991). *Breaking bread: Insurgent black intellectual life.* Boston MA: South End Press.

Hyde, M.J. (1980). The experience of anxiety: A phenomenological investigation. *The Quarterly Journal of Speech,* 66(3), 140–154.

July, F. M. (1988). R*ecruitement and retention of black students in baccalaureate nursing programs: An application of the marketing process on higher education.* Unpublished doctoral dissertation. Georgia State University, GA.

Kahn, E.D. & Robbins, L. (1985). Social-psychological issues in sex discrimination. *Journal of Social Issues*, 41(4), 133–134.

Kapoor, P. (1992). *A chance of double lives: Study of black female graduate experience.* Paper presented at the Annual Midwest Pop Culture Association and Midwest Cultural Association, Indianapolis, IN.

Langellier, K. M. & Hall, D. L. (1989). Interviewing women. In K. Carter & C. Spitzack (Eds.). *Doing research on women's communication perspective on theory and method.* New Jersey: Ablex.

Lanigan, R. L. (1979). The phenomenology of human communication. *Philosophy Today*, 23(i), 3–15.

Merleau-Ponty, M. (1968). *The prose of the world.* In C. Leford (Ed.). Evanston, IL: Humanities Press.

McCombs, H. G. (1989). The dynamics and impacts of affirmative action progress on higher education, the curriculum, and black women. *Sex Roles.* 127–144.

Moore, W. E. (1992, May). Race relations in academia. *Black issues in higher education.* p., 48.

Nelson, J. (1989). Phenomenology as a feminist methodology: Explicating interview. In K. Carter & C. Spitzack (Eds.). *Doing research on women's communication perspective on theory and method.* New Jersey: Ablex.

Orbe, M. (1993). *"Remember its always whites ball": A phenomenological inquiry into the African-American male experience.* Unpublished doctoral dissertation, Ohio University, Athens, OH.

Patton, M. Q. (1990). *Qualitative evaluation and research methods.* (2nd ed.). Newbury Park, CA: Sage Publications.

Polkinghorne, D. (1983). *Methodology of the human sciences, systems of inquiry.* Albany: State University of New York Press.

Rodriguez, R. (1992, February). Retention programs seen moving to academic departments. *Black issues in higher education,* p. 28–29.

Stevick, E. L. (1971). Experience of Anger. *Duquesne studies in phenomenological psychology.* PA: Duquesne University.

Silvers, R. J. (1982). A silence within phenomenology. In V. Darroch & R. J. Silvers (Ed.). *Interpretive human studies.* Washington, DC: University Press of America.

Stewart, D. & Mickunas, A. (1990). *Exploring phenomenology.* (2nd ed.). Athens: Ohio University Press.

St. John, E. P. (1991). What really influences minority attendance? Sequential analysis of the high school and beyond cohort. *Research in higher education* 32 (2), 141–158.

Van Manen, M. (1990). *Researching Lived Experience Human Science for an Action Sensitive Pedagogy.* New York: State University of New York Press.

Van Sertima, I. (1993). *African presence in America before Columbus.* Kwanzaa guest lecture. Athens: Ohio University.

Wallace, M. (1990) *Invisibility Blues from Pop to Theory*. New York: Verso.

Walls, B. (1992). Rodney King rebellion. Chicago, IL: African American Images.

Wiley III, E. (1993 May). Intellectual pursuits, examining the role of black thinkers in a contemporary world. *Black Issues in Higher Education*, p. 12–15.

Wyche, J. J. & Frierson, H. T. (1990). Minorities at majority institutions. *Science* 229(4972), 989–991.

SISTUHS BREAKING DOWN BARRIERS: BLACK WOMEN EXPERIENCE CORPORATE AMERICA

6

SHE WORKS HARD FOR HER MONEY

THE EXPERIENCES OF AFRICAN-AMERICAN WOMEN IN THE WORKPLACE

Pamela Y. Dykes

It's not what you know, it's who you know.

The above is a common phrase which alludes to the belief that one does not get in the door, become successful and make it to the top without the help of someone else. In professional and business circles, this person who helps others is called a mentor. In recent years, both popular and academic literature has drawn attention to the benefits that mentoring relationships can offer proteges, mentors and organizations (Carbone, 1992; Ragins & Cotton, 1991; Burke, Kram,1983; McKeen & McKenna, 1989, 1990; Thomas, 1989; Tepper, 1995). Research indicates that mentorship is related to career progress, organizational influence and advancement in organizations (Ragins & Cotton, 1991). According to Thomas (1993), mentor-protege relationships can be critical to helping a junior staffer meet key requirements for career advancement. Although research on mentor relationships is growing, the body of findings about mentoring is still rather limited (Burke, McKeen & McKenna, 1990).

Some scholars suggest that these developmental relationships,— another way to describe mentoring,—are particularly important to women and minorities. For members of marginalized groups who might face race or gender related obstacles to advancement in organizations, mentors serve as either advocates or buffers in certain sensitive situations (Ragins & Cotton, 1991). Although mentoring relationships have been the focus of recent studies, none of those research efforts has been devoted to studying the effects that such developmental relationships have on African-American men and women.

Organizational scholars have taken a few individuals, usually white males, and used them as the norm for their research (Nkomo, 1989). Only recently have we begun to study the experiences of women in management, and even this body of literature focuses mainly on white women (Nkomo, 1989). We have amassed a great deal of knowledge about a limited number of groups, yet we treat our theories as if they are universal (Nkomo, 1989). Given how much change is taking place in our culture and in organizations, especially with respect to ethnic and gender diversity, it seems propitious to investigate how women of color develop relationships with mentors.

Background of Study

The terms mentoring and developmental relationships were mentioned in the introduction of this chapter to describe the type of relationships on which I wish to focus. However, the concept of mentoring has been described and defined by organizational scholars in many different ways, which is why it is necessary to discuss and define what mentoring is and how it will be used in this chapter. This definition will serve as the lens to focus the reader on the key concepts related to mentoring and how this term will be used in relation to the research.

Mentoring can be best defined by combining the definitions of several organizational scholars. Collins (1989) defines mentoring as a one-on-one relationship between a more experienced person and an inexperienced person. Bolton expands on this concept to describe further what a mentor does, which is to provide guidance and support to help develop the novice in many different ways. In addition, Thomas (1993) contends that in a mentoring relationship the senior employee provides the junior employee with highly diverse support. The combination of all of these definitions would be the best way to define mentoring.

Although much has been written in scholarly journals and popular magazines, what do we really know about mentoring? First, we know that the mentor plays a crucial role in the development of newer employees, and studies also suggest that these mentoring relationships are beneficial to the mentors as well. Moreover, research indicates that most successful managers are also successful mentors to others (Burke & McKeen, 1990). According to Burke and McKeen, there are several professions in which one historically has learned the trade from mentors (e.g., athletic coaching, university teaching, medicine and various artistic forms). Writings by many scholars describe the type of support a mentor provides (Bullis & Bach, 1989; Thomas, 1989; Shapiro, 1978). Thomas and Kram (1988) state that the type of instrumental career support that a mentor supplies includes advocacy for promotions, performance feedback, coaching, protection, and challenging work assignments. Finally, studies have begun to look at how mentoring relationships are developed and the various types of mentor protege relationships.

Types of mentoring

Although scholars have suggested many ways to classify developmental relationships, these relationships usually are defined as formal mentoring or informal mentoring. Formal mentoring is a relationship encouraged in some way by the company, such as the relationship between supervisor and someone who works for him/her, or a relationship that develops through a formal mentoring program in which junior employees are arbitrarily teamed up with senior employees. Informal mentoring is a relationship established between a senior employee and a junior employee to enhance the development of the less tenured person; this relationship develops naturally between the two individuals without any encouragement or interference from the company.

Even though both types of mentoring relationships have had positive results, research has shown that the most successful of the two is the informal developmental relationship (Thomas, 1989; Burke, McKeen & McKenna, 1990). Such developmental relationships are now thought to be so effective to management and the career development of employees that companies are beginning to implement formal mentoring programs with the intent of fostering such informal mentoring relationships among their employees (Burke, McKeen & McKenna, 1990). The design of these programs has been influenced by published empirical research and personal anecdotes of informal mentoring relationships in a variety of organizations.

Once the importance of mentoring had been established, a large body of research began to emerge concerning the effects of gender on mentoring (Burke, McKeen & McKenna, 1990). For historical reasons most mentors are men. And while mentors have been identified as an important factor in the success of men, studies suggest that mentors might be even more critical to the career success of women (Burke, McKeen & McKenna, 1990); yet, women are likely to have a more difficult time finding mentors (Burke, McKeen & McKenna, 1990). One explanation of women's inability to find mentors is the shortage of women occupying high organizational ranks. However, according to the previous studies (Burke, et.al, 1990; Thomas, 1989), there are also perceived gender differences which make it complicated for women to develop mentoring relationships with men.

Burke (1990) suggests that the reason for women's inability to find mentors is that there are barriers which prevent women from developing cross-gender relationships. One such barrier is that the pair must manage the closeness of the internal relationship as well as the perceptions of their relationship by outsiders. Some contend that women bring a unique set of competencies and needs to the relationship which men are not equipped to address. Whether the above examples are accurate or not is less important than the fact that the individuals might internalize stereotypical gender perceptions that can create barriers between men and women and prevent them from developing mentoring relationships.

These barriers to developing a relationship become further complicated, particularly for African-American women, when race is added to the gender problems. Thomas (1989) states that minorities and women often face barriers to developing these types of relationships. He asserts that the barriers to cross-race developmental relationships can be attributed to a number of racial taboos which have an adverse affect on the way people interact in the workplace. He contends that an organization is the seat of irrational life and that in the United States feelings of racial identity powerfully shape unconscious fantasies and fears (Thomas, 1989). Just as a superior and subordinate can enact the unconsciously experienced dynamics of a parent and a child, whites and blacks can enact the history of race relations, with all its difficulty and promise, in their everyday interactions, in the microdynamics of supervision and mentoring (Thomas, 1989). One might assume that a logical solution to the above barriers and the deleterious effects of racial taboos would be for African-American men and women to mentor each other. The assumption that mentoring between and among African-American men and women would naturally occur is based on the historical context in which African-American men and women have been partners in many crucial respects.

Historically, African-American culture was built on a foundation of strong kinship and community ties that can be traced back to African origins (Hopson & Hopson, 1994). There was a guiding principle of group survival that put above all else the preservation of the collectivity (the community). That alliance was tested first by the cruelties and enforced separations of slavery, later by racism, economic struggles, and misguided social welfare policies (Hopson & Hopson, 1994). Despite these obstacles, the love and loyalty within so many African-American families and communities endured, becoming the mainstay of their existence in a hostile world (Hopson & Hopson, 1994). Until the 1950s, these strong marital and community relationships prevailed (Reynolds, 1994). In the 1950s, approximately 75 percent of African-American households were headed by married couples (Long, 1995). Now the idea of a strong relationship based community has been replaced in many instances by hostility between the genders (Reynolds, 1994). One of the factors that might be affecting marital relationships between African-American men and women is that there is a perceived view that African-American women have more job opportunities than African-American men (Davis & Watson, 1982).

As noted by Gaiter (1994), some African-American men resent that African-American women today have more job opportunities than they do. According to Wynter, African-American women outnumber men almost two to one in the workplace and the numbers are rising (1994). These feelings of resentment have led to the popularity of several myths among African-American men that apparently explain why African-American women are getting ahead. One such myth is that African-American women, unlike African-American men, have been aided by white men. For example, there is a feeling among many African-American males that African-American women succeed because white men prefer working with African-American females (Gaiter, 1994).

The subtext to this myth is that the attitudes and behaviors that abet women in the workplace, such as assertiveness and confidence, are looked upon negatively when African-American men display them (Wynter, 1994). Ambitious, direct and assertive Black males are often seen by white supervisors as aggressive, suspicious and arrogant, and therefore as harder to work with (Roberts, 1994). In short, this myth promotes the arguable view that African-American women are seen as more compliant and easier to get along with in the workplace.

Also, according to Davis and Watson (1982), African-American men hold to the myth that the progress of African-American women in corporations is related to the fact that they are considered a two for one deal. That is, hiring an African-American woman doubly fulfills the company's need to have more members of under-represented groups. Understandably, most C.E.Os would not admit to this as a reason for the success of African-American women, preferring to maintain that jobs and promotions are granted solely on merit. Ultimately, the negative views African-American men hold about African-American women, which can only be reinforced by such workplace myths, inevitably must affect negatively the once strong relationships between African-American men and women.

Unfortunately, African-American women experience a double whammy in the labor-force. A double whammy is the effect of racism and gender discrimination that African-American women face because they are members of two minority groups. This also serves to separate African-American women from both white women and African-American men (Wynter, 1994). According to Ella Bell (1994), African-American women often feel that they have the support of neither African-American men nor white women within organizations, leaving African-American women feeling isolated in the workplace. So although African-American women have had some successes in the work-force, even their achievements seem to have negative repercussions. These repercussions are especially evident in African-American women's relationships with co-workers, particularly African-American male co-workers.

In comparison to their male counterparts, more African-American women over the last twenty years began to attend college. This trend is even more obvious now as Reynolds (1994) observes that, today, African-American women outpace African-American men educationally. For every one hundred African-American women who complete their college education, only sixty-seven African-American men get college degrees (1994). This educational gap between men and women carries over into the workplace, as African-American men often lack the necessary skills to compete effectively with African-American women.

Problem Statement and Research Questions

As we approach the 21st century, the growing presence of African-American men and women is bound to influence the American corporation (Davis & Watson, 1982). It is now recognized that despite the successes that African Americans have made in the work place since the 1960s, racial inequalities still persist (Hacker, 1995). Furthermore, sustained interracial contact occurs primarily in the workplace, as most Americans live in homogeneous communities with little social interaction across racial lines. Organizational researchers' inattention to the dynamics of intra-racial work-centered relationships has impeded our understanding of the influence of race on organizational processes and the problem of managing diversity in the workplace (Thomas, 1993).

Given the increasing numbers of African Americans in the workforce, the evidence of ill-will between African-American men and women, and the failure of the organizational communication literature to address the African-American experience and problems, this study seeks to answer two questions: How do African-American women understand mentoring within the corporate environment? What internal and external forces hinder mentoring relationships between African-American men and women?

As more African Americans enter the managerial ranks in corporations, we must seek answers to these questions. As long as there seems to be feelings of resentment and competition between African-American men and women within corporations, no one will benefit. African-American men and women need to find ways to improve their communication in order to foster better developmental relationships with each other in the workplace.

Methodology

Phenomenological inquiry, the systematic study of human lived experience, is the approach this study will take. The aim of phenomenology is to translate lived experience into textual expression. The text, in turn, becomes a site of reflective re-living and reflective appropriation (Van Manen, 1990). Ideally, phenomenology reconstructs evocative description of human actions, behaviors, intentions and experiences as we encounter them in real life (Van Manen, 1990). Moreover, phenomenology provides a forum for the otherwise muted voices of society to articulate their lived experiences from their own perspective.

This interpretive study is phenomenological in nature because of its attention to the lived experiences of African Americans. The unmuting of African Americans' voices in an organizational setting offers an opportunity for them to describe the experiences of minorities in the workplace. What this analysis seeks to achieve is an understanding of African Americans' lived experiences in organizations by analyzing interviews to determine the codes and concepts which animate and inform their communication.

Given this study's phenomenological nature, thematization is the primary method of analysis. Themes are defined for this study as a recurrence of the same meanings or ideas throughout the interviews; themes are a repetition of words, sentences or key phrases and the presence, of nonverbal cues which indicate a focus by the co-researchers on certain meanings or ideas (Chuang, 1995). This definition of themes will guide the classification of meanings and experiences from the co-researchers interviews.

Method

To explore how African-American women communicate and experience the workplace, I interviewed eleven African Americans who had been identified by various informants and business contacts as having successful careers. Of the eleven participants interviewed, three were college administrators, two were consumer foods executives, two were senior level managers in the insurance industry, one was an organizational trainer for an oil company, one was an orthopedic surgeon and one was a service contractor for a major computer conglomerate. The participants ranged in age from 27–46. There were 6 men and 5 women. This thematization, however, only reflects the voices of the 5 women interviewed. The participants were similar in many ways, as all were college educated and all had a high level of self esteem and strong personal motivation.

The participants in the study came from different business and professional contexts. The orthopedic surgeon worked in a small private practice with a group of doctors; there were four men and one woman and they were from different cultural backgrounds. The organizational trainer worked for a large oil company and held a middle management position. In his division, which was comprised of about 300 people he was the only person of color. The college administrators held various positions at a medium sized midwestern university, one individual was the vice president of administration. The remaining participants worked for very large sales organizations and although they acknowledged the presence of other African Americans within their organizations, African Americans were the minority in the organization.

I interviewed the participants during the month of August 1995. These interviews ranged from 20 minutes to one hour, resulting in over 200 minutes of tape recorded experiential description, and over 50 pages of transcribed text.

The interviews were conducted using a topical protocol which allowed me to hold a conversation with my informants but required me to cover all topics concerning mentoring during the course of the interview (see appendix). I chose a more conversational approach because this allowed the participants to speak freely which enabled them to tell me stories about their work experiences.

Six of my interviews were conducted over the telephone and the remaining five were conducted in the co-researchers offices. During the course of the interviews I took detailed notes and all interviews were audio taped and fully transcribed. The subsequent step was to reduce the data from the co-researchers into major categories or themes. What follows is an identification of the essential themes drawn from my co-researchers interview texts.

Thematic Analysis

Contextual realities of the work environment: Politics and Games

The co-researchers all worked in different occupational settings but their statements about the general work environment, success and the means of achieving success were quite similar. They described work as being political and competitive, and they stated that it takes much more than hard work to survive and get ahead. All of the co-researchers said that they thought some younger employees believe that if they just worked hard they would automatically move up the corporate ladder. A participant explained this belief by saying:

> Well I think that there are some people who believe that if you just work hard you will automatically move up the corporate ladder, and certainly you cannot excuse working hard and doing your job well, but it takes a whole lot more than hard work to get ahead (C2: 72–74).[1]

Another co-researcher expressed a similar view:

> Some younger African-American employees think that just because they have a degree and got hired, all they have to do is do their job and they will automatically advance. Actually, I was just like that but once I was overlooked several times for promotions I began to question why. I found out that I had to do more than the technical aspects of my job but I had to learn the other side as well. The other side involved attending cocktail parties, pressing palms with the right people and promoting myself which meant talking about the work I was doing to the right people (I2:58–67).

They agreed that there are politics involved in all aspects of life and that the workplace is not exempt from such politics. Office politics as defined by the co-researchers were the unspoken rules and norms of the company. They observed that it is important to know who the important people in the company are and, regardless of their official position, where they fit in the power structure.

---

1. To preserve the anonymity of the participants, interviewees' remarks will be cited using the following system A1:2-3, where A represents the interviewee, 1 represents the page number of the typed transcript and 2-3 represents the line numbers where the remarks can be found.

The power structure might or might not be the same as the actual organizational structure. One participant illustrated this by giving the following example:

> Politically speaking you have to know the difference between the appointed leaders and the leaders who are appointed by the group. For example, in this setting there are deans and administrators and they have a certain place in the hierarchy but the people [who] are more powerful in the department might be the eminent scholars (K4:156–166).

Other similar examples included knowing whether the vice president of the company was more important than the territory manager who was the son of the president of the company, or knowing whom to go to when you need something done.

They stated that the political structure of the company is the first thing a new employee must master, but since this information is somewhat inaccessible a new employee must learn this information on his or her own. They talked about ways to learn about the office politics but they all agreed that the best way to find out this information is through a mentor who knows the political system within the company or industry. They affirmed that a mentor would play an important role in teaching younger employees how to anticipate and manage the office politics and how to handle certain situations. One co-researcher bluntly noted that a mentor is someone who tells you about the office politics.

> I play the game. I use the term game because work is a game and playing the game is a big part of paying your dues (I1:21).

While acknowledging the political nature of the workplace, others perceived work to be more of a game. One participant observed: "I just think its important to understand the game, the rules of the game, and the players in the game." Another remarked similarly: "I do those outside activities because they are a part of playing the game." For those using the game metaphor, a mentor was analogous to a coach in that he or she was responsible for teaching a younger employee how to play the game, what the rules of the game were, and what consequences result from not playing properly. Other co-researchers combined politics and games to comment critically on why

African Americans too often fail in the workplace. One made this point well: "While we understand politics because we play them in the racial environment we haven't learned to apply them in the workplace."

The co-researchers recognized that to become successful in the workplace you must compete in the game with other coworkers, but they also agreed that competition goes beyond the office. They pointed out that it would be a mistake for African Americans to think that if they did their job better than their peers then they would automatically get promoted because there were other factors to be considered. Other factors such as the level of participation in non-work related activities include playing golf, attending cocktail parties and eating lunch with other coworkers. The co-researchers stated that participating in these types of informal activities was just one aspect of playing the game. Other aspects include getting to know the right people, knowing what their hot buttons were, and how to toot your own horn. They lamented that although many African Americans realize the importance of learning office politics and how and when to compete in the game, it is still difficult for African Americans to meet the key people who can teach them how to survive in the workplace.

Mentoring involves building relationships

Meeting key people was described as the first step to mentoring; however, all co-researchers agreed that mentoring was a process of establishing relationships with the people who could mentor them. The mentor-protege relationship was described as being somewhat of a give and take between the mentor and protege which required mutual trust. This includes networking with people across the organization who were not in one's particular department and developing relationships with them. One person said that he thought this type of networking was crucial to the growth of younger employees and was a big part of career development.

However, they all felt that responsibility for this relationship was on the mentee (i.e., the recipient of the mentoring). They said that it was important for mentors to make themselves available to younger employees but it was necessary for the mentee to be receptive to the guidance from the mentor. In some cases it was preferred that the mentee take the initiative since this showed the mentor that he or she was receptive to and wanted support from a mentor. The people who acknowledged that they had a mentor explained that they established relationships with individuals who became mentors to them, which indicated that they sought out and developed relationships with their mentors. A good example of this is captured in the following statement:

> I found out who the important people were in many different departments and established relationships with them. These individuals eventually became mentors to me (A2:107–108).

According to the co-researchers, another way to establish relationships was to become successful in your current position. Participants remarked that mentors will appear once a younger employee establishes himself or herself as a mover and shaker within the company. The participants who had mentors stated that after they were hired and had some successes in the workplace people who would eventually become their mentors noticed this or took a personal interest in them and approached them to offer their help. What this means is that younger employees must prove themselves before their superiors will risk serving as their mentors. Another co-researcher stated that her mentor saw something different in her and liked her candor and eventually became her mentor.

I have not had a mentor but I know what one is: The characteristics of a desired mentor

Mentoring was described by the co-researchers as being an informal relationship between a younger employee and an older employee which was not an elaborate process. One person's statement captures how the entire group described mentors:

> A mentor is someone who is usually older both in age or tenure, they are usually two or three levels higher and their word means something in the company. I think sometimes we think that mentoring has to be this elaborate process, but mentoring can be as simple as being there for new employees and providing them with guidance and support. As a matter of fact, those formal programs never work because they are not natural (H3:126–130).

Some stated that a mentor in some cases does not have to do much more than set a good example for others (just be a good role model).

They maintained that being a mentor involved developing relationships with newer or younger employees and making yourself available to them. They described the mentor as providing bits and pieces of information, here and there .

In most cases the co-researchers reported that, although they did not have a mentor, they knew what a good mentor was. A mentor was described by the co-researchers as someone who was successful himself or herself . Success was defined by the co-researchers as a high achieving individual two or three levels above them in the company hierarchy who could lead by example. Good mentors must have a good understanding of the work environment and good sense about people in general. And good mentors must be respected by members of upper management as well as their peers.

Others stated that some mentors don't necessarily have to be on the "A" list, but through their negative and positive experiences within the company, they could help younger employees by sharing this information with them. In short, they might not be as successful themselves as others higher in the organization, but from their past successes and mistakes they knew what to do and what not to do to become successful. Often these people who were African-American tenured employees were not extremely successful within the company, but because of the experiences they had been through they were considered to be an asset to younger employees. They stated that it was beneficial for them to work with African-American mentors because they understood the fight (meaning discrimination and racism in the workplace), and they could identify with them. One person stated:

> He mentored me because he understood what it was like to be an African American in this business. It is important for African Americans to reach out to each other and coach each other through difficult situations. To put it bluntly, white people, although I have run across some who have been sensitive to racial issues, they really can't identify because they have not had to fight those battles, but African-American mentors usually understand the fight (C2; 36–42).

They saw a good mentor as someone who had the ability to lead or guide people through various situations and inform them on particular aspects of the company. The types of guidance that a mentor provides was described as coaching them in the decision making processes, alerting them to the unspoken politics and rules of the company, identifying key people in the company and explaining their personalities and expectations. They believed that a good mentor provides a protege with career support such as advocacy for promotions, and they represented a mentor as someone who is able to put in a good word for you. They said that a good mentor was someone who could look out for your best interest while letting you make your own decisions and mistakes. The co-researchers also stated that it was important for a mentor to assist mentees with career development by giving them feedback in the form of constructive criticism. According to the co-researchers, it was imperative that a mentor be open, honest and not be afraid to express him/herself. Finally, a good mentor as described by the co-researchers should help you identify your weaknesses and help you develop those weaknesses.

Obstacles to Mentoring

When asked specifically who contributed to their career success, many of the participants stated that they did not have a mentor.

> I have not had a mentor (A4:203–4)
>
> I was basically on my own (J1:42).
>
> I had to blaze my own trails (F3:128).
>
> The one thing I lack in my career is a mentor, I have always wanted someone who could help me (C4:2 57–58).

They also felt that their inability to find a mentor was consistent with the experiences of other African Americans. They claimed that there are both internal and external barriers which make it difficult for young African Americans to find mentors. Internal barriers were described as behaviors and/or self-perceptions that mentees displayed which militated against their finding a mentor. For instance, co-researchers referred to some African Americans as often coming to the job with chips on their shoulders, with an attitude which suggested that they perceived themselves to be qualified, and as believing that someone owed them something . This attitude prevents them from recognizing the need to have a mentor, and it also impedes their ability to establish relationships with people who might be beneficial to their careers.

Another internal barrier is that some African Americans believe stereotypes and myths perpetuated by members of the majority culture. One such myth is that African Americans are incompetent. Although there might be African Americans in the workplace who were not competent, this myth is not true for all African Americans. By believing those myths, many African Americans in the workplace tend to be somewhat standoffish as if they did not want to be associated with the other African Americans because it might reflect negatively upon them. Other comments were opposed to this view, as some co-researchers felt that the blacks were cliquish and stayed to themselves which, in their opinion, prevented them from meeting people outside their cultural group. One person described this by giving the following example:

> I've found that Afro-Americans in our organization go to a kick-off meeting or a conference and I'm generalizing but they tend to stick together, they don't get out and talk to other people to get new ideas or to find out what they are doing, they tend to just be together...this is bad because they are not expanding or they are not growing in any way because they are not getting out of their comfort zone (E3:152–E4:164).

Other co-researchers also felt that this cliquishness prevented African Americans from realizing career and personal growth.

Another internal barrier was described as the assumption that all African Americans were competing for the same position, as if there was only one job. And many of the co-researchers felt that this view affected African Americans negatively for a number of reasons. It prevented African Americans from working with other African Americans because they felt that there was only one job or position that African Americans could compete for; therefore, if they assisted you this might somehow decrease their chances of getting that job or position. One participant stated:

> African-American men and women are allies when we are up against the masses but when we are competing for that one position we are enemies (D2:201–203).

They also felt that this belief stifled African Americans and prevented them from reaching their full potential because they did not strive to be the best employee but the best Black employee.

External barriers were described as the experience of being isolated or excluded from key groups of people. They felt that they were often isolated from non-African-American managers who perceived them to be different, which suggests that white mentors don't mentor blacks because they don't feel comfortable with the differences. One co-researcher stated:

> Often people mentor others who are of like kind and quality and unfortunately, we are not like most who are in the position to mentor us (G2:76–77).

These perceived differences also precluded white mentors from including African Americans in various informal conversations, activities and professional projects that would potentially allow them to get to know African American and thereby change those perceptions (debunk some of those negative perceptions and myths). For these reasons the co-researchers saw this as a harmful and self-perpetuating cycle. One co-researcher said sometimes we are the stereotype and sometimes we become the stereotype because of the way we are treated. She explained by telling a story:

> For example the other day I was at the kick-off and my counter parts who are all white males were standing in a circle talking. Now they could have been talking about anything from their families to work issues. Well I walk over to them and as soon as I walk over to them they stop talking. Well if they continue to do this I'm going to begin to take it personally and think they don't want to be around me. Therefore I will stop trying to socialize with them and if I do then they will start saying she's unfriendly or she has poor communication skills. However in reality I did not become standoffish until I was excluded (G2:88–100).

Vision and Future Implications

Finally, although the workplace was defined as political and competitive, the participants still managed to blaze their own trails to become very successful in their respective careers. And they felt that they had been placed in positions within the company that would enable them to help other African Americans. Because of this opportunity, they wanted and felt obligated to share their experiences with younger African Americans to help them in their careers.

They also felt that the workplace was more conducive to the fostering of positive relationships between African-American men and women overall. They stated that under the old system African-American men and women were conditioned to work against each other. However they all acknowledged that it was more important for African Americans to stick together in the workplace than to work against each other. They admitted that although they once were competitors in the workplace, African-American men and women must now become allies and work together to establish the foundation of positive work relationships that will be beneficial to all.

Conclusion

The lack of organizational literature concerning mentoring does little to explicate the experiences of African-American women. This chapter seeks to highlight those experiences, and to show that African-American women and men actively participate in supportive relationships with each other. Although most of the persons interviewed for this study admit that they were not privy to the benefits that mentors offer their mentees, they realized the significance of mentoring relationships in the work environment as well as in interpersonal relationships. According to these co-researchers, there are fewer obstacles to mentoring others today than there were when they entered the workforce seeking mentors. In other words, there are structural as well as personal barriers facing African Americans that prevented them from being mentees, but they have overcome those obstacles and feel it is their duty to share this information with younger employees. In light of this, this project seeks to highlight the potential for affirming relationships among African-American men and women in the workplace. In this way, the study hopes to advance knowledge of the communicative practices of African-American women in the workplace, which for too long have been overlooked by organizational communication scholars.

Appendix

Interview Protocol

I. Opening

Standard introduction, purpose of the study, explanation of anonymity (confidentiality), and oral permission to audiotape the conversation.

II. Your Career

1. Highlight your career path/track.
   a. current position
   b. length of time in this position
2. What was instrumental in helping you advance the way that you have?
   (probes, including the presence or lack of mentors in your career. If they don't mention a mentor I will bring it up at this time.)

III. Mentors

3. How would you define mentor?
4. What are the qualities of a good mentor?

IV. Others and Mentors

5. Name someone who has benefitted from a mentor. Give some examples.
   (probe for them to tell stories)

V. Self and Mentor

6. In what ways have you benefitted from a mentor? Give an example.
7. Describe your mentor.
8. Tell me about your relationship with him/her.
9. How did this person become your mentor?
10. Was this person African American? If yes, what impact did his/her ethnicity have on his/her ability to mentor you?
11. What were some of the things your mentor taught you?
12. Has working with a mentor ever been detrimental to your career?

VI. Professional relationships in the organization

13. Who else do you go to for support in the organization? Examples.
14. Describe your relationship with others in the organization.

15. What is your perception of the relationships between African Americans in your organization?
16. Are the African Americans in your organization allies or adversaries? Examples.
17. Are the women in your organization allies or adversaries?
18. What is the perception of African-American women/men in your organization?

VII. African Americans and mentoring

19. How receptive are African-American men/women to receiving guidance from a mentor?
20. How do you perceive an African American's ability (i.e. power, influence) to mentor others?
21. How willing are African-American men and women to be mentors to others in your organization?

VIII. Closing Questions

22. Is there anything else you would like to tell me about mentoring in your organization.
    (Fill in any demographic gaps at this time)

References

Burke, R.J. & McKeen, C.A. (1990). Mentoring in organizations. *Journal of Business Ethics. 9,* 316–332.

Burke, J., McKeen, C. & McKenna, C. (1990). Sex differences and cross-sex effects on mentoring some preliminary data. *Psychological Reports.* 67, 1011–1023.

Carbone, L. (1992). Breaking the glass or just window dressing? *Management Review.* 16–22.

Cazenave, N. (1983). Black male-Black female Relationships: The perceptions of 155 middle-class Black men. *Family Relations, 32*, 341–350.

Cooks, L.M. & Descutner, D. (1994). A phenomenological inquiry into the relationship between perceived coolness and communication competence. In K. C. Carter & Preschell (Eds.), *Interpretive approaches to interpersonal communication.* (pp. 247–268). Albany, New York: SUNY Press.

Chuang, R. (1996). You are the key (to performance): a comparison of Asian and Euroamerican expatriate/native employees' perceptions of their organizational culture. Unpublished thesis. Ohio University. Athens, Ohio.

Davis, G. & Watson, G. (1982). *Black life in corporate America: Swimming in the main stream.* New York: Anchor Press.

Gaiter, J. (1994, March 8). The gender divide: Black women's gains in corporate America outstrip black men's. *The Wall Street Journal,* p. B1.

Hopson, D., & Hopson, D. (1994). *Friends lovers and soul mates: Better relationships between Black men and women.* Simon & Schuster.

Kram, K (1983). Phases of the mentor relationship. *Academy of Management Journal. 26, 4.* 608–625.

Long, C. (1995). *Dearest brothers love awaits, much peace, your sisters: African American women talk about sex love and life.* New York: Bantam.

Nkomo, S. (1992). The emperor has no clothes: Rewriting race in organizations . *The Academy of Management Review,3,* 487–513.

Ragins, B. & Cotton, J. (1991). Easier said than done: Gender differences in perceived barriers to gaining a mentor. *Academy of Management Journal. 4,* 939–951.

Reynolds, A. (1994). *Do Black women hate Black men?* New York: Hastings House.

Roberts, S. (1994). Black women graduates outpace male counterparts: Income disparity seen as a marriage threat. *The New York Times.* p. B12.

Spaights, E., & Whitaker, A. (1995). Black workforce: A new look at an old problem. *Journal Of Black Studies, 3,* 283–296.

Tepper, B. (1995). Upward maintenance tactics in supervisory mentoring and non-mentoring relationships. *Academy of Management Journal, 4.* 1191–1205.

Thomas, D. (1993). Racial Dynamics in cross-race developmental relationships. *Administrative Science Quarterly 38.* 169–194.

Thomas, D. (1989). Mentoring and irrationality the role of racial taboos. *Human Resource Management, 28.* 279–290.

Tucker, C. (1984). Black women in corporate America: The inside story. *Essence.* 1–66.

Van Manen, M. (1990). *Researching lived experience: Human science for action sensitive pedagogy.* New York: Suny Press.

Wynter, L. (1994, January, 19). Double whammy hinders double minorities. *The Wall Street Journal.* p. B1

7

METAPHORS FOR NEGOTIATING WORK AND FAMILY

BLACK PROFESSIONAL WORKING MOTHERS' DUAL ROLES

Audrey Curtis Hane

Traditionally, the labor force participation of black married women has been high and continuous, regardless of age, education, occupation, income of husband, and the presence of young children (Wallace, 1980). As daughters, sisters, wives, mothers and grandmothers, black women have had to integrate the dual roles of wage worker and houseworker (Higginbotham, 1984). In most cases, it is the wife/mother role that is central to these women's identities, but increasingly the employment role has become prominent in their lives (Moen, 1992). The work identity is especially important to black women who have achieved occupational mobility and have gained professional status (Morse, 1983).

One way of gaining a better understanding of the identity construction of black professional mothers is to examine their language choices as they talk about their role combination. Therefore, this chapter is aimed at examining the ways in which black professional mothers talk about their attempt to balance their professional and domestic responsibilities. The central focus is on language and language patterns that evidence how these women experience and express their lives. Metaphoric analysis is used to illuminate the identities that have been created through role combination.

A Language-Based Approach to Understanding Black Professional Mothers' Identity Construction

Because language is a powerful sense-making tool, studying black professional women's talk is a useful way of understanding the reality of their lives (Koch & Deetz, 1988; Morgan et al. 1983; Putnam, 1983; Redding & Tompkins, 1988). The power of language rests in the fact that it both reflects and shapes our behavior. Acting as a "social mirror," language reflects the organization and dynamics of our world (Adams & Ware, 1979). For instance, black professional mothers' talk reveals the sociocultural expectations they try to meet, including the tasks of sustaining cultural and moral values and preserving social order through duties involving support, nurturance and relationship maintenance (Spitzack & Carter, 1987). Not only does language reflect social values, attitudes and prejudices, but it reinforces them as well (Adams & Ware, 1979).

The basic symbols we use to understand and express ourselves can affect the way we view ourselves (Bate & Taylor,1988). What we say, individually or in groups, has the power to alter our personal gender identifications, identity, judgments and values. In other words, our tendency to talk about things in a certain way may lead us to think about and enact them in a particular manner. The power of language rests in the fact that it not only reveals our lives but also shapes and reshapes them, affecting how we think and behave throughout life.

Because of the powerful influence communication can have in reflecting our worldviews and in shaping our lives, researchers can gain a better understanding of black professional mothers by examining their communication patterns. Studying their language choices can be useful in developing insight into the way in which they understand and reveal themselves. One specific approach to studying black professional mothers' identity construction entails the use of metaphoric analysis.

Metaphoric Analysis

In order to point out the power of metaphor, scholars have noted the interdependent relationship between metaphor and reality. Burrell, Buzzanell, and McMillan (1992) suggest that metaphors reflect reality. Jamieson (1980) adds that recurrent patterns observable in surface language reflect deeper structures of reality. In other words, metaphoric analysis can provide a way of knowing black professional women's lives. By exploring the metaphors women use, researchers can understand how women view themselves (Morgan, 1983). Specifically, metaphors help to reveal individuals' identities and to make sense of their actions (Morgan, 1983). The understanding gained from metaphoric analysis can be used to discover black professional mother's implicit philosophies of life and coping mechanisms for dealing with life events.

Insight into black professional mother's lives can be gained because of the way in which metaphors function. Metaphors offer a vocabulary for thoughts and feelings that may be difficult to articulate. In other words, a woman might rely on a metaphor to describe a life experience that is impossible to capture through any other symbolic form. In this way, individuals use metaphors as a way of conveying a reality that others may not have experienced or been able to understand otherwise (Burrell et al., 1992).

In addition to reflecting reality, Lakoff and Johnson (1980) argue that metaphors define and create reality by focusing our attention on some aspects of reality and hiding others. The sharper dimensions potentially shape behaviors, attitudes and values while the less prominent features fail to influence behavior significantly. Recognizing which features have been privileged allows researchers to examine the way in which reality is created and brought into existence through language use.

Before examining the language choices of black professional women who combine multiple roles, it is important to understand the context in which these women function. The following discussion highlights some of the challenges black women face in both roles.

Challenges Facing a Black Female Professional

Black women as professionals share certain problems with professionals in general like obtaining degrees, meeting licensing requirements and receiving favorable performance reviews. In addition, they share concerns specific to African Americans, including difficulties in hiring and professional advancements due to racial discrimination.

Furthermore, if they are discriminated against on the basis of gender, they may find themselves in the "double bind." The black professional woman experiences racial, sexual, and professional discrimination, often being viewed as black first, a woman second and a professional third (Morse, 1983).

Collins (1990) offers an example of a black woman professional who was treated in this type of discriminatory way. A young manager graduated with honors from the University of Maryland. Before she was scheduled to fly to Cleveland to present a marketing plan for her company, her manager made her go over it three or four times in front of him so that she would not forget it. Then he explained how to check luggage at an airport and how to reclaim it. The woman responded by asking him if he would like to tie her money up in a handkerchief and attach a note to her in case she got lost. Although most professional black women do not encounter such blatantly discriminatory incidents, they may have to endure other racially related challenges.

One of these challenges includes becoming a target for hostility. For example, Collins (1990) shares the case of Leanita McClain, a black journalist raised in segregated Chicago public housing who eventually became a feature writer for a major Chicago newspaper. In an editorial entitled "The Middle-Class Black's Burden," McClain says that she is uncomfortable being middle class because she is in a marginalized position. She explains, "My life abounds in incongruities... sometimes when I wait at the bus stop with my attache case, I meet my aunt getting off the bus with other cleaning ladies on their way to do my neighbors' floors" (Collins, 1990 p. 61). With this experience in mind, it is no wonder that she adds, "I am a member of the black middle class who has had it with being patted on the head by white hands and slapped in the face by black hands for my success" (Collins, 1990 p. 61). Even though McClain is a successful professional, her race and gender render it difficult for her to gain true acceptance.

A black professional woman may also receive a hostile response if she is perceived as a competitor in the labor force by black males, white males, or white females (Morse, 1983). In other cases, a black woman's professional achievements are belittled as she is criticized for devoting too much time and energy to her work and not spending enough time with her family (Campbell, 1986).

When trying to determine the challenges faced by black women, it is important not to establish a dichotomy between their experiences as working professionals and their experiences as working mothers. Collins (1990) encourages us to use a both/and stance rather than an either/or dichotomy when examining the lives of black women. This stance suggests that the experiences of black professional working mothers cannot be viewed in isolation as either being a work experience or a mothering experience. Rather, when examining the lives of black professional working mothers, a researcher must consider the fact that black women are both workers and mothers. Viewing black women from the worker/mother stance leads us to examine the challenges associated with simultaneously filling both roles.

Challenges Facing Black Working Mothers

Black working mothers share many challenges with working mothers in general. They are concerned with providing care for their children, offering support for their spouses if they are married, and maintaining a pleasant home environment. While each of these tasks is single-handedly demanding, they become extremely challenging when one considers that working women have less time and energy to devote to their childrearing and household duties.

Black mothers face some additional issues. Protecting black children remains a primary concern for African-American mothers because black children are at particular risk. They must protect their children not only from physical dangers like disease or violence, but also they must guard their children against the psychological threats of racism.

> Black working mothers are also sometimes engaged in conflict resulting from their husbands' unfavorable attitudes toward them working. Staples (1973) contends that black males frequently desire to have a working but submissive wife. He further states that many black women who are employed demand to have a "voice" in family affairs. Often, marital problems may result from this conflict in role expectations.

Black professional women face added expectations because they are often held in high esteem in their multi-faceted roles of worker, wife and mother (Morse, 1983). In the black family and in the world of work, they are expected to excel at their job while serving as supportive wives and mothers to their families (Morse, 1983).

As can be seen by the previously outlined challenges, fulfilling the role expectations for black professional working mothers can often be difficult. One of the ways black professional working women attempt to cope with their demanding roles is to share their experiences with other people, particularly women. When asked to communicate their role management experiences, black professional women offer a variety of responses. Some women liken the experience to juggling, maintaining a balancing act, or walking a tight rope. Others describe it as an attempt to weave a tapestry, nurture a garden, or run a marathon. Still others may characterize the experience as a tug of war.

The descriptions women offer of their attempt to meet the challenges associated with their varying roles depends on the context surrounding the roles and the role expectations. Regardless of these differences, the descriptions reveal that attempting to manage the various roles entails a sense-making process that is defined symbolically through language. Furthermore, that sense-making process is accomplished by comparing the role management to other acts with which the women are familiar.

The fact that symbolic activity functions as an ordering process for individuals' social realities is recognized (Ball, 1985; Burke, 1957, 1962, 1965; Cassirer, 1946; Eisenberg, 1984; Lakoff & Johnson, 1980; Langer, 1951,1962). Symbolic interactionists, in fact, assert that humans "interpret and act upon the basis of symbols" (Blumer, 1972). In other words, symbols are viewed as the essential medium through which individuals create their social reality (Morgan, Pondy, Frost, 1983). The constructed reality is actively maintained through the communicative experiences of individuals who enact meaning through their behavior (Putnam, 1982).

For this study, as well as many others conducted from the interpretive perspective, the aim is to understand how the taken for granted aspects of everyday life are constituted and made real through symbolic processes. This is accomplished through a meaning-centered focus which examines the way individuals make sense of their world through communicative behaviors. One approach to gaining such an understanding is to examine people's use of metaphors since metaphors help people structure their symbolic realities by allowing for comparisons to be drawn between less familiar phenomena and more common phenomena. The comparison serves to illuminate, clarify and order the less familiar in terms of the common place. With this in mind, metaphors provide people with what Burke calls a "strategy for dealing with a situation" (1957, p. 256). Examining these metaphors provides insight into the way black professional working mothers conceptualize the meaning and importance of their daily lives, their family patterns, their work demands and their self-concepts.

Metaphoric Analysis of Role Management

A metaphoric analysis of the way black professional working mothers communicate their role management began with an attempt to identify the types of metaphors used when they were talking about their lives. In hopes of locating metaphors, I gathered material about black professional working mothers including biographies, books analyzing role management for professional black women, popular African-American publications, and discussions from a panel organized to discuss role management. I identified metaphors by looking for statements in which black professional working mothers juxtaposed pairs of symbolic concepts as a way of describing their role management since metaphor is often defined as a juxtaposition of symbolic concepts (Black, 1962, 1979, 1981; Leff, 1983; Richards, 1965; and Ricoeur, 1974–1975). Once the metaphors were identified, I then analyzed the rhetoric in an attempt to explain the significance of the comparison so that the women's sense-making could be understood. Since metaphorical meaning arises when the attributes of one phenomena are projected onto another (Lakoff, 1986), I identified attributes of the commonplace phenomena as they related to the less familiar phenomena. Thus, the attributes of everyday activities, like juggling, balancing, and playing tug-of-war, were used to gain insight into the women's role management. I examined unique aspects of the comparisons and looked for recurring themes that provided insight into the way women organized their lives and how their lives are shaped and determined by relations extending beyond them. This type of analysis offered insight into both the women's organizational and home life. The description is presented in the women's own language and thus retains the implications of their world independent of the researcher (Koch & Deetz, 1981).

An examination of the metaphors used by black working women to describe the delicate interaction of their family and work lives will hopefully produce the data necessary for concept development and theory building in this area. In particular, the development of the models of womanhood may be enhanced by this increased understanding of black women's lives.

Role Management Metaphors

Five different role management metaphors emerged from the examined texts. Each metaphor represents a unique way of conceptualizing the role management process. While this representation of metaphors is not exhaustive, is does highlight the ways in which several black professional women with children characterize their role combination. In order to gain greater insight into the women and their language choices, each role management metaphor, including those of juggling, balancing, walking a tightrope, playing tug of war and becoming a superwoman, is examined in greater depth, beginning with an examination of the juggling act.

"Juggling Act"

Black professional mothers agreed that in combining work outside the home with family responsibilities they expended a lot of energy. In order to keep everything in motion as they maneuvered life's responsibilities, they often found themselves engaged in intense activity. Capturing this level of activity, black working mothers spoke of their juggling acts, describing a type of movement which required skill, awareness, and proper planning.

Amy Hilliard-Jones, the director of market development for the baked goods division of Pillsbury Co. grew up expecting to work and have a family. Still, she admits that having it all requires a "skillful juggling act" (Ebony, 1992, p. 78). "You have a job to do; you have a household to maintain, children to raise" (Ebony, 1992, p. 78). She further explains, "I always have many balls in the air" (Ebony ,1992, p. 78). She emphasized that a supportive husband, an occasional housekeeper and good care providers for her two children, Angelica, five and Nicholas, two make her life manageable. She asks that she and her husband never schedule to be out of town during the same time, that the children help with household chores, and that she be allowed time for herself to exercise. Despite the conflicts and sacrifices, this executive mother is quite happy with her life choices. "Nothing is more gratifying than coming home from work and having those two little munchkins wrap their arms around my legs and say, 'Mommy, I'm so glad you're home. Mommy, I love you.'" She adds, "I would not trade having children for anything in the world" (Ebony, 1992, p. 81).

While Jones seems successful in her juggling act, other women do not manage as well. Bebe Moore Campbell (1986, p. 86) explains:

> Nineteen seventy-nine was a fast juggling act; some balls were in the air and some were hitting the floor. My marriage was four years old and failing. My fledgling career as a freelance writer was expanding, but my highly visible job was stressful. My three-year-old daughter was thriving. I was a mother, a wife, an employee, a moonlighter with big dreams. Outwardly, all the pieces of my life seemed to be in sync. I was the epitome of 'You've come a long way, Baby.' I was the feminist dream come to life. In reality, the balancing of the roles caused me more tension than I realized. Some of the balls were cracking as they hit the ground, and one of them was me.

In the descriptions shared by black professional mothers, it is significant that the use of the juggling metaphor is oriented towards measuring the women's ability to manage multiple roles. The women evaluate themselves, mentioning that they sometimes drop balls and thereby suggesting that they are not always successful at handling the various demands placed upon them. Due to the nature of this metaphor, failure is unavoidable because even the best jugglers are unable to keep the balls in motion indefinitely.

Despite this outlook, the women's descriptions suggest that there are ways of increasing the likelihood of successful juggling. For instance, they respect the possible necessity of eliminating a ball in order to keep the others in the air. The implication is that the juggler wields the ultimate control, enabling her to delete or add roles and duties at her discretion. We should keep in mind, however, that the most valued juggler is normally the one who can successfully keep the greatest number of balls in circulation. Women should be aware that their choice of this metaphor to describe their role management is sending a message that it is appropriate to judge women by the number of roles they can manage.

The visual image of three or more balls circling through the air while maintaining distance from one another highlights the sense of segregation inherent in this metaphor. Each ball, which represents a different role, is intentionally separated from all the others and is doomed should it collide with another. While some women may conduct their lives in a manner which segregates their roles, others have deeply integrated lives, rendering this metaphor a less accurate description of their experiences.

While some of the women spoke of their attempts to manage multiple roles as a juggling act, others referred to their attempts to strike a harmonious and satisfying arrangement between their responsibilities. Rather than emphasizing simultaneous attention to the varying demands of their lives, these women described their attempts to find balance, a strategy which emphasized the creation and maintenance of parity.

Maintaining a Balance

Black professional mothers expressed pride at being able to successfully meet their professional and personal obligations; however, they realized that in order to do so successfully, they had to maintain a balance between the physical and mental energy they devoted to each arena.

Earlene Hardie Cox, director of IBM's Credit Corporation, says that the most difficult aspect of being an executive mother is "trying to keep a balance" (Ebony, 1992, p. 81). She adds that "it is difficult to balance the needs of two children and a husband, as well as manage a staff of 14 attorneys and accountants" (Ebony, 1992, p. 81). In commenting on the balancing act, she says, "I have never been offered or asked to do a job that I had to turn down because of my family. And I don't feel that my children have had to suffer because I work. I personally need to work, and not just because of money. I have always worked, and I enjoy it. But I also love my children and my husband very much. It is a way of life for both parents to work" (Ebony 1992, p. 81).

Cox advises working mothers to take time for themselves (Ebony 1992). She personally spends three to five hours a week playing tennis. She views the time she spends on herself as a way of preventing losing herself in the demands of her career and family.

The balance metaphor implies that a black woman can be successful in both the professional and domestic arenas. In doing so, she is not restricted but rather is able to give her best to both her career, her family, and herself. The key, however, is in striking the appropriate balance that allows a working mother to contribute both at work and at home without neglecting the other. The realities of many women's lives suggest that achieving such a balance is a difficult task, and for a woman to successfully do so, she must be a part of an organization geared to supporting working mothers as well as part of a highly supportive home life.

Drawing on some of the same characteristics as the balance metaphor, including the need to find an equilibrium in one's life between work and home duties, another role management metaphor, that of walking a tightrope, emphasizes the difficulty of finding such a balance.

Living on a Tightrope

Black professional mothers articulated the complexity of attempting to manage multiple roles by drawing on the tightrope metaphor. Their choice of this metaphor expressed not only the difficulty of meeting the multiple responsibilities associated with one's career and homelife, but also of facing various people's attitudes and expectations of a woman who chooses to combine a career with her mothering duties.

Bonnie, a manager, wife and mother, said several years ago she and her husband were "living on a tightrope" because of the demands of their careers (Campbell, 1986, p. 52). She was a manger of a crew of radio technicians and her husband was a photographer. The grueling schedules imposed by their jobs left Bonnie and her husband with little energy for themselves, each other, their children, or their marriage. They often heard themselves asking, "Why don't you bring a little of that work energy into the house?" (Campbell, 1986, p 53). On several occasions, they came close to saying, "I can't take it anymore." They were referring not to each other but to the stress.

Bonnie and her husband found themselves in a work life that included late hours, extensive travel, and after-hours socializing with coworkers. When they returned home, they were often in a state of collapse, and rather than spending time together, they were forced to prepare for the next day's work (Campbell, 1986).

Their problem was not so much that they were working hard and coming home exhausted as it was that they weren't living up to each other's expectations. Bonnie had believed that in her two-career marriage she would be able to care for her children and her household more gracefully than housewives had ever done before because her chores would be shared (Campbell, 1986). Her husband had secretly believed that he would be exempt from those duties. In fantasizing about his career, he'd never pictured himself changing diapers and washing dirty dishes. The balance Bonnie was trying to achieve may not have been so simple as finding an equilibrium between her work and home duties but may have been more complex and having to do with balancing her expectations of her work role against her husband's traditional attitudes of what women's role ought to encompass.

The use of the tightrope metaphor indicates that Bonnie sees herself in a temporary, but highly precarious position for we know that the time a tightrope walker can remain on the rope is limited. When Bonnie uses this metaphor to describe the management of her roles, she indicates that the tension between her and her husband's role expectations places her in an unstable position. This description also expresses her desire to resolve competing role expectations, just as the tightrope walker seeks to complete his or her act and return to steadier footing.

The tightrope metaphor not only indicates the urgency of the situation in which a woman who is attempting to combine roles finds herself, but also implies that the act of managing both professional and personal roles is as difficult as walking on a rope hundreds of feet from the ground. When we think of a tightrope walker, we picture someone with unusual talent and courage; however, the fact that they are part of the circus suggests that they may have a freakish nature, and therefore, they often receive minimal respect from the audience. A possible negative implication of this metaphor is that it suggests that women who are trying to manage several roles are in a precarious position and may be as unusual as a circus performer.

As opposed to the tightrope metaphor, other women drew on the rope imagery, using the tug of war metaphor to express their experiences with role combination.

"Tug of War"

The tug of war metaphor was used by black working mothers with professional careers to highlight the constant adjustment needed to make role combination manageable. Analysis of this metaphor reveals the friction that role struggles can cause between family and organizational members.

One professional black mother stated, "I'd never disclosed to anyone the kind of tug of war my husband and I engaged in as we struggled with work and domestic roles. Perhaps that was why I'd always felt so isolated and maladjusted, thinking that other dual-career couples were somehow sailing through the heady process of living together as equals while my husband and I struggled" (Campbell, 1986, p. 9).

Depicting the role struggles experienced by black men and women through the image of tug of war is particularly useful because it highlights the fact that roles are reciprocal (Crosby, 1987). In other words, it takes two to make a role. It is also an useful image because it highlights the friction that role struggles can cause between spouses and family members. Although the notion of working wives has been commonplace rather than the exception for black families, the dual-career marriage roles of the emancipated black woman and the liberated black male are ones to which many black men and women are still adapting. The social and psychological changes necessary for these new roles have not yet fully developed (Campbell, 1986). There has been resistance to change as well as confusion about the ways to address new needs and incorporate new values. The result is that dual career couples find themselves in a transition period, tugging back and forth, in an attempt to establish agreeable new roles.

While a husband may be satisfied living in the traditional home, the wife desires to live in the liberated home where she is not solely responsible for the household duties. When the couple finds themselves with differing expectations, they may be literally pulled apart. The ensuing emotions may include shock, pain, anger, and puzzlement.

The tug of war metaphor points to the opposition experienced by an independent woman when her husband feels threatened by the role she assumes. The shifting of the rope as it is tugged by the husband to the side of traditional values and then pulled by an independent wife to the side of liberated thinking represents the clashing of the new and old systems. The value systems are in conflict because men have a vested interest in the old values while women recognize the new values must be adopted in order for them to be able to continue in both the public and private realms.

Switching from metaphors which depict action to those that draw on labels or descriptions, some black professional women compare their attempt to combine professional and familial responsibilities to trying to be a superwoman or superstar.

Superwoman

Reflecting the perceived challenge of working in both the private and public spheres, some women's language choices revealed the experience of being elevated to a superhuman status due to the attempt to work inside and outside of the home. One black woman executive noted that in trying to combine roles she became a kind of "superwoman or superstar" (Morse, 1983). People loved her when she gave what was desired and hated her when she failed to perform as expected, similar to the reactions experienced by professional athletes. The result for the black executive was that she felt overworked, underpaid, alienated, isolated, uncertain and powerless.

Black women are often told that electing to be a working mother is a fine option but that they better be prepared to be a superwoman or supermom. While this label is often given to working mothers, one should be aware that it is no more of a literal description, and therefore no more of a viable option, than are those which depict black professional working mothers juggling or walking a tightrope.

The superwoman metaphor emerged from the "super slave woman" image during the slavery era when the constraints placed on black women did not allow them to adhere to the cult of true womanhood (Morse, 1983). The "super slave woman" was a matriarch who arose as a consequence of her strength and independence which she was forced to exert to save her family and her community. As a result, black women came to be perceived as women of super strength and perhaps even domineering or castrating.

While the superwoman image is not as negative today, the message that black professional working mothers should be able to do it all is burdensome. Some black women are actually convinced that they can successfully play the roles of caretaker and problem-solver on the job and then accept additional roles at home. With this in mind, they fail to recognize that they may need to limit their responsibilities or seek assistance from support systems. Adopting the superwoman role is a result of a failure to communicate with those at home or at work about the expectations placed upon them. Additionally, it draws attention away from husbands and employers, the division of family obligations, and the structure of corporations, placing the burden of adjustment on the woman, and thereby eliminating the need to make adjustments elsewhere. As a result, black professional working mothers who embrace this metaphor may allow themselves to unfairly and unnecessarily accept an excessive work load. Therefore, black working mothers must be aware of the dangers of accepting this metaphor. Rather than being persuaded that it is possible for them to single-handedly manage work duties and household duties, black professional women must be encouraged to set limits and seek available support both on the job and at home.

The role management metaphors used by black professional working mothers, including those of juggling, balancing, walking a tightrope, engaging in a tug of war, and becoming a superwoman, can be grouped into three categories, allowing for a greater understanding of the implications associated with each metaphor. The three categories will be examined in order to gain additional insight into the women's language choices.

Categorizing Role Management Metaphors

The metaphors found in the literature in which black professional working mothers describe their role management fall into three categories. The first category focuses on a metaphor which can be interpreted as detrimental to the cause of women who are trying to expand their role as wife and mother to include the role of working professional. The metaphor which is burdensome to women is the superwoman comparison in which black professional women are made to believe that they should be able to do it all. This attitude negates the need for organizations to be sensitive to working mothers' needs or to a family network willing to share household and childcare responsibilities, leaving black professional working mothers overburdened as they take on several roles. The superwoman metaphor, rather than calling for societal structures to accommodate the needs of working mothers, stands in the way of family and organizational changes by suggesting that black women must learn to accept all the responsibilities associated with the various roles they play.

The second category of metaphors suggests that women managing multiple roles are able to function within the societal system as it presently exists by either prioritizing or sacrificing. The metaphors of juggling and balancing are used as the women describe their attempts to serve both as professionals with career goals and as wives and mothers dedicated to their families. The need to juggle or to balance responsibilities arises because corporate America has not yet made the necessary adjustment to accommodate working mothers and the traditional American family has not yet fully adjusted to a wife and mother with career demands.

The final category of metaphors depicts the struggles women are involved in as they attempt to shift organizational and familial expectations in order to create new values for women's roles. The metaphors of walking a tightrope and participating in a tug of war highlight the courage and strength needed by women who attempt to change societal structures and values. The question we must ask ourselves is what type of hardships black professional mothers will have to endure before they are able to successfully change societal structures as well as employers' and family members' attitudes and expectations. Hopefully the tug of war will be won and the walk across the tightrope will be completed with only a minimal amount of emotional, physical and psychological injury to black professional mothers.

Conclusions and Implications

The challenges facing black professional working mothers are a reality that must be faced. Our responsibility as rhetorical critics is to look at the current situation and to provide insight and support to black women to enable them to thrive under the circumstances. One means for doing this is to evaluate the symbolic language they use to organize their social realities. By analyzing the metaphors black professional working mothers use as guides for managing their various roles, they can be made more keenly aware of the strengths as well as the possible limitations of the language they use to make sense out of their demanding lives.

Hopefully, this chapter has helped us realize that the superwoman metaphor is burdensome and unsupportive of women's goals. Furthermore, working mothers may realize that metaphors like juggling and balancing are requiring them to unnecessarily prioritize and sacrifice in order to meet their goals due to structural limitations. Finally, the value of metaphors like tightrope walking and engaging in tug of war may be seen when black women realize that these comparisons highlight women's struggles to change expectations and societal structures.

In conclusion, this study serves only as an introductory look at the experiences of black professional mothers. In order for us to gain a more complete understanding of their attempt to combine motherhood with the pursuit of a career, the lives of more women need to be examined. As more black professional mothers become the focus of study, it is hoped that the accumulation of knowledge will create a society in which black women can choose to be active in both the public and private spheres, restricted only by limitations of their own capabilities and vision.

References

Adams, K. & Ware, N. (1979). Sexism and the English language: The linguistic implications of being a woman. In J. Freeman (Ed.), *Women: A feminist perspective* (pp. 474–486). Palo Alto, CA: Mayfield Publishing Co.

Ball, M.S. (1985). *Lying down together: Law, metaphor, and theology.* Madison, WI: University of Wisconsin Press.

Barnett, R.C. & Marshall, N.L. (1992). Worker and mother roles, spillover effects, and psychological distress. *Women and Health, 18*, 9–33.

Baruch, G. & Barnett, R. (1987). Role quality and psychological well-being. pp. 63–73 In F. J. Crosby (Ed.), *Spouse, parent, worker*, (pp. 63–73). New Haven: Yale University Press.

Bate, B. & Taylor, A. (1988). *Women communicating: Studies of women's talk*. Norwood, NJ: Ablex Publishing Corporation.

Bird, G., Gerald, B. & Scruggs, M. (1984). Determinants of family task sharing: A study of husbands and wives. *Journal of Marriage and the Family 46*, 345–55.

Black, M. (1962). *Models and metaphor.* Ithaca, NY: Cornell University Press.

Black, M. (1979). More about metaphor. In A. Ortony (Ed.), *Metaphor and thought* (pp. 19–43). Minneapolis: University of Minnesota Press.

Black, M. (1981). Metaphor. In M. Johnson (Ed.), *Philosophical perspectives on metaphor* (pp. 63–82). Minneapolis: University of Minnesota Press.

Blumer, H. (1972). Symbolic interactionsims: An approach to human communication. In R.W. Budd & B.D. Ruben (Eds.), *Approaches to human communication* (pp. 401–419). New York: Spartan Books.

Bowen, G. (1991). *Navigating the marital journey.* New York: Praeger Publishers.

Burke, K. (1957). *The philosophy of literary form.* New York: Vintage Books.

Burke, K. (1962). *A grammar of motives and a rhetoric of motives.* New York: World Publishing Co.

Burke, K. (1965). *Permanence and change* (2nd Rev. Ed.) New York: Bobbs-Merrill.

Burrell, N., Buzzanell, P., McMillan, J. (1992). Feminine tensions in conflict situations as revealed by metaphoric analyses. *Communication Quarterly,* 6, (2), 115–149.

Burris, B. (1991). Impact of class and marital status on family/work priorities. *Social Science Quarterly* 72, 50–66.

Campbell, B.M. (1986). *Successful women, angry men.* New York: Random House.

Coffman, S.L. & Eblen, A.L. (1987). Metaphor use and perceived managerial effectiveness. *Journal of Applied Communication Research, 15,* 53–66.

Collins, P.H. (1990). *Black feminist thought.* New York: Routledge.

Cowan, R.S. (1983). *More work for mother: The ironies of household technology from the open hearth to the microwave.* New York: Basic Books.

Crosby, F.J. (1991). *Juggling.* New York: The Free Press.

Crosby, F.J. (Ed.) (1987). *Spouse, parent, worker: On gender and multiple roles.* New Haven, CT: Yale University Press.

Edge, D. (1974) Technical metaphor and social control. *New Literary History,* 6, 135–147.

Eisenberg, E.M. (1984). Ambiguity as a strategy in organizational communication. *Communication Monographs, 51,* 227–242.

Etter-Lewis, G. (1993). *My soul is my own. Oral narratives of african american women in the professions.* New York: Routledge.

Galinsky, E., & Stein, P.J. (1990). The impact of human resource policies on employees: Balancing work/family life. *Journal of Family Issues, 11,* 368–383.

Hocker, J.L. & Wilmot, W.W. (1991). *Interpersonal conflict,* 3rd ed. Dubuque, IA: Wm. C. Brown.

Hoffman, L.W. (1989). Effects of maternal employment in the two-parent family. *American Psychologist, 44,* 283–292.

Hughes, D., & Galinsky, E. (1988). Balancing work and family life: Research and corporate application. In A.E. Gottfried & A.W. Gottfried (Eds.) *Maternal employment and children's development: Longitudinal research* (pp. 233–268) New York: Plenum.

Jamieson, K. (1980). The metaphoric cluster in the rhetoric of Pope Paul VI and Edmund G. Brown, Jr. *The Quarterly Journal of Speech, 66,* 51–72.

Johnston, W.B. (1987). *Workforce 2000: Work and workers for the 21st century*. Indianapolis, IN: Hudson Institute.

Joseph, G.I. & Lewis, J. (1981). *Common differences*. Boston: South End Press.

Kimbrough, M. (1991). *Accept no limitations: A black woman encounters corporate America*. Nashville: Abingdon Press.

Koch, S. & Deetz, S. (1981). Metaphor analysis of social reality in organizations. *Journal of Applied Communication Research, 9*, 1015.

Lakoff, G. (1986). A figure of thought. *Metaphor and symbolic activity, 1*, 215–225.

Lakoff, G. & Johnson, M. (1980). *Metaphors We Live By*. Chicago: University of Chicago Press, (pp. 1–24).

Langer, S.K. (1962). *Philosophical sketches*. New York: New American Library.

Langer, S.K. (1951). *Philosophy in a new key*. New York: New American Library.

Lewis, D. (1977). A response to inequality. *Signs. Vol. 3*, #2, Winter.

Lewis, S.N.C., & Cooper, C.L. (1987). Stress in two-earner couples and stage in the life-cycle. *Journal of Occupational Psychology, 60*, 289–303.

Lopata, H. & Pleck, J. (1983). *Research in the interweave of social roles: Families and jobs*. Greenwich, CT: JAI Press.

Malson, M., Mudimbe-Boyi, E., O'Barr, J.F. & Wyer, M. (1990). *Black women in America*. Chicago: University of Chicago Press.

Moen, P. (1992). *Women's two roles*. Westport, CT: Auburn House.

Mom is the Boss. *Ebony*. September, 1992, 72–76.

Morgan, G. (1980). Paradigms, metaphors, and puzzle solving in organization theory. *Administrative Science Quarterly, 25*, 605–622.

Morgan, G., Pondy, L., Frost, P. (1983). Organizational symbolism. Greenwich, CT: JAI Press, Inc., (pp. 3–33).

Morse, R. (1983). *The black female professional*. Howard University: Institute for Urban Affairs and Research.

Oresick, P. & Nicholas, C. (1990). *Working classics*. Chicago: University of Illinois Press.

Osborn, M. (1977). The evolution of the archetypal sea in rhetoric and poetic. The *Quarterly Journal of Speech. 63*: 318–363.

Putnam, L. (1982). Paradigms for organizational communication research: An overview and synthesis. *Western Journal of Speech Communication, 46*, 192–206.

Putnam, L. (1983). The interpretive perspective: An alternative to functionalism. In L. Putnam and M. Pacanowsky (Eds.), *Communication and organizations: An interpretive approach*. Beverly Hills: Sage. (pp. 31–54).

Redding, W. & Tompkins, P. (1988). Organizational communication: Past and present tenses. In G. Goldhaber & G. Barnett (Eds.), *Handbook of organizational communication*. Norwood, NJ: Ablex. (pp. 5–33).

Rexroat, C. & Shehan, C. (1987). The family life cycle and spouses' time in housework. *Journal of Marriage and the Family, 49*, 737–750.

Richards, I.A. (1965). *The philosophy of rhetoric.* New York: Oxford University Press.

Ricoeur, P. (1974). Metaphor and the main problem of hermeneutics. *New Literary History, 6*, 95–110.

Scarr, S., Phillips, D. & McCarney, K. (1989). Working mothers and their families. *American Psychologist. 44*, 1402–1409.

Sidel, R. (1978). *Urban survival. The world of working class women.* Boston: Beacon Press.

Spitzack, C., & Carter, K. (1987). Women in communication studies: a typology for revision. *The Quarterly Journal of Speech, 73*, (4) 401–423.

Staples, R. (1973). *The black woman in America: Sex, marriage, and the family.* Chicago: Nelson Hall.

Thedge, L.B., Wortman, C.B., Downey, G., Emmons, C., Biernat, M., & Lang, E. (1990). Women with multiple roles: Role-compatibility perceptions, satisfaction, and mental health. *Journal of Marriage and the Family, 52*, 63–72.

Vannoy-Hiller, D. (1989). *Equal partners. Successful women in marriage.* London: Sage.

Vaughn, M. (1988). Interpretive research in organizational communication and the rhetorical critic. *Communication Reports, 1*, 68–75.

Wallace, P. (1980). *Black women in the labor force.* Cambridge, Massachusetts: The MIT Press.

8

"THERE'S ALWAYS A LINE OF SEPARATION"

THE FIGURING OF RACE, GENDER, AND CLASS IN THE CONSTRUCTION OF CORPORATE IDENTITIES

Jeanne L. Porter

Though African-American women have always participated in the workforce as slaves, farmers, domestics, skilled and unskilled laborers, they are now entering the professional and managerial ranks in larger numbers (Scarborough, 1989). The African-American woman who finds herself in positions of leadership in organizations and businesses finds herself distinctly situated in a social setting that implicitly defines her as different (Stivers, 1993). According to Myers (1991), "Black women carry the dual stigma of being female and black in a society that devalues both" (p. 8). Race, class and gender are social stratification variables that serve to socially situate, limit and ultimately control people within the broader society (Berger, 1963; Stivers, 1993). So it is, then, that African-American women enter into the corporate setting or other white male dominated organizations carrying a set of socially-constructed characteristics that define her as being different and, according to prevailing notions, "less than."

How does the African-American woman deconstruct the prevailing image that society has given her, and become effective in organizations in which she is in the minority? The purpose of this chapter is to gain insights into the ways that African-American women adapt, survive and succeed as leaders in predominately white male organizations.

Using the Symbolic Interactionist perspective, I will attempt to answer four key questions. (1) How do African-American women see themselves as a result of being leaders in white male organizations? (2) How do African-American women leaders see their role in these organization? (3) What reference groups do African-American female leaders identify with or use as social support systems? (4) What factors go into the definition of the situations for African-American female leaders?

Overview of the Symbolic Interactionist Perspective

Symbolic Interactionism finds its philosophical and historical roots in Social Darwinism, German Idealism, the Scottish moralist, the American branch of Pragmatic philosophy and functional psychology (Reynolds, 1993). From these diverse antecedents, the interactionists synthesized their perspective and view about the nature of humans and their social experiences. The Interactionists stressed that humans are agents who act upon and shape their environment; that selves and minds are social products; that realities and worlds are socially created by human beings; that language was the key to making social interaction possible (Reynolds, 1993).

Though Symbolic Interactionism was influenced by such thinkers as Charles Pierce, William James, John Dewey and Charles Horton Cooley (Reynolds, 1993), credit is given to George Herbert Mead as the "major source of the interactionist movement" (Littlejohn, 1992, p. 171). Herbert Blumer was Mead's "foremost apostle" (Littlejohn, p. 171) and is credited with organizing and disseminating Mead's ideas.

Basic Concepts in Understanding Symbolic Interactionism

Basic to understanding the Symbolic Interactionist perspective includes the notion of object, objects and language, acts and social acts, self as object and self as process. The notion of object refers to the way in which people perceive and act upon their environment. Objects are provided by us through language but can also be created by us as we use language. Humans create the objects through the process of interacting and creating shared meaning.

Mead (1934) emphasized language as essential for the development of the self. The self has the characteristic that it is object to itself, distinguishing it from other objects. The self is not the same as the physical body; it is not based in biology or biological functions; and it is not present at birth. Through language, the self emerges out of social experiences.

Mead (1934) also described the self as process, distinguishing between the acting, spontaneous and creative part of the self (the I) and the conventional, passive part of the self (the me). Finally basic to understanding Symbolic Interactionism is the process known as the social act. To the Interactionist, people are actors not reactors; and social action is lodged in acting individuals who interact (Blumer, 1969). Littlejohn (1992) describes the social act as a three part process: "an initial gesture from one individual, a response to that gesture by another (covertly or overtly), and a result of the act, its meaning, which is perceived or imagined by both parties" (p. 171).

Additional Symbolic Interactionism Concepts

Roles, reference groups and the definition of the situation must be defined as key to the Symbolic Interactionist perspective. Humans' roles and identities are created and maintained by social interaction. According to Mead, people are able to assume one another's viewpoints by taking the roles of others. We take the role of others by imagining our selves as others see us. Specifically, roles are clusters of duties, rites and obligations associated with a specific social position (Berger, 1963). With respect to roles, humans engage in role making and role taking. In role making, the person constructs their own activities in a situation so that it fits their definition of the situation. In role taking the person takes the role of the other and is the primary way to see self as others see it.

There are two ways to look at Mead's concepts of generalized others and significant others. First, Littlejohn (1992) defines the generalized other as the unified role from which the individual sees the self. Berger's (1963) notion of reference group can also be used to explain the generalized other. The generalized other is the social group that gives the individual his or her concept of self. Significant other represents the reference group whose opinions and beliefs we value in defining self.

Finally, definition of the situation is one of the tenets of Symbolic Interactionism. It is the interpretation or meaning we give to our immediate circumstances; it is the reality as perceived by people. People use past experiences to make sense out of their current circumstances and use this sense making to make decisions and order their actions in present situations.

Now that the historical perspective, key concepts, and ideas of Symbolic Interactionists have been given, I will use their perspective to provide a number of insights into the contemporary African-American leadership phenomenon.

Method

For this preliminary study, in-depth interviews were conducted with three African-American women who manage departments in predominately white male organizations. The organizations included a national law firm with 2500 employees worldwide; a financial analysis staff of a midwestern Public Utility; and a Construction engineering staff of a large automotive manufacturer. The women's ages ranged from 35 to 40, and their titles were Director of Human Resources, Manager of Compensation Analysis, and Remediation Group Project Manager. The educational background of the women ranged from bachelor degree to post Master's degree. These women worked in departments that were predominately white male. The questions used in the interview are given in the notes section of this chapter.

Black Women's Corporate Identities

The Self as Seen by African-American Female Leaders

Each of the African-American women that I interviewed saw themselves as competent and capable. One means that each of the women leaders used to maintain this sense of competence was to work hard and produce great results. Even thought each of these women were highly educated (two have Master's degrees) the prevailing notion was that they had to work harder to prove themselves and be more knowledgeable. One leader stated, "unfortunately there is always this implied perception that we are not as competent as anybody else, even though [our] credentials are far greater than everyone else. [We] end up living this tension."

Another means used by these Black female leaders to maintain a sense of self was to consciously and intentionally control interactions. Each of them talked about letting the men at work "see in me what I want them to see." They were very deliberate in their interactions. One example comes from the Human Resources Director. She would call meetings in which the president of the law firm had to attend. In this way, she maintained visibility and at the same time became associated with the types of decisions in which the president was involved. Soon she found herself "being invited to all meetings of importance." This strategy is an example of the mutual influence of environment and actor stressed in the Symbolic Interactionist perspective.

All three women were clear about how the organization perceived them. Only one of the women appealed to the data from her written performance review to substantiate her perceptions. It appears that the women leaders had become adept at reading the signals of the organizations. The women believed they were seen as stern, demanding, high performers, competent, capable and able to manage multiple priorities and demands. Their continued presence as leaders in their organizations was proof enough for them as to how the organization viewed them.

The Role of the African-American Female Leader

Each of the women in the interviewed group was clear on her formal role in the organization. Each of these women believed she was in her organization to provide a technical service to the organization. Their role was to implement those services by providing data, counseling, or management decisions. Each of them was clear not to mix up or confuse their formal roles with informal interactions in the organizations.

Each of them maintained very strict and clear boundaries. One interviewee stated "once the men got used to me, we established a good working rapport but it is still professional and all business; our interactions are somewhat distant because there is always a line of separation. There is never any doubt as to who is in charge." The notion of a line of separation came out in each interview. One leader stated that "even though her job put her in the same economic class as her work counterparts, she is less likely to interact socially with business people of that social strata."

The Reference Groups for African-American Female Leaders

As can be seen from the previous section, the black female leaders in this study maintained professional distance from their counterparts at work. Consequently, none of them were willing to build social support systems at work. Myers (1992) defines a social support system as "those helping agents or individuals within their environment whom Black women identify as those who provide social support and feedback in solving problems or during periods of crisis" (p. 17). One interviewee explained that these support groups weren't sought out at work, because there was no "common ground" between them and the white men they worked with. It appeared that each leader in our group felt it was important to maintain that distance between them and the white men at work; building social support networks with their co-workers was perceived as "not safe."

So to whom did these women leaders turn in time of problem solving or crisis? Each of them described their social support system as friends who had similar backgrounds; and family members who had similar experiences. One leader belonged to a Black professional networking group for executives called Blacks in Management (BIM). She was the only female leader in this group. She described the type of support she received from this group: "I would have conversations with they guys in BIM and give them the situations I was facing at work. They would help me to build alternative scenarios and reconstruct appropriate behaviors and responses."

Defining the Situation

Each of the African-American female leaders in the study worked in predominately white organizations that were traditionally all male (financial analysis, legal, and construction engineering). These departments and organizations confronted each leader with specific expectations. Usually these expectations created powerful pressures to perform and to respond in appropriate, organizationally sanctioned ways. Each of the leaders talked about the expectations on her high performance. One leader described intense planning meetings in which "questions are being shot at me; I've got to be able to answer on the spot and substantiate my numbers; there are high expectations."

Another one of our leaders described a situation in which her boss had given her an assignment to put together a complex analysis for a confidential salary review. She was unfamiliar with the type of analysis in question, but felt it was one of those situations in which her job would be on the line if she did not do it correctly. She felt she could not go to anyone within the company, so the men in BIM coached her through the analysis and taught her how to put the report together. Each of these examples indicate that the leaders are attune to reading the organization and ascertaining the high expectations for performance put upon them.

Another theme appeared around the perceptions of power in organizations. Two of our leaders were very clear in stating "I try not to be overpowering or aggressive." It appears that in defining the situation in their organizations, it became clear to these women that aggression was not effective for them to use. One leader described how she had to learn the hard way after "wars had escalated" that "aggressiveness" was not going to work for her. She had to learn new ways to get people in the organization to respond. She said, "As in science, for every action, there is an equal and opposite reaction. I had to learn not to react in an equal and opposite manner. If [the white men in the organization] came at me, I could not go right back at them." She had learned from past experiences that this type of behavior led to escalation of conflict that was unproductive.

Another one of our leaders expressed a similar issue. She described herself as possessing inner strength, but worked hard at not being overpowering. In some ways both of these particular African-American leaders perceived their strength or power to be a threat to members of the organization, so they consciously worked to be perceived as nonthreatening. In both of these cases, these African-American women intentionally downplayed power, as if they were implicitly deconstructing images of themselves that were replete with power or aggression.

Summary

This brief picture of our African-American women enables us to see a little more clearly the issues they face as leaders within predominately white male organizations. As Berger (1963) describes reality as being socially created at multiple levels, each of these women has learned that there were many layers of meaning in their organizations. It appeared that each of them maintained a public image and were very intentional in their official discourse at work, and yet they were guarded of their private selves. The organizations in which these women led were instrumental in helping to shape their professional selves. These women had become adept at negotiating interactions at work and were very intentional and strategic in their communication.

Just as it is clear that these organizations affected the women in our study, it is clear that these women are making impacts in their respective organizations. They are performing, producing, coaching, empowering, and most of all—surviving.

Areas for Additional Study

It was the intent of this chapter to use the Symbolic Interactionist framework to explore the African-American female leadership role and thus gain insights into this experience. The paucity of studies and research for African-American women in general, and African-American female leaders in particular, points to the necessity for additional research and study. The general questions offered in this chapter, can serve as questions to guide future research aimed at explaining the leadership experiences of African-American women. Issues of power and prevailing images of African-American women must be explored in organizational contexts.

Additional questions might include: Are the leadership experiences of African-American women different from African-American men or women of other ethnic groups? How do African-American women emerge as leaders in organizations? Is the African-American female process of leadership emergence different from those in the dominant culture or for African-American men? What are the strategies used by African-American women to be effective leaders in organizations?

As more and more African-American women attain leadership positions in public and private organizations, in political and community institutions, the more researchers will need to be able to answer these basic questions for African-American women. Role and process models are needed for aspiring African-American female leaders.

Current theories across a variety of disciplines are somewhat silent on the issues of the African-American woman leader. We must halt the silence and in so doing give voice to the African-American female leader, and allow her experiences to inform and perhaps reframe general leadership theory and practice.

African-American Female Leadership Questionnaire

Name:
Company size:
Title:
Age:

1. How many other African-American women are there in your organization?
2. Describe your other leadership experiences.
3. Use metaphors or phrases to describe your style or brand of leadership.
4. How do you see yourself as a leader?
5. Describe your role in the organization.
6. Who do you talk to the most in your organization? What are the roles of these people? For what purposes do you talk to them?
7. Describe your interactions with white men in your organization.
8. Describe your interactions with white women in your organization.
9. How do you think the organization views you as a leader?
10. Describe or list the people who make up your social support system in or out of the organization.
11. In your opinion, what was the most important factor in you being selected to lead or manage your organization?
12. Do you have anything else to add?

References

Berger, P.L. (1963). *Invitation to sociology*. New York: Doubleday.
Blumer, H. (1969). *Symbolic Interactionism: Perspectives and method*. Englewood Cliffs, NJ: Prentice-Hall.
Littlejohn, S.W. (1992). *Theories of human communication* (4th ed.). Belmont, CA: Wadsworth Publishing.

Mead, G.H. (1934). *Mind, self and society: From the standpoint of a social behaviorist.* Chicago: University of Chicago Press.

Myers, L.W. (1991). *Black women: Do they cope better?* (Rev. ed.). San Francisco: Mellen Research University Press.

Reynolds, L.T. (1993). *Interactionism: Exposition and critique* (3rd ed.). Dix Hils, NY: General Hall.

Scarborough, C. (1989). Conceptualizing Black women's employment experience. *The Yale Law Journal, 98,* 1457–1478.

Stivers, C. (1993). *Gender images in public administration: Legitimacy and the administrative state.* Newbury Park, CA: Sage

SISTUHS AT THE WELL: QUENCHING OUR SPIRITUAL THIRSTS

9

JOURNEYS IN AFRICAN-AMERICAN WOMANHOOD

EMERGING COMMUNITY-ORIENTED SPIRITUALITY

Brigitte Rouson

I am because we are, and because we are, I am.

As Americans of African ancestry continue to explore and center ourselves in traditional African culture, women's understanding of this collective enterprise merits greater attention. The labor of giving voice to such experiences prospers through ethnographic studies, where a subject's own expression is privileged. Using this approach, my related research primarily has focused on two areas. One is to foster an appreciation of the communicative dimension of spiritual practice, not only in ritual assemblies but more specifically in such activities as divination and sacrifice in which priestesses and priests collaborate with spirits in defining life directions. In that vein, I have sought to situate participant expressions about the meanings, roles and responsibilities of traditional African systems adopted in and adapted to the context of African-American cultural experience. That line of inquiry also has led to analyzing discourse that arises in the context of judicial challenges—drawing comparisons between contested traditions that are African-American (animal sacrifice) and Native American (sacramental use of peyote), both of which can be seen as predominantly communicative. Another area of research, addressed here, acknowledges the aspirations and agency of sisters as cultural leaders to sustain a communal ethic. What connects these two areas is a dedication to understanding communication as a basis for systems by which people are made whole, which is to say connected in life-affirming ways.

To appreciate how women of the African diaspora conceive community as they reinvigorate pre-colonial African traditions, a case study was made consulting two priestesses living in Philadelphia. As a knowledge seeker in the academic and the cultural sense, I had multiple encounters with them over a four-year period (1992–1996). Also in that cycle, I interacted occasionally with some of their family members and with numerous African Americans adopting Yoruba and Akan traditions. The current analysis is based on a full complement of related ethnographic work, including participatory research and interviews with other initiates. Three interviews were conducted during 1996 specifically for this writing; another three interviews from previous years also yielded material employed here. This work is further informed by extensive readings of relevant literature, both scholarly and popular. The sections that follow discuss thematic impressions and historical background, contextualize the account of two priestesses relative to other works about traditional African culture in the Americas, briefly highlight the background of the two women in this study, then present their perspectives that relate to the elevation of the communal. Finally, brief conclusions and suggestions for further investigation are offered.

Throughout our history, African Americans have been captivated by issues of the cultural efficacy—retention, reclamation, revision or rejection—of practices in the interest of collective uplift. At the heart of many significant acts and ideas within African America is the yearning to benefit the whole, to possess a wholeness rooted in enduring systems that acknowledge divine being. This impetus is manifested in the many adaptations of traditional African systems (see for example a comprehensive overview by Mbiti [1969], writings on Akan culture by Busia [1991] and Meyerowitz [1985], and writings on Yoruba culture such as Awolalu [1979], Idowu [1994].) Voudou (or "Vodou") and Santeria have been practiced in such areas as Louisiana, New York, Florida, Cuba and Puerto Rico; Angola or "Gullah" traditions in the Carolinas and Georgia; Candomble and related systems in Brazil (Walker, 1990; Hurston, 1990; Teish, 1985; Simpson, 1978; Haskins, 1978; Santana, n.d.; Deren, 1953). Whereas previously most documented organized activity was outside the continental United States, the past 50 years have witnessed the start of Akan communities in such places as New York, Washington, DC, Philadelphia and Atlanta, creation of a Yoruba village in South Carolina, theological archministry in New York and formation or continuation of many houses of devotion to traditional African systems in various parts of the USA (Santana, n.d.; Mason, 1993; Mason & Edwards, 1985; Dinizulu, 1974, 1987; Sarpong, 1993). In similar fashion, African Americans have been galvanized by various interpretations of Islam, often with considerable attention to notions of African origins and racial uplift (McCloud, 1995, pp. 1, 13–14, 33–34). Efforts grounded in Judaism and Christianity also historically exhibit such yearning. Illustrative are interests and events related to the founding—inside a woman's home—of the African Methodist Episcopal Church; mobilization of African Americans in the migration out of the South (to the North and to the West) and campaigns for migration to Africa, including Garveyite Orthodox Christianity that sought to connect with Ethiopian Orthodox and other Africans in the Orthodox tradition; establishment of other groups influenced by a biblically grounded Ethiopianism; and extensions of Black Power in the conception of Black Theology and womanist thought (Jones, 1990; Barrett, 1988; Cone & Wilmore, 1993). Although far from exhaustive, these developments indicate the high priority African Americans place on a spirituality of the commons, of common people who prize their connectedness—rather than a tradition favoring individualism and isolation. Moreover, this way of being has great resonance with what relevant culture and spirituality scholar-activists see as quintessentially African or Black. (See, e.g., Richards [Ani], 1985)

Studying such diasporan experiences calls for probing the ways in which cultural leaders formulate the basis for existing in community. That basis might be considered a matter of cultural authenticity, meaning that womanhood (and manhood) are determined by cultivating the potential for being true to one's communal self and intentionally consistent with the purposes of collective self-preservation and advancement. My primary concern here is to expand the spaces for women committed to African spirituality to set forth their grounds for evaluating how people, particularly African Americans, relate to African identity. Thus, with each phrasing of questions and interpretation of responses, this project is about learning how, in one large urban center, women who have adopted traditional African systems at the level of priesthood express themselves to offer a wider audience (beyond adherents) counsel on ordering relations. This piece moves toward articulations by and for women of the African diaspora drawn from unique positions of cultural leadership.

The task at hand is to document how these women speak as spiritual-cultural authority figures that privileges the communal. This emphasis may be found by examining women's expression for evidence of how they apparently conceive, and labor for, bonds linking them with others, both adherents and persons who are strictly speaking outside the tradition. Women's own way of voicing the importance of these traditions, not only for themselves but for African America, can and should be taken as an important instance of speaking about community formation philosophy and grounding it in practical experience. This writing attends to what is being said by women who are active in renewing African traditions in the U.S.A., as it evokes commitment to life sharing that infuses everyday practices.

Self-Disclosure

In the stream of African-centered life, storytelling—of which scholarship is one esteemed form—benefits from self-examination and from engendering reciprocal opportunities for examination by those who will receive and interpret, and who may participate in calling into being the particular communication (Asante, 1990, 1987). No pretense is made that one's own experiences and views can be almost entirely divorced from research. Indeed, it is vital that there be forthright cues as to the author's cultural location.

This project has many sources of interest and perspective. Perhaps foremost is the loss of my father to the spirit world in my young adulthood; my eyes were opened as relatives and friends in our African-American Catholic faith community affirmed that his spirit remained in sometimes tangible ways. A more light-hearted curiosity was sparked even earlier by my mother's tales of her New Orleans childhood amid Creole speakers, and her amusement as an adult when people—having learned what city she claimed as home—would come asking her to work "roots" or make a love potion.

Invaluable insights stem from earlier religious study pursuits of my husband, the explorations of friends and colleagues, and the encouragement of several of my professors. Most striking has been a continuing recognition of the strength of African elements still present in Catholicism and Orthodox Christianity, and a sense of genuine synthesis achieved in various adaptations of African systems in the Americas. This understanding contradicts the still pervasive deficit model imposed on African peoples' culture and capacity, and on the continuing challenges that have been raised to acknowledging our divinity and even humanity. Traditions not popularly seen as consonant with European "civilization" or colonization have been routinely disparaged or set apart as quaint, perhaps freakish. This project flows from my own investment in reawakening the consciousness of living traditions of wholeness and community-making, not as purely universal, but as specific to expressing and shaping African-American womanhood in contemporary culture.

Omissions and Openings

Although a focus on women is rare in research on African spirituality, it is rarer still in reports of American experiences adapting traditional cultures in this land. Moreover, the approach in scholarly literature is not usually one in which African-American women enjoy great latitude to speak for ourselves. In the case of Akan and Yoruba alike, published work has not focused specifically on presenting in their words the experiences of women who grew up in the USA. In an unpublished paper, Leila Brown offers significant insights about Akan women in Washington, D.C. who participate in the Bosum Dzemawodzi. Brown (1993), presented and analyzed several women's comments. She found that these women in their own voices give priority to being community-centered and maternal, affirming the important roles of men while in no way viewing themselves as subordinate. My own related paper (1993) illustrated that women who have sought knowledge of Yoruba have expansive concepts of community and communication, particularly divination; their experiences run counter to most notions of subordination based on gender. A later work (Rouson,

1994), seeking to contextualize sacrificial practices of African Americans in Akan and Yoruba, concludes that rituals and roles are understood to mediate relations in community that extends to ancestral and divine spirits. Among those the study relied on are African-American women priests, including Nana Korantemaa Ayeboafo (one of the two priestesses given voice here) as main consultants. However, it did not concentrate on presenting women's perspectives.

A number of published works develop useful analysis about how African-American women may embrace African cultural presence and uphold its definition as, and dedication to, community building. Raul Canizares (1993) and Joseph Murphy (1988) furnish descriptive and theoretical perspectives on initiation and participation in Santeria, the African-Caribbean tradition that has strong roots in Yoruba. Given the paucity of published writing about traditional African religion in the USA, these men make valuable contributions by setting personal experience into historical-cultural context. The writings of Canizares, Cuban-born, and Murphy, European-American and of Catholic background, are spiced with anecdotal information that speaks to the power of women who helped lead them into "new world" Yoruba practice. First-person accounts and instruction offered by others such as Philip John Neimark (1993) and Awo Fa'lokun Fantunmbi (1991), are two similarly situated men who combine a personal and general focus, leaving for others the study of women's experiences.

A few works bring a refreshing emphasis to the voices or perspectives of women of African ancestry who are synthesizing African traditions in the United States. Among them is Karen McCarthy Brown's *Mama Lola.* (1991). Brown vividly recounts her journey as a European-American woman growing into a spiritual family. She developed a relationship under the leadership of a Haitian-American priestess whom Brown initially met while doing ethnographic work for a museum, and who eventually initiated her in Haiti into "Vodou". In equal measure, she retells stories of her own encounters alongside autobiographical stories passed on by the woman called Mama Lola or Alourdes. Brown's own initiation experiences and the voice of Mama Lola, woven together with historical and fictional narratives, speak to how a woman of African ancestry perceives her task of binding people together in a community that crosses lines of race, national origin and religious upbringing. Brown suggests that this challenge of building spiritual community is particularly difficult in New York, where members of a cultural community do not necessarily live or work near one another and are bombarded "with messages that counsel self-interest and self-reliance" (p. 47). Even with the priestess's local blood relatives, "the bonds...are not as durable as they would be in Haiti" (p. 47). Clearly constructed as the experiences of a priestess who emigrated to the United States and of a woman scholar/curator who emigrates culturally, these accounts point toward but do not intentionally seek to define experiences of African-American women, women of the diaspora who were born and raised in the USA.

Jessie Gaston Mulira's (1990) chapter on "Voodoo" culture in New Orleans reproduces vivid descriptions by folklorist Zora Neale Hurston, writing about her initiation there in the 1920s (pp. 40–44). Although Hurston was the only initiate under this priest at the time, there was no sense in which she was isolated. Numerous aspects support an interpretation of the ritual practices being mainly about the community invoking the spirits and using symbolic practices to bring her into the circle. Mulira also devotes considerable attention to famous Voodoo priestess and queen Marie Laveau and mentions other women priestesses (pp. 49–56, 61). Aside from quoting Hurston, Mulira's piece relies mainly on historical and anthropological material by male authors.

Mary Arnold Twining (1991) describes the cultural synthesis achieved by women of the Sea Islands in arts and crafts. Her treatment is enriched by relaying some of the women's own descriptions of their work (e.g., pp. 132, 136). She further notes events that indicate the purposefulness of their work in fostering family connection. In a labor equally interpretative and documentary, Twining contends:

> [W]e can reject the notion that if the makers of the patched cloth (or other material culture traits) do not identify the item as to its original function and designation, it is not then truly 'carried over.' Sea Island quilts document African cultural continuity. They are deeply conscious, however, of another more immediate, more intimate significance of the quilts: that is, the communication of affection between family members and the celebration of their family history. Thus the quilts relate to family events as symbols of the continued caring from one generation to another. Rites of passage such as marriage, births of children, young people leaving home to go to school, are often signalized

> by the making or completing of a quilt which accompanies the departing family members to their new situation as a reminder of the ties of kinship which connect them to the parent family. (p. 137)

Such analysis affirms the centrality of communal aspirations and practices for women, and suggests a way of identifying this center even where women are not explicit about African continuity or specific related purposes. By contrast, the present case study taps into more explicit accounts by women of their purposes and understanding. It also seeks to articulate spiritual aspects of the phenomenon, which are not discussed directly by Twining.

The present work owes a tremendous debt to a remarkable first-person account by Luisah Teish (1985), purposely intended as a handbook for women, rather than directed to scholarly audiences. As a preface to description and prescription, Teish makes evident that through African-based spirituality she honors the female perspective, a broad notion of community, and the importance of everyday practice:

> The voudou has special appeal to women. Because it is the child of matristic traditions, it recognizes spiritual kinship; encourages personal growth; respects the earth; and utilizes the power of sexuality and women's menstrual blood.... Our foremothers knew things that modern science is still struggling to "explain." Our ancestors had access to the collective unconscious centuries before Jung's mother got pregnant. Through ancestor reverence we erase the "Exorcist" tapes and learn to relate to spirits as friends, as members of the family.
>
> Because the Voudou is African-based, it views spirituality as an integral part of everyday life. Because the Voudou of New Orleans was nurtured by a "servant class," its magic is practiced as household acts. Because it survived uprooted from its motherland, it teaches adaptability. Because its truth is found in the oral tradition, it teaches respect for the elders.... (1985, p. xi)

Many of the elements that Teish invokes are instructive for present work, suggesting possible parallels in experiential perspectives of women in a certain named system (Avoudou) traced to parts of the Americas, but with an acknowledged traditional African base (Yoruba). In particular, Teish's words confirm the centrality of extended community and wisdom born of praxis.

Two journeys

In distinctive yet parallel ways, the two women in this essay each exercise leadership in adaptations of Yoruba and Akan traditions. One was initiated in the USA., one on the African continent. They know and respect one another, greeting each other warmly when they find themselves in the same place and speaking positively each when the other's name is mentioned. They share an immense concern for future generations and love of teaching. They are undaunted by experiences of estrangement, being somewhat set apart by others, whether this takes shape as admiration or fear. This fearlessness rests on conviction that they have entered into a larger and more enduring community in which divine energies and ancestral spirits are fully present. They cultivate the authentically African, which is to say communal, experience in their own and others' lives.

Iya Omo Wumi Ogundeisi is a woman in her mid-60s, mother of seven (two daughters, five sons), teacher in a public elementary school, civic leader, former wife, and a priestess for 29 years. As we meet again in 1996, Iya stands tall and has a commanding presence that is maternal, intense, intellectual. Raised Christian in the Episcopalian church, she left at age 22. Moved to seek a reading by a Yoruba priest, she was impressed with its truthfulness and began studying the tradition. She was among the earliest African-American priestesses. Iya gives readings to assist people in understanding their lives and paths, arranges and conducts ceremonies, speaks and promotes educational activity. She participates in an Egbe association that is working toward establishing a landed community in the Southern USA, dedicated to a return to African culture and its revitalization. Invoking a commonality of values with the Akan (including the Ashanti, or Asante) people, the group speaks of this as the Sankofa principle. One of Iya's sons, Sekou, is a Yoruba priest, as is her former husband; they, too, are actively involved in educating interested people about the tradition.

Nana Korantemaa Ayeboafo is a woman in her mid-40s, the head of a shrine, consultant and teacher of cultural traditions such as drumming, and a former professional dancer. She is a mother to one daughter in the communal parenting tradition of African peoples, sometimes acknowledged as the "other mothers" tradition of the diaspora in which the role is somewhat similar to that of an aunt; following this tradition, she held a wedding in her home for her daughter, whose birth mother enthusiastically participated. Of medium stature physically, Nana is energetic, reflective, curious, positive. As a Christian in her youth, she was in the Holiness church, but in her young adult years turned to studying meditation and knowledge sometimes described as "new age." On a trip to Ghana in 1974, she was performing dance and experienced spirit possession. Initiated a priestess three years later, she trained a total of seven years in Ghana. Nana leads ceremonies, maintains the Asona Aberade Shrine in her home, teaches and performs drumming, and provides cultural instruction for students, arts teachers and others. In recent years, she participated in rites in Ghana and took part in planning ceremonies in the USA for the renowned Nana Okomfohemaa Akua Oparebea, the high priestess of Larteh's Akonnedi Shrine under whom she trained. In 1996 Nana Korantemaa was a key organizer of ceremonies in the USA to mark Nana Oparabea's passing and also participated in traditional rites in Ghana. She also has traveled to Brazil and moved toward initiation in a venerated sisterhood there, to Beijing for the fourth international women's conference, and to the African continent for a gathering of trade women from 44 nations.

To listen to these women is to begin to know that understanding and being are one. Their journeys in spirituality, and more broadly in culture, bear witness to the endurance of a valued African-centered and womanist principle: loving the whole and cultivating an understanding of extended community. Common to their lived experiences is the process of gaining the communal self: recognizing and mourning loss, followed by reclaiming and remaking cultural practice. Theirs is a journey where road maps, publicly spoken directions, manufactured vehicles, and even destinations that pay homage to a particular social order of capitalism and materialism are not valued in deference to the desire to bring people, principles and processes of wholeness and health.

Naming Loss, Reclaiming Culture

Iya Omo Wumi and Nana Korantemaa alike lament a cultural loss that they feel has crippled African-Americans and by extension American society. Yet they candidly concede both the rewards of reclaiming tradition and the difficulty in remaking oneself while still relating to others who lack more than a tourist's interest in traditions in which they deeply engage.

Clearly more intent on appraising the prospects for collective uplift than religious righteousness, Iya declares,

> We are the road openers. We have had to open doors that had been closed to us.... The Black church historically had the same struggles... We say we want more than the religion. We want all that we have lost.... To save our young people, there's only one answer... You can't fight TV, MTV, rap, one hundred kinds of cigarettes or juices, Internet, Sega Genesis, ultra reality—it's so big until it just sweeps 'em off their feet.... The most important thing any man or woman can have is a way of life—that's what the African-American community has lost: the way children address adults, talk to one another, know ways problems can be answered outside of hurting or killing—that comes from having the culture. It keeps bringing them back.... I have seven children, and I think that if there's nothing else I want to give my children, I've always wanted to give them the culture. I truly believe our way of life is the most powerful thing on earth, period. If I can just make a few other people see that, I can open the world. (1996)

The way Iya seeks to open those doors to the spirit world for others, however, has shifted since our first meeting in 1992. She no longer perceives a calling to reach out to nearly everyone who may be considered part of African America, even on a local level.

> I don't know if I serve a community; rather, I try to be available to a select group of people that want to go in the same direction as I go—with a common desire to take back that which is ours, Sankofa.... for future generations, to assure ourselves that what is important for our children, for people, will always be, into infinity. (1996)

For Iya, purposeful departure was required from the Christianity she had known as a source of identity personally and collectively. She shows little patience for ongoing commitment to precepts or practices claimed as Christian, insisting that

> I did not come, my ancestors did not come here with Jesus; we came here with different languages, cultural bases, but still hav-

ing the common thread of the continent. Jesus was given to us to replace that. There's no way I could take that religion of the master. Our people have gotten so good at becoming infused... I'm sorry; the religion of the master just can't be mine. No matter how I tried, it would still be the master's. I even told my sister that. The religion of the master has kept us on our knees for over 200 years. I remember singing, 'Let us praise God together on our knees.' You can't go to war on your knees.... I have to say to God, 'I can't bow down right now, there's some business I've got to take care of.' (Iya Omo Wumi, 1996)

Consistent with this translation of purpose, Iya urges a historically generated veneration and practicality:

> It's real important that we begin to honor ourselves... [I]f we all went back to our roots, we would be free. You're on this side. You deal now. White people look at us as if we are less than human beings—trying to erode our following our own culture. We have a power that is unimaginable. (1996)

This sense of power is not without its tensions; as Iya notes, in her interactions with close relatives, she is unapologetic about her departure from Christianity.

Nana Korantemaa perceives the role of cultural "custodian" in part as requiring respect for a full range of spiritual orders, while seeing Akan as life-giving for those involved (1993). Speaking of her own transformation, Nana notes that when in about 1970 she "really started to identify with African culture, it gave me such a sense of self, of fulfillment" (1996). This personal dimension of change is fully consonant with the collective sensibility, for as Nana ponders her relationship with other African-Americans who observe Akan traditions somewhat differently, she considers that what binds all together is not simply a realization of common ancestry, but a "strong desire to bring a sense of pride and respect to a people who are constantly being told: 'You are nobody. You don't do or have the capacity for anything'" (1996). Nana is conscious and explicit about countering folk thought represented by such sayings as, "Grass don't grow where the niggers go" (1996). In describing her own experience, she imbues the fear of new encounters and of transition with a collective character, stating her conviction that

> Within our genes, all of that experience is there—even enslavement. So to re-identify is to go back through that passage. It

> takes your breath away. It means crossing into an area that is unknown or that is not readily remembered. And so there is that fear, that instability of not being here or there. I felt it was practically the end of the world. . . . I remembered running outside trying to catch my breath. I didn't see it was because of re-identifying through drumming, dancing. I felt I must get past this. It was that kind of experience for me. (1996)

Going "back through that passage," through moments of terror that raise historically powerful sources of bonding through shared pain, Nana suggests, leads to renewal of deep, shared understandings. Even emotions are recast:

> People say, was it hard for you to accept that, to do that? Many people don't want to go that deeply. I felt they were exhibiting shallowness of character [if they did not understand]. However, now I see that there was an intense, psychological readjustment that was happening here. It was like, let me not put that thought into it. I won't 'go there,' as the young people say. I would tell someone to deep breathe, to know that whatever was happening within yourself is not the end of the world. . . . I really believe we don't learn anything new; we have the lessons within us. . . . Experience or information helps us to remember. . . . It's memory in every part of you . . . (Nana Korantemaa, 1996)

To know how one recognizes the lessons, takes up the culture and moves forward, both women willingly teach about the basics of the traditions into which they have been drawn.

Elements of Connection

To define one's community in keeping with African cosmology presupposes an expansive notion of being as well as communication. In Yoruba and Akan cosmology, Supreme Being is manifested in numerous aspects, sometimes generically termed deities or divinities. Also important are ancestral spirits, characterized as the "living dead" (Mbiti, 1969). Relating to these entities by word, gesture, deed or other sign is as necessary, continuous and revitalizing as breathing. Nana Korantemaa begins a description of her spiritual community by recalling,

> Number one . . . we believe there is one Supreme Being who has created like mortal people and . . . a reality of psychic and spiritual entities—those who reside in the different elements, natural elements like water, fire and the like, as well as . . . general spirits, as well as the ancestral spirits. . . . (1993)

The Abosum (generally pronounced aw-bo-soom or oh-bo-soom) are divine, while the Nsamanfo are ancestors. Other entities exist whom Nana considers outside of the Akan community because they are not directly summoned by Akan people and are not thought to influence the people's activity (1993). These might include divinity figures or supernatural forces in other traditions.

An Akan community is structured as a family, Nana emphasizes. Spiritual energies provide the role characterization and functions for members such as the *obrafo,* who acts as executioner in sacrifice and the linguist or *okyeame,* who speaks for the head of a shrine and for certain spirits (1993). People who are not specifically in Akan communities are thought to participate in its beneficial acts. Nana explains,

> And that is, again, part of the most significant reason for reclaiming traditional spiritual concepts, traditional rituals. There's a community, there's an identity that we reclaim, so that we're not lost, desolate people again taken from our heritage, taken from [our land] . . . so that we claim that. . . . [E]verybody doesn't have to be involved in indigenous African religion to be a part of the larger community. (1993)

In Yoruba tradition, Iya Omo Wumi envisions "God" as composite. By interacting with spirits whom the Yoruba call the Orisha—essentially, deified ancestors, those claimed for the spiritual ancestry of an entire people—"we're dealing with every aspect" and thus with the totality (1992). Continuity is embraced collectively rather than pursued solo, although this reality translates to different forms of assembly, not all of them with several gathered in the same bodily form. For Iya, there is little need to display specific symbols on a daily basis (such as wearing a cross) or necessarily go to one site to commune with the spirits;

> I am totally complete within myself. My church is a part of me, It's in my heart, it's in my head. . . . I'm in constant contact—be-

> lieve that—with the forces. [T]hey're always with me. I'm always utilizing their messages, their constant... direction, and all I've got to do is listen and hear.
>
> They are more powerful in death than they were in life. Because they are always with us. They're that wall you feel when you're walking and you go into a place and get that feeling, I shouldn't be here, or there's something in here I don't like... something's wrong. God, there's something wrong. That's that life force, that family I'm talking about that's talking to you. (1992).

The wisdom of everyday, every moment experience sustains through calling on a collective presence. Phenomena related to racism are, of course, a major concern that generates differing approaches to defining community. For Iya, European Americans or those identified as "White" are outside what she considers community since leaving the Episcopalian church. She dubs them collectively "the master," a cultural point of reference marking historical relationship that African - Americans must leave behind in belief as well as practice. A different opinion is voiced by Nana, who instructs

> Racism is truly not our concept. This concept of being a human family is the African way; Africans' doors were open. People were welcomed—because to a large extent, you looked like me, you walked on two legs, you had five fingers, there was a nose and ears; you were not an animal, so I didn't have a fear of you. You were welcomed. (1996)

Nonetheless, recalling oral history she learned in Ghana, Nana Korantemaa points out that informed by experiences of colonialism and now contemporary racism, she and African cultural custodians generally guard access, even as they generously offer healing to those who seek it out.

A parallelism between the human and spirit worlds informs the understanding of gendered ancestral and divine spirits, and gender distinction also carries significance when adherents act in the tradition. As an example, the Akan shrine of Larteh, Ghana, where Nana learned strikes quite a contrast to American culture. By tradition in Africa, there has been a female section and a male section, each with somewhat distinct responsibilities. In such arrangements, for instance,

> The female section deals with ritual observances of the [Abosum], possessions, the herbs, and training for priests and priestesses. The male section deals with land disputes and the judiciary processes of a community. So the shrine itself is an integral part of a community, basically used to create or to maintain the balance between the seen and the unseen world, worlds. (Nana, 1996)

Although this structure is not necessarily replicated in USA Akan communities, the form and its underlying concepts of gender complimentarity merit further investigation in the study of diasporan women's experiences that inform contemporary culture.

As a Yoruba, Iya Omo Wumi notes that she is directly linked with the spirit of femininity known as Oshun, "because when I was born that was the Orisha which called me as one of her children." (1992) Each summer, Iya presides over a river ceremony in Philadelphia to honor Oshun. Akan priests also serve certain spirits and are responsible for training initiates who have been called by those spirits; the Abosum whom Nana serves are from the female side. It is noteworthy that Nana's training came from a rare woman, Nana Okomfohemaa Akua Oparebea, a nonagenarian queen mother who passed early in 1996. Nana Oparebea's decades of travel to the USA sought to bring African Americans home to a reliable source of understanding in connection with a motherland culture. As such, for whatever inclinations there may be to shape Yoruba or Akan in this land as patriarchal, in keeping with other cultures, there are grounds for reconceiving and resisting. Gender, as one characteristic shared by humans and other spirits that shapes women's experience and investment in a communal ethic, thus is deserving of study.

Bonding Through Practice

"More than ancestry, all of us pour libation as a way of prayer because all of our African ancestors poured libation. That is what Nana Oparebea brought to us; she is responsible for us being a family" (Nana Korantemaa, 1996).

Through ritual ceremonies, readings to inform and counsel an initiate or client, and a host of practices, the world and the way of the Yoruba or Akan tradition are regenerated continually. A powerful proverbial convention holds that only by calling names of the departed and of deities are they assured continual life. The relationship consists in mutual exchange of work, substance and understanding—understanding in its literal meaning as support and its figurative sense as knowledge.[1]

Nana Korantemaa distinguishes her own congregational practices from those of the "Black church" as rooted in the cosmological, "acceptance that there is an intangible world existing perpetually," and "whatever is done, there is a correspondence in the tangible world with a physical act" (1996). As an example often reproduced in contemporary settings outside of ritual;

> Pouring of libations is a prayer; there is a divine force and spiritual entities always listening that make up that congregation—and that we are living a future life as we exist today; and that future life, where ancestors are present is right here in the present, we just don't see it. (Nana, 1996)

The ethical correlates of this understanding are highly instructive for everyday practice, as Nana counsels:

> If I'm in dialogue with you, and say something to offend you, I'm not just offending you but also the spirit world—and I will experience response not just tomorrow but in the next moment. I could stub a toe... The concept of being all of one family, not just blood lines [means I show] more honor and respect to you. It extends beyond people who are [identified as] Akan (1996).

Indeed, Nana's inaugural experience, possessing a spirit while performing African and Caribbean dances with an American dance company in Ghana, brought consciousness raising through strong sensation. While in spirit possession, she spoke in a Ghanaian language that neither she nor the other dancers—all of whom were American—knew. It was phenomenal not only for immediate impressions, but for its value leading her into more communication with

---

1. For this and many related insights, I am indebted to Klaus Krippendorff for his leadership in constructivist and semanticist scholarship. (See, e.g., Krippendorff, 1989)

Akan people and into becoming part of an Akan community who then worked to form community in the United States among African Americans;

> Because I was doing a dance that really did not have anything to do with the Akan pantheon as I knew at that time. However, because we were drumming and singing, the energy mounted. And so it changed my perspective in terms of how connected the different dimensions are, and how multidimensional people or beings; we have access to all those.... Well, after the experience of actually channeling an Obosum, another energy, I wanted to know what had happened to me. And it was explained to me that this was an entity, it has these qualities and it has called you to work for, to work through you for other people, those that are in need of psychic healing, spiritual healing. And so if you are prepared to study in depth about it, then we can continue from here. Or if not, we will look at different ways that we can appease the energy, ask it to release you. However, we can't guarantee that it won't come and call you again.... So after that experience, every time I got in an area where there were religious [activities] going on, and drumming, with lots of people, then I would go back into...these states. And then afterwards,...I had a little more information...[B]efore going [back to the USA], they gave me some information and things to do. (1993)

Her encounters were not to be interpreted individually or in isolation, only socially and in the context of people already immersed in the culture. This feature illuminates a particular way in which ritual operates as a community-making endeavor. In particular, animal sacrifice and ceremonies have significance such as that ascribed to Catholic communion. Its unifying effects are not confined strictly to adherents, according to Nana Korantemaa;

> [W]ithout actively taking a part in, but understanding the representations of the rites and rituals, I believe that it is important for each and every person to identify with those activities that strengthen them, you know. And we are all individual and unique. And depending on what part of your journey on this planet you're in, that may not be something that you actively have to be a part of at this point in your life. However, because it is a part of your heritage, you may benefit from understanding

> it and not denying it. . . . And so, in that respect, the feasting is just not for a separate few, but that it is available to everyone regardless of their religious convictions.

Similarly, Iya Omo Wumi finds an investiture of communal responsibility in divination and moment to moment awareness of spirits' presence. In Yoruba practice,

> We have concrete ways of communicating with the Orisha. For the Orishas also give us...signs and messages. Many times what the Orisha tells us are things that are far off, that may not be coming for six, eight, ten months, a year. Egun [ancestors] give us the immediate, right now. . . . They can also see things that are far off. But basically the Orisha give us long range. . . . When I got initiated into the religion, I had one child, my oldest son. I have seven children now. And, one of the things I was told in the reading that I got during my initiation was that I was going to have a daughter and I would have several other children afterwards. At that point, I didn't see having any more children. . . . They're right on time. . . . Whatever they say, you can go to the bank on it. For they don't lie. They've never, ever told me something that didn't come to pass. (1992)

Younger initiates and non-Yoruba clients now rely on her for readings, as they mutually grow in respect for tradition that has joined people across generations. Iya, while choosing not to disparage non-Yoruba approaches such as psychic consultation, finds divination particularly accurate, moving, and valuable for its function of drawing people into African tradition and binding them to one another. While in Akan it may mean gazing into a vessel, in Yoruba it often involves casting cowrie shells and interpreting the signs with stories passed down over many years. The practice has convinced Iya that

> Religion—Ifa—is so awesome. I often think how did the people create it? They must have been touched by God. I'm in awe of it all the time—when I read someone; the things I tell people, to bring, to do, and they see me later . . . it's just amazing how the ancestors can speak to one person and tell me [what they need to hear]. (1996)

Naturally, change is a constant. Nana Korantemaa sees an ongoing transition process that is reflected in ritual: "when I plan a ceremony...here I'm knowing that in some way I'm combining old with new...in healthy societies, that's the way it is." (1996) Becoming a "new Africa," Iya believes, will require new codes and new modes of communication, with even greater emphasis on "contextual clues." This stems from appreciating that "We're such an expressive people. I believe that's true in everything that we do. We're going to make it ours. We're going to be progenitors. When I come back in, the groundwork will [have been done]" (Iya, 1996).

Domesticity Revisited

Strong consciousness of a cultural base empowers women to fulfill priestly responsibilities as a call to wholism. Their attention to investigating and incorporating Yoruba or Akan traditional elements, to being mothers, and to keeping the home all flow from the cultural leadership that they live. Iya repeatedly instructs, "I'm not a religious person. I'm a cultural person. I must know about language...food...clothing...all these things" (1992). "It's not just religion—that was the hook that brought many of us in; but culture is total, encapsulating how we eat, dress, birth children, raise children; languages, art—everything that makes someone a living being." (1996) Her immersion in Yoruba has such depth that Iya says without hesitation,

> It's livin'. It's existin'. It's being able to be a whole human being and to take the rough and the good, the hard times and the good times and put them in their place, to be able to survive them and to live, to give my children a role model which is exemplary, that although they may have their stages and their phases, they know that they must live as an African in America. They must practice, and advance the whole cultural environment. This is their life...(1992)

Domesticity in this context is not a limitation to the household or even to a historical role. It is simply a ground on which to stand, a dimension of all one's dealings. Yet the home is significant in the building up of community, as dwelling spaces that are also symbolic spaces.

According to Nana Korantemaa, in her early forays into African culture, "Colors, artifacts gave me a sense of empowerment, of harmony I didn't find in my mother's house or my friends' house." (1996) Confirming that it is more than personal sentiment or idiosyncrasy, she recalls that subsequently when people entered her home, they have frequently volunteered that they find an atmosphere of peace and spirituality there; this is true even of those who before arriving, did not know her as an Akan priestess (1996). Especially memorable was the wedding ceremony she performed in her home (and shrine) for the young woman who recognizes Nana, as a biological parent, as well as mother. For both women, seeing oneself as mother and home maker poses no contradiction with seeing oneself as priest.

Endings and Excursions

The world of two Philadelphia women as priestesses of Yoruba and Akan tradition is centered in an African spirit, calling them to live and teach a communal ethic. This is evident in their personal journeys and conviction that cultural loss and reclamation are central, their consciousness of community defined by cultural and spiritual concepts, their continuation of traditional practices that aim to maintain and heal relationships in and across human and spirit worlds, and their own brand of domesticity bearing little resemblance to phenomena of women burdened by being home-bound. Further study might fruitfully gather and compare experiences of more women, with attention to the relationships participants in these traditions have to female deities, specific experiences in translating gender concepts from the African to the American context, and perceptions of gender issues as they compare among African traditions as well as across traditions relating experiences to those of women in Christianity, Islam, Native American or other cultural systems. Most important is to make spaces, and the commitment to listen well, to women whose courage leads them to reclaim African traditions on the soil of a "new world."

References

Awolalu, J. O. (1979). *Yoruba beliefs and sacrificial rites.* London: Longman.

Asante, M. K. (1987). *The Afrocentric idea.* Philadelphia: Temple University Press.

Asante, M. K. (1990). *Kemet, Afrocentricity and knowledge.* Trenton, NJ: Africa World Press.

Barnes, S. T. (Ed.). (1989). Africa's *Ogun: Old world and new.* Bloomington: Indiana University Press.

Barrett, L. E., Sr. (1988). *The Rastafarians: Sounds of cultural dissonance.* Boston: Beacon Press.

Bascom, W. (1991). *Ifa divination: Communication between Gods and men in West Africa.* Bloomington: Indiana University Press.

Brown, L., Rouson, B., De Gannes, G., & Godbolte, C. (1993). Four paths to one God. Unpublished manuscript, presentation to American Academy of Religion, Mid-Atlantic Region, March, Philadelphia, PA.

Brown, K. M. (1991). *Mama Lola: A Vodou priestess in Brooklyn.* Berkeley: University of California Press.

Busia, K. A. (1991, c. 1954). The Ashanti of the Gold Coast, pp. 190–290 in D. Forde (Ed.), *African worlds: Studies in the cosmological ideas and social values of African peoples.* Oxford: Oxford University Press, for International African Institute.

Canizares, R. (1993). *Walking with the night: The Afro-Cuban world of Santeria.* Rochester, VT: Destiny Books.

Deren, M. (1953). *Divine horsemen: The living gods of Haiti.* New York: MacPherson & Company.

Dinizulu, N. Y. O. (1974) *The Akan priests in America.* Long Island, NY: Aims of Modzawe.

Dinizulu, N. Y. O. (1987) *Nana says.* Jamaica, NY: Aims of Modzawe.

Fatunmbi, A. F. (1991). *Iwa-pele: Ifa quest - The search for the source of Santeria and Lucumi.* Bronx, New York: Original Publications.

Haskins, J. (1978). *Voodoo & hoodoo.* Bronx, NY: Original Publications.

Hurston, Z. N. (1990, c.1938). *Tell my horse: Voodoo and life in Haiti and Jamaica.* New York: Harper & Row.

Idowu, B. E. (1994, [reprinted, original c. 1962]). *Olodumare: God in Yoruba belief.* New York: A & B Books Publishers.

Krippendorff, K. (1989). On the ethics of constructing communication, pp. 66–96 in B. Dervin, L. Grossberg & E. Wartella (Eds.) *Rethinking Communication,* Vol. 1. Newbury Park: Sage.

Jones, E. F. (1990). *In search of Zion: The spiritual significance of Africa in Black religious movements.* Bern: Peter Lang.

Mason, J. & Edwards, G. (1985). *Black Gods—Orisa studies in the New World.* New York: Yoruba Theological Archministry.

Mason, J. (1993, 3rd ed.; 1985). *Four new world Yoruba rituals.* Brooklyn, NY: Yoruba Theological Seminary.

McCloud, A. B. (1995). *African American Islam.* New York: Routledge.

Mbiti, J. S. (1969). *African religions and philosophy.* Oxford: Heinemann.

Meyerowitz, E. L. R. (1958). *The Akan of Ghana: Their ancient beliefs.* London:

Mulira, J. G.(1990). The case of voodoo in New Orleans, pp. 34–68 in J. E. Holloway (Ed.) *Africanisms in American culture.* Bloomington: Indiana University Press.

Murphy, J. M. (1988). *Santeria: An African religion in America.* Boston: Beacon Press.

Neimark, P. J.(1993). *The way of the Orisa: Empowering your life through the ancient African religion of Ifa.* San Francisco: Harper.

Richards, D.M. [renamed Marimba Ani]. (1985). The implications of African-American spirituality, in M. K. Asante and K. W. Asante (Eds.), *African culture: The rhythms of unity,* pp.207–231. Westport, CT: Greenwood Press.

Rouson, B. M. (1994). *Sacrifice and Synthesis: African-American Akans and Yoruba Reconstructing Communication and Community.* Unpublished manuscript, Master's thesis, Annenberg School for Communication, Philadelphia, PA.

Santana, A. (n.d.). *Voices of the Gods: African religion in the U.S.A.* [Film on videotape]. Brooklyn, NY.

Sarpong, N. A. N. (Osunyomi) Afolabi'. (1993). *They have come to reclaim their children.* Rosedale, NY: The Akan-Yoruba House of Nana Aba Afolabi'.

Simpson, G. E. (1978). *Black religions in the new world.* New York: Columbia University Press.

Teish, L. (1985). *Jambalaya: The natural woman's book of personal charms and practical rituals.* San Francisco: Harper.

Twining, M. A. (1991). Baskets and quilts: Women in Sea Island arts and crafts, pp. 129–140 in M. A. Twining & K. E. Baird (Eds.), *Sea Island roots: African presence in the Carolinas and Georgia.* Trenton, NJ: Africa World Press.

Twining, M. A. & Baird, K. E. (Eds.). (1991). *Sea Island roots: African presence in the Carolinas and Georgia.* Trenton, NJ: Africa World Press.

Walker, S. (n.d.). The Afro-Brazilian Candomble: An African spiritual microcosm in the Americas. [Monograph] New York: Schomberg Center for Research in Black Culture.

Walker, S. (1990). Everyday and esoteric reality in the Afro-Brazilian Candomble. *History of Religions,* 30, November, pp. 103–128. Chicago: University of Chicago Press.

10

AUNT HAGAR'S DAUGHTERS

THREE WOMEN IN THE NEO-PENTECOSTAL TRADITION*

Deborah A. Austin

My decision to collect the personal narratives of three Black female ministers was born of longstanding interests. I have been fascinated with women in ministry since my mother refused to attend church with my family one Sunday when I was ten years old, noting that she "did not believe in women preachers." I was very confused by the content and passion of her statement. Having witnessed the strength and leadership ability that she and other women in my church possessed, I had no idea there were restrictions on women in the church. After becoming an adult, however, I realized that women, denied access to major religious offices and positions, had carved out special places for themselves.

Those special places are noted in a twenty-year study completed by C. Eric Lincoln, author, poet, and professor emeritus of Religion and Culture at Duke University and Lawrence H. Mamiya, professor of sociology at Vassar College. Lincoln and Mamiya's (1990) research, recorded in a 400-page volume, notes that over 30 million African Americans report that they are members of the Black church. Of these 30 million members, 70 percent are females. However, ninety-

* This chapter originally appeared as "'In the Middle of Everyday Life:' The Spaces Black Clergywomen Create," in *JITC* , Vol 22:2, Spring 1995; used and slightly modified with permission.

six percent of the pastors are male (p. 304). Thus, an almost exclusively male leadership characterizes the Black Church, whose membership is predominantly female. The pulpit is "man's place" and the pew is "woman's place." In response to this segmentation, women in the Black Church have developed some of the strongest networks of service organizations in the world.

> Women serve in myriad roles in black churches as evangelists, missionaries, stewardesses, deaconesses, lay readers, writers on religious subjects, Sunday school teachers, musicians, choir members and directors, ushers, nurses, custodians, caterers and hostesses for church dinners, secretaries and clerks, counselors, recreation leaders and directors of vacation Bible schools. Women are also designated "mothers of the church," an honorific title usually reserved for the wife of the founder or for the oldest and most respected members. In some black churches, pastors usually consult with the church mother before making an important decision because she can exercise countervailing power among some key members (p. 275).

While some Black women were carving out places as lay persons, others were striving for acceptance as ministers. The first official challenge to restrictions on Black women ministers in a Black denomination came with Jarena Lee's petition (1986) to be ordained by the African Methodist Episcopal Church in 1809. Today, almost 200 years later, only four percent of the ministers in the Black Church are female.

This new understanding of the place women played in the life of the Black church led me to listen intently to stories told by and about women in ministry—women who were accepted and supported, women who were denied ordination, women who were refused the right to preach even when they were ordained. I began to wonder about these women. Why did they want to be ministers when so many people were opposed to their existence? How did they develop and maintain their identities as members of groups who generally opposed their inclusion? I thought about the stories that I heard, told in small circles of women or in religious communities, and felt that they must be more widely heard. Thus, I asked three Black Baptist clergywomen, whom I shall call Beverly Ray, Janice Jones, and Hermena Monroe, to serve as informants about their own experiences. They do not comprise a representative sampling of all Black clergywomen. Residing in central and southeastern North Carolina, they attended a 1991 women minister's retreat at which I was present. I was thoroughly engaged by the stories they told about the spaces they carved out for themselves.

The Spiritual Life Stories

As my three informants told me about their lives and their call to ministry, the similarities and differences in their stories struck me. Two of them, The Rev. Beverly Ray and The Rev. Hermena Monroe, told stories of the physical and emotional healings at the center of the process by which they felt God called them to ministry. The third, The Rev. Janice Jones, spoke of her concern about the unmet emotional and spiritual needs of the clients in her law office, of persons in her native Bajemi (the names of all places are fictitious) who encouraged her to prepare for and enter the ministry, and the sermon describing the good shepherd that she felt was a description of her. Each of these women said she believed God had chosen her to help meet the physical, spiritual, psychological and emotional needs of the people; they went about preparing themselves for those tasks.

These women's stories were filled with accounts of dreams, visions, and premonitions typical of women's confessional and spiritual biographies (Braxton, 1989). In the manner of Puritan and Quaker conversion narratives, these women's accounts of their access to the Holy Spirit through visions and the inner voice were vehicles for defining themselves in opposition to the limitations placed upon them. Because they had power that they felt came directly from God, they were able to defy limitations placed on them by their specific denominations, communities and families. These dreams and visions, Braxton asserts, also served as a way of distancing themselves from the life around them and creating private spaces in which they could create their own identities and voices:

> The black female, denied a public voice, became the recipient of the promise of a divine gift... The inner voice sets up a tension between her inner self and external religious authorities, a tension she will use to carve out an identity and a voice for herself. (p. 58).

"And Your Daughters Shall Prophesy"

The controversy surrounding clergywomen and their need to tell the story of who they are and how they came to be that way is not new to the Black Church. Women, as acquainted with the Bible as men, knew of the scriptures that admonished them to be silent in church (I Timothy 2:11–14; I Corinthians 14:34–45). However, they also knew about a special promise to women.

> And it shall come to pass afterward, that I will pour out my spirit upon all flesh; and your sons and your *daughters shall prophesy*... and upon the handmaidens in those days will I pour out my spirit (emphasis mine). (Joel 2:28–29)

Jarena Lee (1986), mentioned previously as having presented the first ordination challenge to the Black church, used this scripture to strengthen the story of her call to and participation in the ministry of the African Methodist Episcopal (AME) Church in a four part narrative entitled *The Life and Religious Experience of Jarena Lee. A Coloured Lady, Giving an Account of her Call to Preach the Gospel. Revised and Corrected from the Original Manuscript, Written By Herself.* It is almost certain that the impetus for Lee's spiritual autobiography lay in Methodism's nineteenth century attitude toward women in ministry. Writing to several women in the mid 1700s, Methodism's founder, John Wesley, gave women permission to pray publicly and testify to their faith experiences. They were allowed to exhort (urge people to hear the gospel, repent and be saved) and expound (explain the meaning of a scripture), but only in small groups. Carolyn Gifford (1989) suggests that Wesley, known for his pragmatism, appeared to have been more concerned about using all possible resources to build the struggling Methodist Church than women's rights. Seeing that women were "leading souls to Christ," Wesley sought ways to circumvent the Methodist Church's prohibitions against women's preaching (p. i.). Writing to Sarah Crosby in 1769, Wesley instructed:

> In public you may properly enough intermix short exhortations with prayer: but keep as far from what is called preaching as you can: therefore never take a text; never speak in a continued discourse without some break, about four or five minutes. Tell the people, "We shall have another prayer-meeting at such a time and place." (qtd. in Gifford p. ii.)

As Wesley watched phenomenal growth at the hands of these women and other lay ministers, he decided to permit lay preaching on the grounds of the extraordinary call of God. I am convinced that this was one of the most historically significant steps for women in ministry. Because the call to ministry was a deep personal experience, no one could really challenge the legitimacy of God's special revelation to any individual. Women, as well as men, constructed narratives that legitimized their calls.

Daughters of Eve

As I struggled to interpret my informants' stories, I noted that as one of its pivotal points, each of them referred to the oppression the tellers experienced at the hands of both men and women. From my stance inside the Christian tradition, I believe these acts of oppression are based on the propagation of the Judeo-Christian myth of Adam and Eve. This myth, which provides explanations of humanity's origins and the etiology of sin and evil in the world ultimately emphasizes

> Eve's disobedience, the sin brought into the world by her irresponsible actions, the compounding of that sin through the temptation of Adam, God's subsequent punishment of both parties, the blame she alone must face because of her primary role in that sin, and the implications of that sin for her daughters (Macom 1986, p. 51).

Over the centuries of Judeo-Christian history, religious and secular discussion of the positionality of women has referred to this myth of Adam and Eve in the Garden of Eden. Critics, pastors, theologians and others have commented over the years that had Adam "plucked that fruit" and then encouraged Eve to do the same, a very different doctrine of sin and perception of women would pervade Western civilization (Phillips 1984, p. 57). However, as Old Testament scholar Phyllis Trible (1978) notes, the traditional interpretation of this story persists:

> God, who is male, created man before woman, which makes man superior to woman; woman is created for instrumental goals (to be man's helper), which makes man's goals, needs, and desires prior in importance; woman is taken out of man's rib, which makes her very existence derivative; woman receives her

> name from man, and so is answerable to him; woman tempted man to disobey, and so is responsible for the presence of sin in the world; woman's punishment, (the pain of childbirth) is more severe than man's punishment, which indicates that her sin is greater; because woman has proven herself simple-minded, gullible, and untrustworthy (if not purposefully evil), thereby allowing both sex and death to enter the world, God has given man the right to rule over her (p. 73).

The Rev. Beverly Ray's experiences recall these attitudes and beliefs. She talked about her struggle to be licensed and ordained in her family's church in Roury, North Carolina. Her pastor and many members of the congregation believed that men held the sole right to pastoral leadership. However, their sexist beliefs did not deter her belief in a God of equality. She attributed her ordination to the secret prayer on behalf of her pastor.

> He came from a long line of male preachers who taught him women are not to preach. His grandfather—a very, very, very, very prestigious pastor—had been adamant about that. But I was praying. "Don't let him rest, just don't let him rest. I don't want him to get a good night's sleep; sleeping all night to get up in the morning to raise hell with me. No, don't let him rest until he does what You say do." I don't understand what happened. When he got up that Sunday morning, he told the congregation sometimes God converts and other times He convinces. I have no idea how God convinced him, but God did convince him that women are called to preach. Not only did he license me, he ordained me within a year.

Hermena Monroe's story of oppression was much more animated than Ray's. She was physically removed from the pulpit in her church in the presence of her husband and children. She vehemently asserts that her husband, who claimed to love her dearly, was unable to protect her from the church's religious zealots. As she engaged me in dialogue about my own story, she noted that many well-meaning persons (her in-laws, my mother) misconstrue the writings of the apostle Paul, using I Timothy 2:11–14 and I Corinthians 14:34–35 as the basis for oppressing women.

Janice Jones, accustomed to seeing women in ministry in her native Bajemi, did not experience the kind of oppression that Ray or Monroe experienced until she came to the United States. She vividly remembers being told in a Texas church that she, as a woman, must not walk into the pulpit area. This admonition was foreign and suspect. At home, she had never been subjected to the prejudice stemming from some tradition's concept of women as secondary and derivative. She had been encouraged to develop the ministry gifts that others felt she had. In fact, upon hearing of her decision to enter seminary, Jones' pastor fully expected her to take over the pastorate at his retirement.

I was especially intrigued by Beverly Ray's account of a situation she believed stemmed from jealousy as much as prejudice. She recounted in vivid detail her pastor's replacement of her as Bible Study teacher with a male minister who was much less prepared academically and who did not even profess to have the gift of teaching as she did. She began the class with six or seven people in attendance. By the end of the month, more than one hundred people were coming. In spite of this and other instances of overt sexism, Ray said she believes that women's first priority should be their homes. Male ministers, she noted, have wives to take care of their homes.

> When Nioshi was young, I would sit in the back of the church to give her room to move around without disturbing the service. What would I have looked like in the pulpit with my child running wild? I could not sacrifice my child for ministry.

At this juncture, Ray's remarks are reminiscent of those made by the mother of African-American historian Elsa Barkley Brown (1986) when Brown expressed the desire to enter graduate school. Her mother wrote her a lengthy letter admonishing her that her primary responsibility was to her husband and children. However, included in that letter was a check for tuition. What might women like my mother, Beverly Ray, and the mother of Elsa Barkley Brown be saying about their hopes and dreams for themselves and all women?

One of the most difficult tasks in describing and analyzing Black women's history is actually centering the experience of these women. This centering, asserts Barkley Brown, goes beyond questions of whether or not we have learned to analyze in particular kinds of ways. It is also about "coming to believe in the possibility of a variety of experiences, a variety of ways of understanding the world, a variety of frameworks of operation, without imposing consciously or unconsciously a notion of the norm" (p. 921). It becomes necessary, then, to "pivot the center," and validate and judge experience by its own standards without need of comparison or even adopting that frame as one's own. Barkley Brown pivots the center by using the framework of African-American women's quilting (p. 922). She notes that the "off-beat" patterning that creates the impression of several patterns moving in different directions or multiple rhythms in the context of the design (p. 922) reveals a symmetry that does not come from uniformity as it does in European Americans quilts. This symmetry comes from diversity.

This symmetry in diversity has implications for the economic, political, social and religious histories of Black women. Just as contrast is used to structure or organize the strips of cloth that compose a quilt, the lives of Black women can incorporate, with relative ease sometimes, the most diverse experiences and resources. From this perspective, I remembered conversations with my mother about her struggles as a single mother. Concerned that we were properly cared for and that we become upstanding citizens, she would not tolerate indecency, but "would see us in the grave before she saw us in jail." We knew that she would not kill us, but she was adamant about the quality of our public and private behavior. Rearing us without our father was no easy task, and her discipline seemed to assure that we would make appropriate wives for men who would not leave us to rear our children alone.

Beverly Ray also struggles as a single mother. She spoke of the financial problems that have characterized her life without her husband and of her fears that Nioshi, now a college student, might become involved with "the wrong crowd" and ruin her chances for an economically secure life, a concern magnified by the stereotype of the preacher's kid. Persons familiar with church tradition know that preacher's kids are reported to be among the most unruly children in society. According to community gossip, these children are "left to run wild while their fathers are out saving the children of others." Ray's allusion to sacrificing her child for ministry was her way of signifyin(g) on male ministers and presenting her concern for the well being of the children as well as the adults in congregations.

This concern for the well being of children is found in the other two narratives as well. As a marriage and family counselor, Janice Jones speaks most passionately about the welfare of all children in general and Black children in particular. She says she believes that one of the most important dynamics in the development of a child's self-esteem is the observation of the love between his or her parents. For her, therefore, it is critical that she and her husband model this kind of love in the communities in which they minister.

> Who we are speaks to the church about relationships. Walter is very open about his feelings for me. His openness says to people, especially men, it is okay to talk about how you feel. That is a unique gift for the Black church since the world thinks Black people don't have relationships. We are the kind of Black couple who is not supposed to exist.

Although the Black church is known for providing emotional and spiritual support for Black women rearing their children alone, churches should put more emphasis, Jones says, on children's need for their fathers. She believes that highlighting the need for increased openness and dialogue in intimate relationships will encourage couples to get married and stay married. She does not celebrate single motherhood or fatherhood, noting that the absence of either parent creates dysfunction that harms children.

Even though Hermena Monroe "sacrificed her family" for ministry, she believes that God will bring them back to the church. For her, the church is a special place where family members ought to worship together. She spoke of experiences in her husband's church.

> When we married, I joined his church. Families should worship together. But they treated me cruelly. He supported me but he said he could not protect me. They told me to get out of the pulpit. I did not belong there. If I didn't move, they would remove me bodily. While my husband and children watched, they lifted me out of the pulpit. Put out of that pulpit, I went to a church in a different town. I sacrificed my family: "she who puts husband or children before God is not fit for the kingdom." One son stayed at Mt. Hermon with my husband. After all, that was his family church. A son and daughter went with me. The children saw too much. They don't go to church now. God will work that out.

Thus, all three women bring a love of family to their stories. Family is priority for them as individuals and ministers. Ministers are not to "save the whole world and lose their own families," even if it means, as in the case of Hermena Monroe, sacrificing them for a little while.

Aunt Hagar's Children

Early on, I was concerned about the reasons these women did not more aggressively critique sexism in their churches. Searching for answers led me to an article on the Afro-Christian tradition by Cheryl Townsend Gilkes (1987). Gilkes asserts that analyses of women and Black church traditions must begin with the dynamics unique to the Black church. She, therefore, looked at the roles of women in the Black church through a womanist analysis which proceeds from a critique of most White feminist critics' failure to recognize that the single mode of analysis that feminism has adopted does not adequately deal with forms of oppression other than sexism. Race and economics as well as gender oppress Black women.

Gilkes asserts that one of the clearest examples of womanist analysis in the Afro-Christian tradition relates to Black people's depiction of themselves as Aunt Hagar's children. She notes that both male and female preachers have presented Hagar as

> the archetype of the slave women (and by extension of all suffering black women with children), raped and abandoned by her owner and "buked, scorned, tossed and driven" by his jealous and selfish wife. Langston Hughes's "Aunt Hagar" and E. Franklin Frazier's essay on "Hagar and Her Children" reflect secular appropriations of the Afro-Christian tradition's use of the experiences of Hagar (p. 82).

Gilkes believes that the sermons preached about Hagar and the numerous references to her and her "outside son," Ishmael, provides an image of the difference in the experiences of Black and White people. Many Blacks believe they, like Hagar, are victims of oppression with only God for assistance and support. However, many Black women see themselves as doubly oppressed—as victims of Whites in general and as particular victims of jealousy, abuse, and misunderstanding by White women.

Beverly Ray's encounter with her co-worker Gena and the prayer circles stands out as an example of the personal experience that seems to differentiate the lives of Black and White women. Experiencing deep emotional pain following her divorce, Ray said that she felt as though the prayer circles offered little in the way of healing:

> My soul was still craving, it was still yearning, but I didn't know what for. So I went to a couple of prayer circles with Gena. I was the only Black person there. It was like being at a little tea party. I couldn't relate to them or them to me. It was like "ohhhhh, let's just lift up our little hands and pray," and I didn't want to lift up my little hands and pray. I had some real gut level issues to settle and they weren't dealing with these kinds of issues. Their group and their psyche were different, were very far removed from me.

Although Ray's experiences were foreign to this particular group, I am certain that all women experience the emotional pain that accompanies divorce. However, Ray identified herself as one of Aunt Hagar's children and indicated that her issues and problems were too far removed from those of the White, middle-class women in the prayer circle.

Gilkes also notes that the oppression typical of women's experience is more complicated for Black women. Although Black people have been rendered invisible in a racist society, Black women have been visible in the Black world. Even when they were prohibited from preaching, Black churchwomen created important and necessary roles for themselves. Their involvement in the worship service through prayer, testimony and music makes the church experience different from that of most of their White sisters. Thus, Gilkes contends that although subordination and subservience are problems that Black women face in the Afro-Christian tradition, silence, isolationism and exclusion are not. Even the strongest of the male bastions, Black preaching, depends for its success on connections with the congregation's experiences and assent. Thus, it has been forced to accommodate its community, which is 70 percent female (p. 80–82). Gilkes believes that these decades of involvement make it difficult to persuade Black women to advocate enfranchisement for Black women preachers.

Womanist, in contrast to feminist, is a stance congruent with the attitudes of my mother, Beverly Ray, and Elsa Barkley Brown's mother. I believe they wanted their daughters, who would become Black women, to live comfortably and securely in a world that would, in various ways, hinder the attainment of that goal. However, they tried to assure that we had the resources to attain that goal. Although they may not have been able to engage in feminist or womanist critiques, they were, I believe, aware and resentful of restrictions stipulated by a sexist society. However, they also knew that too overt a critique of a male dominated system would likely backfire. By working within the system—wearing hats as a symbol of submission or subordinating ministry or education to the needs of the family—doors of opportunity would open more easily. Their priority was to ensure that their daughters, whether in a marriage or a profession, did not experience the poverty and pain that filled their lives.

In the Middle of Everyday Life

Because many men had lost interest in work outside centrally located church authority (pulpit), women like Beverly Ray, Janice Jones and Hermena Monroe focused on meeting the spiritual, emotional and physical needs of all people, no matter where and how they encountered them. This caring was central in the flow of their stories. Their ministry used the characteristics of compassionate, loving mothers as they guided their symbolic families (Lawless 1988, p. 152). Jones' narrative indicates that she sees herself as a midwife rather than the masculine image of shepherd. Ray asserts that she understands, perhaps as many male ministers do not, that ministers must deal with people's emotional pain before approaching them about "spiritual things." Their appeal to societal expectations of "a woman's place," has opened doors within the all-male hierarchy of the church, despite some lingering opposition.

Using the convention of the confessional autobiography and conversion narrative—reciting struggles to find the inner light, salvation or grace, and attempting to establish a binding relationship with God (Edkins 1980, p. 42)—Janice Jones, Beverly Ray and Hermena Monroe constructed a view of themselves and the world that cannot be reviewed simply. They are not crusaders, leading large numbers of women into battle against the archetype of the rebellious, simple-minded, gullible Eve. They meet men on their ground, challenging them to "search their own hearts." Without directly asking for shared power and authority—the agenda that challenges the Biblical/denominational prohibitions—these women have found ways to maintain ties with their patriarchal systems *and* acquire positions of authority as ministers. In the midst of the tension between the "God-given inferiority of women" who are to be submissive to men and the belief in individual and spiritual equality before God, these women are finding strategies and images that authenticate their personal and religious power. Paradoxically, much of the mythology that motivates the submission of women is operating for these women *and* the people to whom they minister (Lawless 1988, p. 146)—that is, both accept the stereotype of the nurturing, loving, compassionate, woman whose priority is to care for her family, biological or symbolic. This attitude of nurturance, which swelled the ranks of fledgling churches on foreign mission fields, actually became one of the greatest impetuses to opening the doors to women for full ordination (Willard, 1987 10–11, 170).

Notwithstanding the critique of patriarchal religion, these women believe that the significance of God is not his maleness, but his humanity. God, they claim, spoke with them. They believe that God will speak to any one, male or female, which will accept the challenges of Christ. For these women, accepting the challenge means that women can preach, that women and men must ask new questions about their faith and their families, and that racism and sexism must be confronted and destroyed. These women found the courage to make their stories and life visions known, stories that are much more than the record of spiritual journeys. They help us to explore women's part in history and challenge us with this constant: *men exercise the authority.* However, as Hermena Monroe says, "We (women) will not fight men for their mess. God has plenty for us to do."

> I could not wait for someone to die or move or retire so that I could pastor. I went out on the street corner, where I knew alcoholics gathered. I preached to these forgotten men and women. Each Saturday, more and more men and women came. When it became too cold to preach outside, I rented a building and started Sunday morning worship service. When my resources dried up, I went to the chapel of the local funeral home. On Easter Sunday morning, there was a body in the funeral home chapel. I called some of the men and asked them to go into the chapel and set up my pulpit and some chairs right smack in the middle of the field across the street. On this Easter morning, the Word of God was taken right into the middle of everyday life.

Just as the pulpit was placed in the middle of everyday life in that town, Hermena Monroe, Beverly Ray, and Janice Jones have reconstructed ministry from the pulpit outward. Much remains to be done, but the work of these women suggests that ministry as a male caste is being dismantled.

References

Braxton, J. M. (1989). *Black women writing autobiography: A tradition within a tradition.* Philadelphia: Temple UP.

Brown, E. B. (1986). African-American women's quilting: A framework for conceptualizing and teaching African-American women's history. *Signs 14*: 921–29.

Edkins, C. (1980). Quest for community: Spiritual autobiographies of eighteenth century Quaker and Puritan women in America. In E. Jelinek (Ed.), *Women's autobiography: Essays in criticism.* Bloomington: Indiana UP.

Gifford, C. D. (1987). Introduction. In C.D. Gifford (Ed.), *The defense of women's rights to ordination in the Methodist Episcopal Church.* New York: Garland. (pp i.-xxi)

Gilkes, C. T. (1987). "Some mother's son and some father's daughter:" Gender and biblical language in Afro-Christian worship tradition. In C.W. Atkinson, C.H. Buchanan and M.R. Miles (Eds.), *Shaping new vision: Gender and values in American culture.* Ann Arbor: UMI Research P. 73–99.

Lawless, E. J. (1988). *Handmaidens of the Lord: Pentecostal women preachers and traditional religion.* Philadelphia: U of Pennsylvania.

Lee, J. (1986). The life and religious experience of Jarena Lee, a coloured lady, giving an account of her call to preach the gospel. Revised and corrected from the original manuscript, written herself. In W.L. Andrews (Ed.), *Sisters of the spirit.* Bloomington: Indiana UP.

Lincoln, C. E. and Mamiya, L. H. (1990). *The black church in the African-American experience.* Durham, NC: Duke UP.

Macom, E. A. (1986). *Eve and the rhetoric of re-vision: A feminist archetypal analysis of the archetype of eve as re-visioned in songs of three female popular musicians.* Masters Thesis. U of North Carolina at Chapel Hill, 1986.

Phillips, J. A. (1984). *Eve: the history of an idea.* San Francisco: Harper and Row.

Thorne, B., Kramarae, C. and Henley, N. (1983). Eds., *Language, gender, and society.* Rowley, MA: Newbury House.

Titon, J. (1980). The Life Story. *Journal of American Folklore 93*: 276–92.

Trible, P. (1978). *God and the rhetoric of sexuality.* Philadelphia: Fortress.

Willard, F. E. (1987). Woman in the Pulpit. In C.D. Gifford, (Ed.), *The defense of women's rights to ordination in the Methodist Episcopal Church.* New York: Garland, 170–173.

11

OF GRACE AND GLORY

AFRICAN-AMERICAN WOMEN CLERGY AND THEIR SERMONS

Vanessa Wynder Quainoo

Wide she sings
And speaks . . . to tell
To widen
And knowing reasons
And come tell
And come tell
Wide like grace
Shine in glory
Word in her
He lives
She speaks
new and again.

To explicate the sermon is to engage the hermeneutic. To trace the biography of the sermon is to cast identity into the hermeneutic circle. Be it contemporary or ancient, convoluted or newly framed, gender pushes identity toward basic definitions of difference. When confronted with the question of gender in the pulpit, a plethora of questions emerge: Does the preaching of Sacred texts take on feminine postures when preached by women? Does the femininity give voice to the subtle, previously unseen qualities which have always been present in the text but have escaped the male interpreter of Scripture?

Perhaps, the experiences common to women help to shape female notions of Scriptural meaning? To frame the question at the basic level—what happens when women preach?

Much of the literature affirms that the female voice brings "something" unique to the preached moment, but what of the element of race/culture? How does preaching by women unfold in the African-American Church experience? Again, at a basic level, what happens when African-American women preach?

The purpose of this chapter is to explore the shared lives of African-American Women Clergy as revealed through their sermons. Using this method of sermonic criticism, rhetorical narratives are identified, framed and analyzed, re-positioned, and ascribed meaning in relation to like texts and contexts. While there are important theological implications that surround the issue women's preaching, this chapter is directed along the lines of understanding the particular group of women in question. They happen to be African-American women and to have inherited a tradition of preaching honed within the oral culture of the African-American Church.

I want to frame this question of what happens when African-American women clergy preach with two rather specific foci: Intuition (an overflow of grace) and authenticity (the expression of glory). There are two other factors which inform the method. First, this discussion privileges a Christian theological perspective. After all, the subjects are representatives of such a perspective. Therefore, basic premises of Christian faith are not set into a dialectic. Examples of these premises include an acceptance of Scripture as sacred and wholistic in meaning; adherence to the Christian teaching that Jesus Christ is the Son of God and that He enacts His Person through the Holy Spirit to have active, viable relationships with individuals as free agents; and the Christian preaching is proclamatory, inspired, and prophetic. Also, this discussion does not invite debate over the theological viability of female leadership in the Christian Church and the formal ordination/recognition and episcopal sanction of that leadership.

I take the position of the women who are about to be explored—that they are preachers and they themselves are first to bear witness to that nomenclature. They are validated by their own experiences and in the vernacular of—Let the Church say Amen.

Methodology—Sermonic Criticism and Rhetorical Narrative

Sermonic criticism has two streams of methodological purpose. First, is the notion of progressive revelation which means that once preached, the sermon goes on preaching long after the preacher has finished the sermon. In essence, the sermon "remains" with the preacher and with the audience, evidenced by the repetition of themes and stories "shared" by preachers. But even more remarkable, the preacher "remains" with the audience and with other preachers as she resides in the collective memory of her listeners. They re-tell her sermon, yes, but they also re-tell her. They interpret her identity as one connected to their own and embrace who she is personally as publicly reflected through her preaching.

Progressive revelation has five phases: location of the text within Scripture; location of the preacher's personal experience within the text; inviting the audience to participate by placing their own personal experiences within the text; establishing common theses; sharing experiences during and after the sermon. Progressive revelation demarcates experience as an oral activity. The aspect of orality is what provides the generative quality and enables the sermon to continue revealing long after the preacher has preached.

The second methodological purpose is the allowance for exploitation of feminine style. "A feminine style emphasizes process rather than closure" (Foss & Foss, p. 422). Inherent in the feminine style of preaching is a privileging of collaboration. In essence, a major thrust of the preaching is the notion that "what I'm talking about is well-known to all of us as women" (Bass-Foster, April, 1997).

Intuition and Authenticity

To give structure to the study, I carefully constructed the research question to suggest interest in both the sermon and the preacher by asking broadly what happens when African-American women preach? More specifically, what do the sermons preached by African-American women reveal to us about the preachers and the process? Does the act of preaching create for women a shared space? If so, what is the nature of this space or as queried by the title of this volume what is the nature of the sistuh or sistuhs who share such space?

I then selected from the National Black Evangelical Association's list of Churches which represent the major Protestant denominations in the African-American community nationwide. Because the list is exhaustive and requires delineation beyond the parameters of this study, I selected 5–10 congregations from the five largest denominations represented on the list. The five include National Baptist, African Methodist Episcopal, Church of God In Christ, the Holiness Movement, and Non-denominational Pentecostal.

I secured the video-tapes and audio-tapes of all of the preachers represented, visited approximately 60 percent of the subjects personally, and collected nearly 40 sermons as data. As I studied and analyzed the data, I organized the sermons under four basic sermonic types: proclamation, instructional, poetic and redemptive. Only a few did not seem appropriate with any of the categories, mainly because the sermon was linked to a special occasion such as celebrating an anniversary or commencement.

After more analysis, patterns of language and application emerged. To get at the meanings of some of the tropes, I employed cluster analysis which is isolating the root metaphor resident within a body of work or text and "clustering" major and minor metaphors around that root metaphor. The clusters reveal much about the texts and authors of the texts.

The clusters were divided around the two operatives of the sermonic method. The first is intuitive language which reflects the receptive/passive nature of the preaching process and gives insight into the preparation and construction of the sermon. The second is language which authenticates or points the listener to the origin/source of inspirational thought. Authentic language reflects the demonstrative/expressive nature of preaching. While references are made to many of the sermons, several are specifically referenced as exemplary of the many.

Framing the Message

While it is a fact that women have always preached, the last decades have witnessed an explosion of female lay clergy, evangelists (itinerant preachers who travel from one preaching engagement to the next), ministers of Christian music, education, counseling, and special ministries (such as ministry to teen-age Mothers), associate and senior pastors, and bishops. According to a recent poll in the November 1997 issue of *Ebony*, African-American Women preachers are listed among the "best" religious communicators of our day. Churches with at least 500+ membership hire women 30 percent more now than they did twenty years ago; 1,000 member plus churches are reporting a 40 percent increase for the same amount of time (Kinnon, 1997). Some of the reasons that account for this change may be related to the socio-economic changes in the African-American community. More women are professionals who are returning or joining for the first time a local church and attending regularly. Larger numbers of them are parents and a significant portion of that number includes single mothers who want a caring support network to help in child rearing. Another reason is the mega-church phenomenon occurring in African-American communities throughout the country. Mega-churches are described as typically 700+ member congregations that flourish typically in the urban near suburban areas and provide a power base for economic, social and in some cases political action in otherwise depressed areas. Mega-churches have tremendous money-raising capacity and with talented leadership can turn whole communities around by building affordable housing, safe, adequate child care facilities, clinics, schools and even drug rehabilitation facilities.

To name a few of the positive social agencies represented in the data, a Columbus, Ohio congregation of nearly a 1,000 members has successfully run a drug rehabilitation comprehensive residential program for the past ten years with an annual 2.2 million dollar budget. The facility is so extensive that it takes up an entire city block, complete with dormitories and medical facility. Another church in San Antonio with a membership of over 1,000 purchased an entire shopping mall that had been abandoned by proprietors hard-hit by the sagging economy of the early 80s. The church now operates businesses within the mall, employs a workforce of at least 300 and all of this accomplished in just one decade of existence as a church.

Perhaps most impressive is a 4,000+ congregation in Philadelphia that has purchased a college campus, built a new facility on the campus to house the main worship area, and opened a new Christian college within a time span of 10 years. All of the progressive large congregations include women who figure prominently on their preaching staff, but that is not the whole story of the African-American Christian community. There are hundreds of small churches with 100, 50, even 25 members who quietly forge ahead on the front battle lines of urban intransigence. Many, many of the small congregations have women at the helm or in positions where they are expected to preach regularly.

There are some factors that characterize African-American churches in general: factors such as the tendency of the African-American church to be the primary economic base of the community; the tendency of the church to attract more women than men; and the interactive style of worship in many African-American churches which invites women to participate in the music and spoken aspects of ministry. Even so, the predominant control patterns of the church have mostly been male-dominated. To see women as pastoral leaders offers a distinctively different paradigm for sermonic communication. What are some of the distinctions? In the segments that follow, I address the uniqueness of female pastoral leadership and critically assess the four types of sermonic styles that display intuitive and/or authentic discourse.

Speaking of Grace—Intuitive Language in Sermonic Texts

Intuitive language draws meaning from the root term—intuition which indicates a way of knowing that circumvents conscious reasoning and results in immediate insight. The intuitive speaker assesses complex and multi-leveled information about her audience through sensitive observation. This notion is related to the idea of rhetorical presence. Found in the works of rhetorical theorist Chaim Perelman, "presence" is the backgrounding of inconsequential information and the foregrounding of pertinent information. The intuitive preacher is able to distinguish what things spoken will enable the audience to background certain ideas and focus more intently on other ideas. Perelman's notion of presence is part of his response to the need for a rhetoric that can systematically evaluate epideictic discourse. Pointing out that forensic speaking is measured by proof or evidence and deliberative speaking is measured by prediction, epideictic speaking is much more difficult to measure because it is concerned with values. "Because epideictic oratory, the form of speaking most closely associated with values, was judged on style instead of content, Perelman felt the need for a theory of argument in which values could be assessed rationally...How a speaker achieves assent with an audience became of particular interest to Perelman..." (Foss, p. 123).

In sermonic criticism, the establishment of presence is at the heart of understanding the preacher/congregation relationship. In fact, intuitive expression culminates in presence, but how this takes place is as much a racial/cultural distinction as it is influenced by gender. Having assessed the collected sermons, several uniquenesses about African-American women clergy emerge. First, two sermonic types are predominant as examples of intuitive preaching. The two types are redemptive and instructional and both are intricately woven into the fabric of African-American female expression. What follows are examples of the two types and further explanation as to how they display intuitive application.

An example of redemptive preaching is taken from the sermon "Facing the Past to Face the Present" by Rev. Claudia Copeland, Co-Pastor of New Creation Worship Center of San Antonio, Texas. The sermon which was delivered at a biennial women's convention of about 1500 women began with rapt remarks by Copeland that set the stage for a personal upfront "encounter with truth." Copeland spoke to the audience as "friends" and then as "sisters." She spoke clearly of the Christian message of salvation—Jesus Christ as a real, relevant Helper and Deliverer. She then moved to invite the "sisters" to soul-searching and facing of the past. In her words, "Perhaps one of the reasons why we keep talking about the past is because the past is not over...we have not faced ourselves in the mirrors of our past individual and collective histories" (Copeland, 1995).

While redemptive theology presents a universal appeal, preachers like Copeland contextualize the redemption message so that it addresses racial and gender as well as spiritual concerns. Again, Copeland speaks up-close to her audience when she reminds them of their obligations at home, "Some of you...have some problems at home that are distinctive 'woman problems'; husband won't do right; children cutting up; things falling apart and the roof caving in, but you're here and God has an answer for you...Just remember that God's redemptive plan is always creating opportunities for you to start over again...to renew...to rebuild...God is always creatively redeeming" (Copeland, 1995).

Instructional preaching delineates Scriptural answers to contemporary problems. In her sermon, "Under the Influence" Rev. Cheryl

Sanders, Senior Pastor of the Third Street Church of God in Washington, DC, carefully explains a detailed list of disturbing statistics about the African-American community. She then directs her message to each area of dysfunction with specific solutions from Scripture. While the mixed gender audience of nearly 2,000 persons affirmed her words, specific segments of her sermon were directed toward women. During these segments, Sanders repeated a root term that unified the other portions of her message.

The root term employed was "influenza" and Sanders used the term in several ways. After giving literal definition of influenza, she then turned to the spiritual and cultural applications. To summarize the applications, Christians must choose to live their lives under the influence of the Holy Spirit or they like all people will be influenced toward the negative.

Speaking of Glory—Authentic Language in Sermonic Texts

In the Christian context, to glorify means to extend great honor and praise in worship of Christ. Furthermore, in Christian teachings, God is preeminent and full of glory and without cause for lack of honor. He is supreme and all of the glory belongs to God alone. Glory can also mean the brilliance associated with bright light; that which is resplendent, magnificent. To say that the clergy are affected by their profession is to imply that they who are associated with the "bright light" draw brilliance from its shining. Clearly, the subjects of this study are not seeking glory unto themselves, but rather as they lift up God and others and speak redemptively, they are afferent in their cause. This observation coupled with an apparent femininity and the unique cadences of African-American rhythmic preaching creates a most dramatic presentation of powerful narrative and celebrative style exemplified by the clergy. The femininity is an interpretative that can relate to personal belief and public expression and affirmation of women and/or the female experience. Even the dress of African-American women clergy affirms the socio-racial dynamics of the culture. Many of them wear custom-designed robes bearing kente patterns and African-American symbolism. While most men clergy are expected to remain in cool colors of dark brown, black, gray, and blue, African-American women clergy express themselves in a variety of bright colors, ecclesiastical garb, and creative clergy wear.

This celebrative quality also finds expression in two sermonic types. The first is proclamatory and focuses on the magnificence and vastness of creation. The second is poetic and points out the beauty and positive qualities of women. In her sermon, "Forgetting the Past," presented at a Women's Convention at the New Covenant Christian Center in Boston, Massachusetts, the Rev. Cheryl Bass-Foster handed out artifacts that represented specific "points of reference" from the female perspective. Each woman in the large audience of approximately 500 women received band-aids and sheets of paper. The paper was for writing three areas of personal hurts. The band-aids were used to cover the areas of hurt. For instance, if a person felt she had been rejected then she might place the band-aid on her chest to represent a broken heart. If she had succumbed to worry, then she was to place the band-aid across her forehead etc.... Throughout the sermon, she re-affirmed the beauty of femaleness, gave Scriptural arguments for positive self-esteem and generally encouraged women to be empowered at every level of public and private life.

Summary

To say that African-American women preach out of their own unique experiences is to validate a paradigm of grace and glory. Many African-American women like women everywhere have had to suffer the indignities of sexist violence and oppression. Quite often, when they speak, they do so intuitively, out of reservoirs of strength garnered through the presses of male oppressive dominance and abuse, marital strife, single parenting, unfair employment practices, racial hostility, and lack of proper social provisions such as inadequate housing and insufficient health care and improper nutrition. Many African-American churches sing the traditional refrain, "How I got over, how I got over, My soul looks back and wonders, How I got over." The refrain is both a question and a proclamation. The implication is that life against these and other odds is, in large measure, lived by another code of survival; a spiritual definitive called grace. In the religious context, grace is a metaphor which represents the spiritual strength that enables and empowers the individual to overcome otherwise insurmountable difficulty. It is a strength that is given, not earned or deserved, and it is given in correlative measure of the particular need or difficulty experienced by the individual. Grace is not bound by gender and this study does not suggest such an implication. Nonetheless, women's experiences are unique and addressing the critical questions of sustenance and creativity involves understanding the peculiarities of how women articulate and process their spiritual journeys. To speak or preach by grace, then is to do so intuitively, giving that which has been strictly given and perceived through experience and insight.

Preaching by African-American women is also often marked by authenticity. The root of this term is 'authentes' which means author. Characteristically, the preachers and their sermons reflect the glory of what is known in the religious context as the Divine author. They are sensitive to the spirit of the text and consistently point audiences toward, what is believed by Christians, to be basic truths. In the African-American church this is often referred to as "telling it like it is."

What happens when women preach? And what happens when female voice is resonant within the context of the African-American Church? Further research is needed to understand with greater clarity the rhetorical dimensions of this genre, however, we can say that the lady preachers make very important contributions in the continual march toward equality between the sexes. They also validate women's experiences in very significant ways.

References

Amos, B. (1997, October) (Sermon) Eye of the needle. St. Louis, MO: Victory '97 Convention (for women).

Bass-Foster, C. (1997, April) (Sermon) Forgetting the past. Boston, MA. New Covenant Christian Center (Women's convention).

Cook, S. (1995). *Sister to sister: Devotions for and from African American women.* Valley Forge, PA: Judson Press.

Copeland, C. (1995). (Sermon). Facing the past to face the future. Heritage Village, SC: Victory '95 Convention (for women).

Foss, S., Foss, K. & Trapp. R. (1991). *Perspectives on rhetoric.* Prospect Heights, IL: Waveland Press.

James, C. (1997, October) (Sermon). A miracle within a miracle. St. Louis, MO: Victory '97 convention (for women).

Kinnon, J.B. (1997, November). 15 greatest Black women preachers. *Ebony,* 102–114.

Lambe, M. (1993, August). (Sermon). Witnessing Christ in the city. West Middlesex, PA: National Association Annual Meeting of the Church of God.
Littlejohn, S. (1989). *Theories of human communication*. Belmont, CA: Wadsworth.
McKenzie, V. (1997, May). (Sermon). Do you know who you are? Providence, RI: Brown University Baccalaurate service for African American Students at Brown University.
Mitchell, E. (1988). *Those preachin' women*. Valley Forge, PA: Judson Press.
Ostling, R. (1992, November 23). God and women: A second reformation sweeps Christianity. *Time*, 53.
Sanders, C. (1990, December). (Sermon). Under the influence. Chicago, IL: Church of God Youth Convention.
Warren, V. (1989). (Sermon). We are all here. Chicago, IL: Holy Temple Church of God in Christ.
Young, F. (1990). Virtuoso theology. Cleveland, OH: The Pilgrim Press.

SISTUHS WATCHING AND READING: REPRESENTATIONS IN MASS MEDIA

SECTION 1

SISTUHS ON TELEVISION AND IN ANIMATED FILM

12

"THE MORE THEY CHANGE, THE MORE THEY REMAIN THE SAME"

REPRESENTATIONS OF AFRICAN-AMERICAN WOMANHOOD ON *LIVING SINGLE*

Katrina E. Bell

Introduction

Television representations of African-American womanhood have been the subject of much debate among scholars and Black feminists for at least two decades. These scholars have highlighted the fact that African-American women historically have been portrayed in ways that reaffirm cultural biases about them. The history of African-American women on television reflects what MacDonald (1983) refers to as the medium's continuing failure: the perpetuation of the most disturbing representations of African Americans found in American popular culture, rather than the reversing of often historically based ridicule and misconceptions of this group. Despite such critique by scholars in opposition to the crippling portrayals of African-American women in popular media, the representations still exist. According to Jewell (1993), "while the cultural images of African-American women have changed over time, the cultural images of African-American women have changed only minimally" (p. 35). Jewell and other writers therefore have criticized traditional as well as current media representations that stigmatize African-American womanhood. They argue that the cultural codes operating in the early days of film and television are structurally similar to those operating in contemporary American programming.

In seeking to portray single life in the 1990s, the production teams for the former Fox Television situation comedy, *Living Single* seem to have been successful in providing representations of characters and situations with which African-American audiences can identify. The show depicts young, African-American professionals and their everyday pressures of love, work and friendship. And although several shows that highlight the lives of African Americans remain somewhat on the fringes of mainstream American media programming, there are significant aspects of *Living Single* and the more recent Fox Television situation comedy, *Between Brothers*, that I suspect are particularly resonant with the contemporary African-American experience.

Organization

Thus, through in-depth interviews with regular viewers of *Living Single* about the cultural codes and concepts they recognize, accept and/or reject, this chapter seeks to determine how African-American women negotiate meaning in light of the cultural codes operating in contemporary American media programming that are structurally similar to those operating in the early days of film and television. This chapter is divided into six sections, the first of which discusses the chapter's methodological approach. The second section establishes what I argue might be the appeal of *Living Single* to African-American audiences. The third section specifies the procedure I will follow in this examination. The fourth section lays out Labov's and Waletzky's narrative structure, which will be used to analyze some of the stories told by my co-researchers. The fifth and sixth sections articulate the thematization that I conduct from my co-researchers' stories. Finally, I will suggest some implications of this chapter's work.

Methodological Approach

To explore the representations of African-American womanhood on *Living Single*, I will employ phenomenological inquiry. This tripartite method of description, thematization, and interpretation (Nelson, 1990) is especially sensitive to women's historically muted voices and requires that a thoughtful and detailed strategy be designed to address these issues. Recent qualitative work in reception studies has defined the audience as co-authors in the social production of meaning (Real, 1996). Such an approach to understanding African-American women as audience members and simultaneously as members of interpretive communities is based on the notion that interpretations arise from "a specific orientation toward the social reality that the media serve to represent" (Jensen, 1990, p. 130). This chapter therefore adopts phenomenology's incorporation of subjective reflection as a research strategy and is informed by contemporary research on reception studies. My own ontological assumptions about the experiences of African-American female audiences of Living Single, and specifically those who participated in this work, have resulted in my fascination with exploring how African-American women form interpretive communities. The data that I process here therefore permits these women's expressions to be unmuted, thereby giving voice to this particular interpretive community.

My narrow concern, then, is to come to understand how some women interpret their televisual experiences with *Living Single*, as well as how they negotiate what they consider problematic aspects of the show. My broader concern is to begin to illuminate how these African-American women similarly negotiate other aspects of their lives as members of a doubly marginalized group. Here is how this chapter exchanges widespread indictments about hegemony for an attempt to better understand some African-American women's own perceptions of their experiences within the social, cultural, and economic landscape in which they exist. This chapter further rests on the fundamental idea that we structure reality and describe our roles in larger communities based on this reality. We therefore need to understand some of the concepts that African-American women use to structure their lived experiences and ultimately use in the face of representations of African-American womanhood on *Living Single*.

This chapter explores how my African-American co-researchers deal with pervasive representations of African-American women's lived experiences and how they negotiate between media archetypes of African-American women and their admiration for the female characters on the show. (The alternative, they suggest, is to consider television as innately problematic, which would likely eliminate desirable American media programming for African-American women.) Thus, these women suggest that because the African-American woman's self-image is essentially complex and cannot be reduced to a single experience, reductive media representations of African-American womanhood warrant some thoughtful attention.

My methodological approach therefore attempts to understand the deep-seated conflicts in ideology that characterize modern society and that deeply concern African-American women. It also offers my co-researchers an opportunity to talk about media archetypes that are present in *Living Single* and the contradictions that they think exist between their lived experiences and those that are represented on the show, and on television in general. This chapter's methodological approach also allows African-American women's own voices to deconstruct the social institutions that they think marginalize them. In sum, this chapter seeks to determine how African-American women deal with the structural similarities that exist between contemporary media representations of African-American women and those operating in the early days of film and television. And as many feminist readings have attempted to do, this chapter attempts to describe what African-American women think about such representations.

Appeal of Show

The way in which the characters of *Living Single* make humorous the everyday delights and struggles of living in the 1990s, arguably is central to the show's appeal among its viewers. The characters use humor in a way that confronts the problems of trying to live in mainstream America, which perhaps is one reason why many African-American viewers might specifically identify with the show. This subtle illustration of a common, humorous ground between African-American viewers and the show's characters also should not be overlooked. Burke (1937) argues, for example, that popular discourse gives persons motives that psychologically equip them for living under current societal conditions. The comedy presented on *Living Single*, might then supply some African-American audiences with "equipment" to deal with their marginalization. Therefore, African-

American viewers of *Living Single* conceivably could find the show humorous due to its ability to mirror some of their own lived experiences, to poke fun at various aspects of African-American life, and to call into question some of the cultural codes that appear structurally similar to those operating in earlier American media programming. Consequently, the appeal of *Living Single* among African-American audiences is worth exploring further.

The show has managed to make humorous the experiences of six twenty-something African Americans at a time when African Americans have a number of opportunities, yet are still subject to the challenges of being black in white America. The show offers a fresh, positive, and sometimes even cynical look at an otherwise stagnant array of representations of African Americans on television. So, what else makes *Living Single* funny to African-American audiences? What follows is an attempt to present three explanations that support my contention that African-American audiences might find both comfort and humor in the show. This will lay the foundation for my subsequent discussion of some African-American women's particular outlook on the show.

Nearly all people of color at some point in their lives (and arguably at many times in their lives) are faced with the decision of whether to code switch—the conscious decision by persons to substitute one form of speaking for another that they perceive as more contextually appropriate. Code switching is a sensitive issue for many members of marginalized groups, because so-called preferred dialects convey power and dominance (Lustig & Koester, 1993). It is one practice that the characters on *Living Single* approach with humor. These characters often code switch to humorously emphasize their speech and to mock underlying assumptions that African Americans do not have a command of the English language—that they do not know how to speak English "properly." One character on *Living Single* code switches regularly. Although the contexts of the code switching vary, it appears that these acts attempt to defy the seemingly requisite code switching that African Americans do in everyday life. For example, character "Khadijah James" can be found switching to what she considers a "white" code as she attempts to impress a potential advertiser for the magazine she edits and publishes. This character also code switches through her use of language that warns the person or persons to whom she is speaking that she might be forced to become "ethnic" if that language choice is required to make her point. The humor here is found in the character's warning that she might be forced to switch to a so-called black code. Khadijah's code switching therefore serves a significant function: It is a tool for empowerment and a threat to the persons to whom she is speaking—which is quite different from the idea that persons who code switch do so in order to account for a deficiency in their own communication competency (Lustig & Koester, 1993).

Living Single's humorous take on the politics of hair is another reason why the show might resonate with African Americans. Gibson (1995) and Russell, Wilson, and Hall (1992) assert that the issue of hair is prevalent within the African-American community. References by these writers to "good" and "bad" hair and to African Americans' preoccupation with it suggest that the show's ability to poke fun at this preoccupation taps into the deep-rooted nature of these "conditions" within the African-American community. The writers of *Living Single* have incorporated, for example, an ongoing anecdote concerning one character's hair. "Regine Hunter," is known for her extensive wig collection and for her openness in wearing such adornment (an openness that has not always been felt by many African-American women). This anecdote points to the humor in many African-American women's supposed obsession with hair. This character therefore makes funny the very idea that an African-American woman could appear oblivious to the politics of hair because she unapologetically flaunts her various wigs as a fashion statement.

The character of "Kyle Barker," also comments on the politics of hair. As an investment broker who has received criticism from his colleagues for wearing dredlocks to the office, this character maintains the style as a way to express pride in his ethnicity and as a refusal to accept some of the ideologies established by corporate America. So, as *Living Single* taps into the current conditions that influence the organizational politics of hair, here too it points to the historically-based conditions that influence the politics of hair in the African-American community. And regardless of African-American viewers' positions on the cultural politics of hair, the issue arguably resonates with many of their lived experiences. The politics of hair therefore might have historically created and perpetuated divisions among African Americans who put a value on the length and texture of African-American hair, but *Living Single* confronts the issue in a way that is both pointed and funny.

Finally, *Living Single* uses humor to challenge directly some of the stigmatizing representations of African Americans that mainstream America media have disseminated since the early days of film and television. The show seemingly is a barrier breaking presentation of these six young, upwardly mobile African Americans. And indeed it appears to stand apart from much of contemporary American media programming that still depicts African Americans in shallow and sometimes ridiculous roles. One way in which *Living Single* accomplishes this is through its subtle attack on the status-seeking depictions of African Americans that were prevalent in 1970s shows such as *The Jeffersons* and *Good Times*.

Media programming in the 1970s often depicted African Americans as seeking a status in life that was far from their reach, but nevertheless sought after voraciously. *The Jeffersons* was based on the idea that "George" and "Louise" had finally made it by "moving on up" the social ladder. *Good Times* can even be said to represent a family that struggled to get out of the proverbial "ghetto" and into a more comfortable position in society. The family's dreams of doing this were nearly realized when the Evans' daughter "Thelma" married a soon-to-be professional football player. Of course the family's dreams were shattered when "Keith" tripped on his way down the wedding aisle, breaking his leg and any chances of their rescue from life in the housing projects of Chicago. Building such status seeking into the plots of these and other shows might have contributed to the representations of African Americans as wishful thinkers and as persons who exert much of their time, energy, and money on trying to "be" somebody.

Living Single seems to reverse these notions about African Americans' status seeking by presenting a few characters who flaunt their clothing and talk of the expensive purchases they make. Kyle's role, for example, is unique in its portrayal of an Afrocentric-styled investment broker who is as good with figures as he is with coordinating an outfit. Kyle seems to reverse stereotypes of overt status seeking by African Americans, because he nonverbally displays his status. This character is often found dressed in designer hats, scarves, coats and suits, or sporting expensive, traditionally African apparel. The humor in all of this usually lies in this character's entrance into the apartment of the four major female characters. Studio audience reactions as Kyle strolls through the door is much like the reaction to the grand entrances of "Lenny" and "Squiggie" on the 1970s situation comedy, *Laverne and Shirley*. Kyle's suave, yet controlled stance, also seems to be the cause of much humor. His "cool pose" and swagger appear to speak of his status—but not in the way that "J.J. Walker's" cool pose on *Good Times* made him appear to be a bit like the Sambo figure from the early days of film and television that Bogle (1992) indicts, along with other stigmatizing representations of African Americans in media. Kyle does not seem to seek status, but embodies status because of his career and because he is pioneering in his own right—a role that has not always been given to African Americans. These characters alone do not exhaust the humor in *Living Single*, but the characters' ability to confront past crippling representations of African Americans suggests another explanation for why African Americans might find that the show resonates with their own concerns and experiences.

However, despite *Living Single*'s appeal to African-American audiences for its ability to make African Americans laugh at themselves and its promotion of less simplified representations of the African-American experience, there are some disturbing aspects of the show as well. It simultaneously seems to perpetuate representations of African-American womanhood that are structurally similar to the stigmatizing representations of women that operated in the early days of film and television. According to Dines and Humez (1995), the lives of African-American women have historically been constructed in the media in a way that perpetuates African Americans' marginalization; African-American women have been denied a widespread and complex presence in mainstream American television programming. So while *Living Single* has managed to create some African-American characters with relatively higher socio-economic status on television, its re-contextualization of the representations of African-American womanhood is worth exploring.

Living Single seems to follow landmark comedies such as *The Cosby Show* in breaking what some scholars refer to as the vicious cycle of representing African Americans as an inferior people—to be pointed to, laughed at, or admired for certain "positive" qualities, such as dancing and sports. Nevertheless, the show warrants critical attention for its reliance on the major archetypes that Bogle (1992) and Jewell (1993), refer to as Matriarch/Mammy, Sapphire, Jezebel, and Tragic Mulatto. Following Bogle and Jewell, I maintain that the characters of *Living Single*, while both contemporary and seemingly resonant with the African-American experience, structurally resemble their respective media archetypes from earlier days of television (and specifically such shows as *Amos and Andy*, *What's Happening*, and *Good Times*). There have been few analyses of how African-American women reconcile these structural similarities with the aspects of certain shows that they enjoy. As Jewell (1993) has called for with respect to media as a whole, it therefore seems necessary to describe and analyze some of the cultural representations in *Living Single*.

It is especially important to understand the ways in which these archetypes have been recontextualized in the 1990s in order to consider their implications for this analysis. Jewell (1993) urges African-American scholars to challenge questionable representations of African Americans and to construct and support more complex and constructive cultural representations of themselves. In the spirit of Jewell's (1993) call, this chapter applies her ideas in its attempt to more critically explore the representations of African-American women's lived experiences on *Living Single*. I argue here that what is considered "positive" and "negative" about these representations co-exist in an ambivalent tension, which locates the place at which this chapter targets the second portion of its analysis.

Procedure

One focus group and two individual interviews were conducted. The focus group was essential because one of the research goals of this study is to understand how African-American women are interpretive communities. As my co-researchers articulated so clearly during their interviews, group dialogue about television characters, storylines, and the like brings to the foreground the way they view the show, articulate their lived experiences and discuss the representations on the show. Observing this dialogue is itself insightful, as is the way the participants of the focus groups respond to one another during the sharing of ideas. The verbal as well as nonverbal cues that are observable from the interaction among my co-researchers, for example, were aspects of the data collection process that could not be found in interviews with individual co-researchers (although face to face interactions are undoubtedly irreplaceable).

Thus, based on my interest in inquiring about how African-American women both identify with and negotiate the representations of African-American womanhood on *Living Single*, the most appropriate strategy for gathering data was through the process of oral history (Gluck & Patai, 1991). These oral histories of regular viewers of *Living Single* allowed my co-researchers to reflect on their viewing experiences, to identify what they consider to be problematic cultural codes, to describe the media archetypes and storylines that they reject, to indicate the representations with which they identify, and to address why they are fans of the sitcom.

According to Gluck and Patai (1991), the oral histories are critical tools for developing new frameworks and theories based on women's lives. The male-centered communication frame, these writers assert, needs to be altered for women's oral history, because "we will not hear what women deem essential to their lives unless we legitimate a female socio communication context for the oral history situation" (1991, pp. 31-32). In other words, operating from a woman-centered communication frame gives insight into how women interpret the world. My aim, then, is to offer my African-American co-researchers an opportunity to articulate their cultural communication frame and its relevance to their interpretations of *Living Single*.

My African-American co-researchers were either referred to me by persons aware of their viewing practices, or they responded to my request to talk with persons who watched *Living Single* regularly. These women satisfied my criteria for being considered regular viewers because they had all watched the show each week from its first air date to the middle of its second season. My interview protocol consisted of discussing my co-researchers' general television watching practices, their perceptions of the characters on *Living Single*, and their expectations for the storylines of these characters. My co-researchers furnished candid responses about their lived experiences and these descriptions allowed me to do what oral history seeks to accomplish: to elicit responses from them that guide the direction of my inquiry, and to allow them to "express themselves as speaking subjects rather than...as objects already spoken for" (Nelson, 1990, p. 225).

Narrative Structure

Understanding what constitutes a narrative involves recognizing that narratives are oral explications of personal experience and occur in a context in which narrators can articulate how they order their lived experiences (Labov & Waletzky, 1967). Thus, I seek to explore how these narratives give insight into the way in which my co-researchers view representations of African-American womanhood on *Living Single.*

Unfortunately, there is considerable disagreement about the nature of a narrative. Aristotle's *Poetics*, for example, claims that a narrative necessarily has a beginning, middle, and end. Labov and Waletzky (1967), however, contend that such structure is necessary, but not sufficient to necessarily constitute a narrative. So although sequence is an essential element of narrative, it alone does not constitute it. It is reasonable that what we as researchers consider the beginning and ending of narratives influences the meaning that we derive from such stories, and ultimately my thematization of this data. These writers identify six elements of narratives. Highlighting these elements will establish the framework I will use to explicate in this chapter the ways in which my co-researchers view representations of African-American womanhood on *Living Single.*

According to Labov and Waletzky (1967), narratives are structured into an abstract, orientation, complicating action, evaluation, resolution, and coda. The *abstract* of a narrative indicates the substance of the story to follow. The *orientation* specifies the time, place, situation, and participants of a given narrative. The *complicating action* is the sequence of the events that develops in a narrative. The *evaluation* is the significance and meaning narrators assign to the action within the story, as well as the narrator's feelings and attitudes with regard to the narrative. For example, the evaluation might reflect a narrator's anger or frustration as she recalls certain details of her story. The *resolution* of a narrative, then, indicates the result of the story and serves as the last point in the sequence of events articulated in the narrative. Finally, the *coda* is the point at which the narrator returns her story to the present (or is forced to do so by another narrator). Narrators, however, do not always articulate a coda, indicating that some narratives remain open-ended.

Labov's and Waletzky's (1967) narrative structure helps to highlight and attempts to understand how stories are told and are linked.

This chapter's analysis of a few of my co-researchers' narratives will allow their stories to assist me in my subsequent thematization of their ideas and to give some insight into how they articulate their lived experiences. What follows, then, is a sample application of Labov's and Waletzky's narrative structure to a single narrative articulated by one of my co-researcher's:

Abstract

> That's a long story.

Orientation

> I guess it goes back to how I was brought up.

Complicating Action

> I mean even though I never... I saw my mom cry... um... maybe twice out of my life. I may have seen her twice.

Evaluation

> Um... but. I've always been the one...

Complicating Action

> when stuff happens in the family... I'm there. And I fix it. And I put it back... and I fix it

Evaluation

> to make it better so that other people will be happy... and disregard my feelings.

Resolution

> That's how it was.

Coda

> But now, I regard my feelings (laugh). I think about me... no not first... but second. I think about other people's feelings first.

Resolution of the Coda

> Now if I don't care about 'em, then they don't know that I don't care.

My hope is that highlighting a few of my co-researchers' narratives that are exemplary of their lived experiences will allow me to identify the commonalities among their interpretive frameworks. My co-researchers' indictments of the representations of African-American womanhood on *Living Single* supports this chapter's recommendation that developing more complex representations of African-American women's lived experiences should be an on-going priority in modern American television programming.

Thematic Method

Van Manen (1990) asserts that phenomenological themes can be understood as the structures of experience. He further proposes that three approaches can be taken to a thematic analysis. Isolating themes first can be done "wholistically" (1990, p. 92), by expressing the fundamental or overall meaning of a text (or, for our purposes, a portion of a narrative). It can be done selectively, by highlighting key statements or phrases that seem particularly revealing about the experiences being described. Finally, uncovering themes can be accomplished with a detailed or line-by-line approach to the narratives under examination. This chapter follows a *selective* approach to thematization, for it seeks to highlight key responses my co-researchers make about *Living Single*. It also tries to consider what these responses reveal about how their own experiences impact the way they view representations of African-American women on this show. The selective approach is also privileged in this study because it provides a strong, initial level of interpretation for this research. Subsequent research could utilize a different thematic framework of analysis.

And although thematization runs the risk of reductively examining the dynamic nature of these experiences, they very usefully specify and describe significant aspects of such phenomena. My thematization was based on organizing the commonalities among my co-researchers' descriptions of their lived experiences and among their views on the representations of African-American womanhood on *Living Single*. This chapter therefore highlights the way these women engage in a self-reflexive process of understanding and dealing with both real life and fictional experiences. And following Van Manen

(1990), this involves the invention, discovery, and disclosure of these phenomena; I incorporate these three goals here.

Thematization

Four themes emerged from my co-researchers' narratives. The themes represent the stories these women told about their lived experiences, the way in which these experiences are reflected on *Living Single*, and in some cases the negotiations that they make between problematic representations of African-American womanhood on the show and their continued admiration for the show. Within my discussions of each theme, I have included an analysis of one narrative that is exemplary of the particular theme under evaluation.

Obligation

Initial discussions of the show and of the women's relationships to it brought up issues concerning the obligation of women and persons of color to speak for their respective groups and to speak publicly about issues related to culture and marginalization. My co-researchers considered this responsibility to be unfairly assigned. Some of the women also noted an obligation to represent all African-American women in many of their discussions with persons who are not members of this group. This frustration was articulated in a number of ways, one of which was the straightforward description of their experiences in situations in which they were the only African-American women present. In sum, academic settings were mentioned as the most frequent site of this frustration, where they are sought out and asked to define African-American womanhood (and what it generally means to be an African American), to speak for all African Americans, and to teach others about it.

hooks (1989) offers an interesting explanation for the frustration some of these narrators experienced in the classroom, suggesting that it is all too common for African Americans to find themselves in this situation. She describes a situation in which only white female students were enrolled in her course on contemporary Black feminist novelists. The dilemma for her white students, she says, was that they did not think they could learn about the topic effectively without

African-American students in the class. Thus, the seeming psychological reliance on African Americans suggests that these white students did not seem to think that they could find their own meaning in the representations of the material covered—and depended on the input of African Americans to direct some of their thinking.

As is the case within academia, my co-researchers argue that *Living Single* and other mass mediated forms that place persons of color and women in leading roles are in a similar position to represent African-American womanhood. Despite the fact that my co-researchers seem to resent being considered spokespersons for women and African Americans, they suggest that the media have more of an opportunity to speak to issues that they feel forced to address in their own lives. Nevertheless, the fundamental difference that they articulate seems to be that media representations unfortunately are viewed as reality, and perpetuates somewhat reductive accounts of African-American women's lived experiences. As an illustration of their frustrations, three of my co-researchers offer a collective account of how academic environments have imposed a spokesperson role upon them:

1: Abstract

> I think, and, you know, I can personally...I get tired of this [in response to idea that shows featuring African Americans are forced to be responsible for representing the entire race].

Orientation

> You know, maybe you're in class

Complicating Action

> and if you're talking about slavery, or some "black" issue,

Complicating Action

> you're supposed to represent the whole black race.

Evaluation

> And I think it relates to what we're talking [about].

Resolution

> I mean, should we always have to...should these four women have to represent all black women?

Evaluation/Coda

I mean that's crazy. I get tired of it. That's not natural for us.

2: Evaluation

I think it should be attempted by those willing to do it. But I don't think that it should be a burden, pushed on everybody who's African American.

3: Evaluation

I think, you know, it's... it's good that they're trying to show variety. But I don't think it's their responsibility... their complete responsibility to show that, okay, this is, you know, this is all black women, or every single black woman.

Orientation

Because, you know, that's another thing that, uh, what I think *Living Single* does.

Complicating Action

It's that it shows a variety of black women.

Evaluation

Because, a lot of times they try to pull us together. You know, that we all act the same.

Evaluation/Resolution

But we're a lot of different women. I mean, I mean, we're all different. We all have our own personalities, you know, our own identities.

This discussion among my co-researchers taps into the frustrations that they express about their seeming obligation to speak for all African-American women in the American educational system, and simultaneously about the media's seeming reliance on archetypal representations of African-American womanhood. My co-researchers therefore consider fostering more awareness of intra cultural distinctions among African Americans as instrumental in the development of a more conscious society and more representative media programming.

Stigmatizing Representations

A second major theme that emerged from my co-researchers' narratives is that they identified some of the roles represented on the show as structurally similar to many of the depictions of African-American women in the early days of film and television. These women assert that *Living Single* is therefore problematic in its evocation of archetypal Matriarch/Mammy, Jezebel, Sapphire, and Tragic Mulatto roles. My co-researchers identified "Synclaire," "Khadijah"'s younger cousin and member of the foursome, as the Tragic Mulatto figure, "Maxine" as the Sapphire, "Regine" as the Jezebel, and Khadijah as the Matriarch. My co-researchers initially seemed hesitant in their articulations of these positions, for the representations that they suggest indeed are structurally similar to those operating in the earlier days of film and television and contradict their simultaneous identification with the contemporary versions of these archetypal roles in Khadijah, Regine, Max, and Synclaire. Ultimately, however, they consider these updated versions as less problematic. In fact, these co-researchers see aspects of themselves in the characters on *Living Single*. One co-researcher, for example, compares herself to the role of Khadijah:

Abstract

> If I had to be someone

Orientation

> I would be Khadijah. I would be Khadijah because I am dominating. I am a control person.

Complicating Action

> I... everyone comes to me with their stuff.

Orientation

> Therefore I know everybody's... most of my friends' business.

Complicating Action

> because they always come to me to ask me for advice.

Evaluation

> Why, I do not know.

Complicating Action

> Um...and I'm like the person that people lean on.

Evaluation

> But, if you notice, Khadijah doesn't have anyone to lean on. She...and Synclaire are cousins, but they're not that tight that Khadijah could go to cry on her shoulders. Khadijah has never cried on that show. Max has never cried on that show. Max didn't even cry when she got fired [from her job with a private law firm]. Synclaire cried. But that's it. Khadijah has never cried.

Resolution/Coda

> And for me...I don't cry at all. It takes a lot for my emotions to build up, or for me to actually express my emotions in front of people.

Regardless, then, of this co-researcher's assertion that Khadijah essentially serves as the Matriarch on the show, she admits the resonance the character has with her own lived experiences and the matriarchal leadership role that she plays in her family and among her friends. The structure of this story also suggests that this co-researcher reconciles her position in these interpersonal relationships by accepting it as a "calling," of sorts. Resigning herself to such a role troubles her, nevertheless, she indicates that because she's a "control person," she actually is comforted by the fact that everyone leans on her and "comes to [her] with their [problems]." Arguably, then, the historical stigma associated with the matriarchal figure is re-appropriated here as a source of control for this co-researcher. To be sure, she manages to negotiate the meanings that are inherent in the role she plays, as well as in the new meaning that she derives from this representation.

Such negotiation was prevalent among my co-researchers. Nevertheless, the representations that they suggest have contributed to the perpetuation of crippling representations of African-American women in the media remain problematic for them. On the one hand, it appears that the mere fact that updated representations of African-American womanhood appear on *Living Single* serves as a kind of resolution of the past. But inherent in this resolution is the recognition among these women that archetypal representations of African-

American women are still widely circulated. In other words, my co-researchers appear to negotiate rather than criticize the meaning that they attach to questionable portrayals of African-American womanhood—likely because the show and the experiences of its characters tap into aspects of their own experiences. Nevertheless, my co-researchers' comments about the more overt representations of African-American women as matriarchal or simple minded doubtless are insightful.

As noted by one woman, the character of Synclaire as the Tragic Mulatto provides the "comic relief" for the show. She points out that there needs to be more substance to this role in order to move the show away from its perpetuation of "dizzy" female roles that resemble those like one of the most memorable roles in television history: "Chrissy" from the 80's situation comedy, *Three's Company*. This archetype hardly reflects the strength and intelligence that many African-American women possess. And according to this co-researcher, such roles reverse the strides that both white and African-American actresses have made toward highlighting the complexity of the women that they play. Interestingly, one co-researcher suggests that Synclaire actually gives the other characters on the show insights about their behavior. These insights, she says, seem shocking to these characters, because they occur sporadically and appear to keep them wondering whether Synclaire is as "different" as they think she is. (Actually, this uncertainty about the depth of this character's "tragic" nature subtly suggests that the character indeed is complex.)

Despite the potential for an underlying complexity for this character, this co-researcher indicates that Synclaire's personality has gained a bit of notoriety among her own friends. They often tease one another by saying, "that's a Synclaire statement," in order to identify a person's comment as off hand or questionable. This co-researcher is concerned, however, that the behavior of some African-American women has been referred to seriously as "a Synclaire," as an indication of their supposed lack of intelligence. Thus, the occasional common sense on the part of this character and the humor that my co-researchers say unquestionably results from her interaction with the other characters, do not prevent one co-researcher from considering Synclaire's tragic figure as "dinginess."

Upon reflection on this theme, it seems that despite the criticisms that my co-researchers levy on some of the characters on *Living Sin-*

gle for offering reductive representations of African-American womanhood, the connection that they have to the show on other grounds creates a balance in their views. My co-researchers therefore seem to deal with the representations that they recognize, by allowing their resonating experiences with the African-American characters on the show to derive their own meaning from the show. Following Real (1996), this "textual poaching" serves as my co-researchers' ability to re-appropriate the problems that they articulate about the show as minor setbacks.

Friendship

This chapter's examination of how African Americans perceive representations of African-American lived experiences on *Living Single* brings it to a third theme. Because the show is based on the friendships among the characters on the show, it should come as no surprise that the depiction of friendship on the show would emerge as an important issue to the women interviewed for this project. My co-researchers' compared the friendships represented on the show with their own friendships with African-American women.

Even though my co-researchers again identified structural similarities between the portrayals of African-American relationships on *Living Single* with those shown in the early days of film and television (such as the Mammy or Matriarch maintaining the stability of her sometimes wayward friends), they focused on the support, nurturance, and sisterhood among African-American women upon which the show focuses. Because these values, they point out, typify their own notions of friendship, the depiction of the characters' friendships on *Living Single* is seen as candid and honest. These representations were identified by my co-researchers in two ways. First, some of them told stories of friendship experiences that they had as African-American women, which would never be depicted on television, because, quite frankly, they are less than dramatic. Second, comparisons were made between the reminiscing by the women on the show of their college days and the women's own college experiences.

One woman, for example, mentioned that her college experience was uneventful in comparison with some of the stories told by the characters on the show. Nevertheless, she says that the autonomy, growth, and friendships that are described in her own college experience indeed are captured in the characters' discussions of their college experiences:

> Abstract
>
> > I remember that [college].
>
> Orientation
>
> > Just going away and being at [college] was an experience.
>
> Complicating Action
>
> > Doing all that stuff for the first time. You know developing those friendships
>
> Evaluation
>
> > It was kind of a carefree attitude.
>
> Complicating Action
>
> > We didn't have to work. There wasn't...like any demand on life.
>
> Evaluation
>
> > You were just in school, to absorb the atmosphere of being there.
>
> Resolution
>
> > That's probably an experience that you'll never forget...and those stories of the stupid things that you did.
>
> Coda
>
> > I live by myself now, and I'm grown.

This narrative was exemplary of the stories told by my co-researchers. They consider the representations of African-American female friendships on *Living Single* and the interaction among the characters to be quite representative of their own lived experiences. The fact that they compare the way in which the characters on the show interact with humor, wit, and in the spirit of sisterhood points to commonalities between their lived experiences and those of the women on the show. In this case, there appears to be little need for negotiation for my co-researchers, who express their admiration for the show's seeming interest and ability to represent the most rich and fulfilling aspects of African-American lived experiences. So, the characters' reminiscing about their college days is indicative of the shared past that my co-researchers value in the show. This is a subject that is reasonable for my co-researchers to address, especially given the fact that *Living Single* is a show about survival and camaraderie in the 1990s. Thus, my co-researchers situate themselves as co-authors (Real, 1996) in the viewing of this show, for they bring as much of their own experiences to their interpretations of the show.

Dating

Dating is the fourth theme that emerged from the narratives of the African-American women interviewed for this project. The women were both critical and accepting of *Living Single's* depiction of dating relationships of the characters on the show. They were critical of the "slightly questionable" ways in which some of the romantic relationships are presented on the show. As one co-researcher points out, it is for such reasons that the women call for more complex representations of African-American dating relationships on the show.

My co-researchers questioned the representations of certain characters on the show as dissatisfied women in need of male companionship. These comments create problems for these co-researchers, for they position certain characters in reductive roles. For example, Regine's role, according to these women, resembles that of the Jezebel. Regine's "man hunt," as another co-researcher describes, not only sheds a shallow light on this role, it sheds a familiar light on African-American women's historical roles in American film and television; the updated version of the Jezebel role is a serious drawback to this character, according to these women. These co-researchers instead would like to see the women on the show represented as truly "single" (as the title of the show suggests) and as content with this status. This would be a significant development in re-visioning women (especially African-American women) in roles that do not rely on male companionship to be complete.

One co-researcher was less critical, however, of the representation of dating relationships on the show, noting that the "game" aspect of dating resonates with her past dating experiences. Her evaluation of her experiences led to her story of the way in which she met and dated her husband:

Abstract

> Other than Max, I don't see a direct contradiction between anything I've done.

Orientation

> I think before I met [my husband] I was more of the Regine type.

Complicating Action

> Looking for the wrong thing in all the wrong places. You know, looking for... I wouldn't really call it instant love, but looking for relationships and trying to find that perfect man at a party, or you know, at the club, or exchanging numbers here or there. That type of thing.

Evaluation

> I mean, I did that and that obviously was not the way to go.

Orientation

> But then with Khadijah, you know, it's like I'm more... I guess along those lines

Evaluation

> because the guy she's with is somebody she grew up with.

Complicating Action

> And they've known each other for years.

Evaluation/Resolution/Coda

> And that's like more... that's more, you know, more of what, what I've been like, or have [been like with my husband], I mean.

This co-researcher seems to use this story, in large part, to provide a meta-analysis of her position and to support her claim that she is far less critical of the depiction of African-American dating relationships on the show. It seems, then, that the African-American woman as "sexual being" is a platform on which my co-researchers articulated their most significant concerns for the representations of African-American womanhood on television. But they appeared to have equally divergent interpretations of the impact that the characters on *Living Single* have in offering problematic representations of African-American women.

Conclusions

There obviously are differing responses among my co-researchers to the issues addressed in this examination of the way in which some African-American women's lived experiences reflect or contradict the representations of African-American women on *Living Single*. What remains constant, however, seems to be the on-going negotiation that my African-American co-researchers make between what they consider problematic representations of African-American womanhood and the way these characters resonate with their own lived experiences. The responses that my co-researchers give are insights into their negotiation of these contradictions and are support for my claim that oral history is a way to allow these issues to be addressed. It should be noted that the narrators' re-conceptualizing of their thinking about the show is constant. The women's interpretations are subject to the particular balance the women seek at any given time between welcoming the humor on the show, relishing in the similarities of the characters' experiences to their own, and recognizing the structural problems that they find with these characters—all which lie at the heart of co-authorship.

Steenland (1988) supports my co-researchers' insights about the power of reductive and stigmatizing representations on television, stating that:

> Rather than fall[ing] back on cliches and outdated stereotypes, television must keep [the] pace with the lives of women today [and] must then, with talent and sensitivity, mirror back to viewers those lives and their stories, so that we recognize the characters on the screen... as authentic parts of ourselves. (p. 82)

Hence, that the women who informed this project indicated that television should more fairly represent their lived experiences and avoid relying on outdated archetypes in its programming is clear. But their assurance that they will remain fans of *Living Single* because they are discriminating enough to re-appropriate this media product, emerges as the most telling comment about how these women interpret the show.

References

Bogle, D. (1992). *Toms, coons, mulattoes, mammies, & bucks: An interpretive history of Blacks in American films*. New York: Continuum.

Burke, K. (1937). *Attitudes toward history*. New York: The New Republic.

Dines, G., & Humez, J.M., Eds. (1995). *Gender, race and class in media*. London: Sage.

Gates, H. L. (1988). *The signifying monkey: A theory of African-American literary criticism*. New York: Oxford University Press.

Gibson, A. L. (1995). Nappy: Growing up black and female in America. New York: Harlem River Press.

Gluck, S. B., & Patai, D. (1991). *Women's words: The feminist practice of oral history*. New York: Routledge.

Labov, W., & Waletzky, J. (1967). Narrative analysis: Oral versions of personal experience. In J. Helm (Ed.), *Essays on the verbal and visual art: Proceedings of the Annual Spring Meeting of the American Ethnological Society* (pp. 12-44). Seattle: University of Washington Press.

hooks, b. (1989). *Talking back: Thinking feminist thinking black*. Boston, MA: South End.

Jenkins, H. (1988). Going bonkers!: Children, play and pee-wee. *Camera Obscura*, 17, 169-192.

Jensen, K. B. (1990). Television futures: A social action methodology for studying interpretive communities. *Critical Studies in Mass Communication*, 7, 129-146.

Jewell, K. S. (1991). *From mammy to Miss America and beyond: Cultural images & the shaping of US social policy*. London: Routledge.

Lustig, M.W., & Koester, J. (1993). *Intercultural competence: Interpersonal communication across cultures*. New York: HarperCollins College Publishers.

MacDonald, J. F. (1983). *Blacks and white TV*. Chicago: Nelson-Hall.

Nelson, J. (1990). Phenomenology as feminist methodology: Explicating interviews. In K. Carter & C. Spitzack (Eds.), *Doing research on women's communication: Perspectives on theory & method*. Norwood, N.J.: Ablex.

Real, M. (1996). *Exploring media culture: A guide*. Thousand Oaks, CA: Sage.

Russell, K., Wilson, M., & Hall, R. (1992). *The color complex: The politics of skin color among African Americans*. New York: Harcourt Brace Jovanovich.

Spender, D. (1985). *Man made language* (2nd ed.). Boston: Routledge & Kegan Paul.

Steenland, S. (1988). Ten years in prime time: An analysis of the image of women on entertainment television from 1979-1988. In A. Kesselman, L.D. McNair, & N. Schneiedewind (Eds.), *Women's images and realities: A multicultural anthology*. London: Mayfield.

Van Manen, M. (1990). *Researching lived experience: Human science for an action sensitive pedagogy*. Ontario: University of Western Ontario Press.

13

"TIRED OF THE WORLD ACCORDING TO YOUNG MEN'S MACHISMO"

BLACK WOMEN'S REACTIONS TO REPRESENTATIONS OF BLACK WOMEN IN MUSIC VIDEOS

Trevy A. McDonald

In the late spring of 1990 a new urban contemporary group, Bell Biv Devoe (BBD), released their first hit single titled "Poison." This group, comprised of three members of the 80s Rhythm and Blues teeny bopper group New Edition, rose to popularity in many circles including children, adolescents and young adults of both genders. "Poison" warns young males to never trust a Black woman with a "big butt and a smile." The song not only became a number one hit on Billboard's Hot 100 Black Singles Chart and crossed over to the Hot 100 Pop Singles Chart, but T-Shirts were printed stating BBD's slogan in all sizes ranging from extra large to child size 10.

BBD's "Poison" is just one example of extreme sexism towards Black women via popular music and accompanying videos. Many of these images, which are primarily produced by male directors and male groups, objectify Black women through camera angles, lighting, extreme close ups of body parts and scant clothing. The goal of this inquiry is to explore Black women's reactions to this objectification of Black women through media.

Music videos became popular in the early 1980s with the birth of MTV (Music Television) in 1981. Maria Viera's "The Institutionalization of Music Video" accounts for their popularity. She states:

> Record companies have traditionally furnished radio stations with free records to play over the air since such exposure yields enormous gains in record sales. The promotional value of music videos also seems to be self-evident—music videos are generally acknowledged to be part of the reason the sales slump of 1979 was overcome (p. 87).

Thus music videos began as a marketing strategy to increase record sales and in effect supplemented records.

The use of Black women in music videos is not unlike her earlier portrayals in other types of mass media. For example, Black women in the films of the 1930s were often depicted in servant roles as "faithful mammies" with no lives of their own. When Black women finally did get their "own life" it was only to serve males as seductresses and temptresses as Lena Horne in "Cabin in the Sky." Pearl Bowser states that:

> A cursory look at the image of Black women in American movies conjures up a host of stereotypes and one dimensional characters pigeonholed by phrases such as mulatto mistress, faithful soul, sultry singer, mammy, high yaller, chocolate dandy, foxy chick. (p. 44)

Sapphire was popularized through the *Amos 'n' Andy* program which aired on television during the 1950s. Sapphire is most known for her sassiness and her ability to tell people off with her hand on her hip and her finger pointed. The films and television programs of the late 1960s and 1970s, carried these themes further to portray Black women as prostitutes and welfare queens. These images are used to oppress Black women according to Jannette Dates and William Barlow (1990):

> Black media stereotypes are not the natural, much less harmless products of an idealized popular culture; rather they are more commonly constructed images that are selective, partial, one-dimensional and distorted in their portrayal of African Americans. Moreover, stereotyped images most often are frozen, incapable of growth, change, innovation or transformation. (p. 5)

Repetitive portrayals of Black women as objects may be viewed by others as incapable of growth if nothing is done to transform these representations.

Even the films of the late 1980s have continued to present Black women in static roles. Spike Lee's *She's Gotta Have It*, for instance, sets out to present a sexually liberated Black woman but falls short of this goal according to Black feminist scholar bell hooks (1989):

> Even though filmmaker Spike Lee may have intended to portray a radical new image of black female sexuality, *She's Gotta Have It* reinforces and perpetuates old norms overall. Positively, the film does show us the nature of black male/female power struggles, the contradictions, the craziness, and that is an important new direction. Yet it is the absence of compelling liberatory reconciliation which undermines the progressive radical potential of this film. Even though nude scenes, scenes of sexual play constitute an important imaging of black sexuality on screen since they are not grotesque or pornographic, we still do not see an imaging of mutual, sexually satisfying relationships between black women and men in a context of non-domination. (p. 141)

This submissive view of Black womanhood is discussed by numerous Black feminist theorists (Collins, 1991; hooks, 1989, 1990; Smith, 1983; Wallace 1990). For example, in the Combahee River Collective Statement, an anthology edited by Smith (1977) it is pointed out that Black Feminism is based in a belief that Black women are valuable, "that our liberation is a necessity not as an adjunct to somebody else's; but because of our need as human persons for autonomy" (p. 274). Stereotypical portrayals of Black women, particularly in the media, serve as an indication of the actual value society has placed upon Black women. The stereotyped representations of Black women in music videos tell audiences that this value is de-limited.

Unlike mainstream feminism, Black feminism does not define the Black man as "the enemy." Black feminists find the Black man a comrade in the struggle to fight oppression. However, when Black male singers, directors, and producers of music videos show us in stereotypical roles, they heighten the importance of the historical struggle for survival and liberation. As Angela Davis points out, "Black women have always embodied, if only in their physical manifestation, an adversary stance to white male rule and have actively resisted its inroads upon them and their communities in both dramatic and subtle ways," (Combahee River Collective, p. 275). In this regard, Black women must seek an authentic voice against their oppressors—Black or white. They must seek their authentic voice by becoming subjects who define themselves and set their own norms. They must reject objectification which serves as yet another means to disempower them. When media continues to subjugate Black women in popular music/videos, specifically those targeted towards them, it does nothing to benefit the struggle, nor does it contribute to an "exploration of parallels between the [sexual & political] dialogue of black women and black men" (Carby, 1987, p. 13).

Examining the popularity of music videos which feature Black women in stereotypical roles then serves as an opportunity for Black women to raise their voices in examining how these representations are viewed.

Background

A content analysis of images of Black women in music videos was conducted. In this analysis, ten hours of *Video Soul* on Black Entertainment Television (BET) were viewed. BET was selected because there is a higher concentration of music videos by Black artists on this network. A total of 91 music videos were aired in the ten hours of *Video Soul* analyzed with some of the videos airing as many as three times. Of the 91 videos, 28 were eliminated because they did not feature Black women. The remaining 63 videos were examined using a sexism scale adapted from Vincent, Davis and Boruszkowski (1987) as a model to analyze the roles portrayed by Black women. This scale consists of four levels with the first being "Condescending." In this level the woman is portrayed as being less than a person, a two-dimensional image. The second level is "Keep Her Place," with strength, skills, and capacities of women being acknowledged, but tradition dictating "womanly" roles. Level three is "Contradictory," which emphasizes a dual role where a woman plays a traditional, subservient role while also displaying a certain degree of independence. In level four, "Fully Equal," the woman is treated as a person (possibly a professional) with no mention of her private life.

The results of this content analysis revealed that 39 of the 63 videos featured Black women as either: sex objects, mindless or subservient (or all three at the same time). These videos were therefore categorized under levels one and two. Thirty-one of the videos in levels one and two were by male artists and two were by female artists. The remaining six videos were by male/female groups. The videos by female artists were in level two. This study provides evidence that some music videos do represent Black women in a negative stereotypical light.

Methodology

An audience study with a group of eight Black women graduate students from a major research university in the Southeast was conducted. The purpose of this study was to examine their perceptions of the roles Black women played in music videos. The women were from a variety of majors (Speech Communication to Medicine) as well as three different age groups (early twenties, late twenties and late thirties). The women's names have been changed to names of Black Feminist Theorists such as Michele (Wallace), Patricia (Hill Collins), Toni (Cade Bambara), Barbara (Christian), Hazel (Carby), bell (hooks), Gloria (Hull) and Angela (Davis). The subjects first completed a media use questionnaire to determine their familiarity with music videos. The women overwhelmingly listened to the radio more than they watched television, which may be a result of their status as students. Also, very few of the women watched music videos on a regular basis. Following the completion of the initial questionnaire, the women were shown three music videos. After each music video they were given time to respond to a series of open-ended questions concerning different images in specific music videos.

Music Video Selection

The music videos utilized for this study were the most frequently aired videos from the content analysis of ten hours of *Video Soul* and were all in level one of the sexism scale. They included: "BBD (I Thought It Was Me)" by Bell Biv Devoe, "You Can't Buy My Love" by Kool Skool and "Just Can't Handle It" by Hi-Five. The remainder of this chapter will discuss in detail the content of the music videos and the responses of the women.

"BBD (I Thought It Was Me)"

Bell Biv Devoe (BBD) consists of three members of pop/R&B group New Edition. The members were fifteen when New Edition was conceptualized in the mid 1980s with their first hit "Popcorn Love," and became popular amongst Black teens. Michael Bivens of New Edition and Bell Biv Devoe fame said in an interview with Donnie Simpson on BET's *Video Soul*, "New Edition was cute, classy; BBD is street, hard and ghetto."

BBD's third hit, "BBD (I Thought It Was Me)," is a phallocentric narrative of a woman who has a one night stand with each of the group's members. The chorus, "I thought it was me who made the girl this way, come to find out she's like that everyday," reinforces the phallocentric themes present in both the song and the video. The extended play version of this single makes a reference to this "girl" having a "do me baby booty." Extreme sexism is apparent in this phrase, not only is the woman objectified here, she is also devalued.

This video is similar to many released today by Black artists in that it incorporated dance/performance sequences with narrative sequences. Other than the woman who has the one-night stands with the group's members, are female dancers presented submissively—in the background. Like most concept videos, the group members serve as actors in the narrative.

The opening shot of the video takes place in a room leading to a roof of a building and is filmed at an oblique angle. An oblique angle involves a tilt of the camera. According to Louis Giannetti in *Understanding Movies*, "Psychologically, oblique angles suggest tension, transition and impending movement" (p. 13). The woman enters wearing a sheer white dress which has a tight fitting halter-type bodice and loose fitting skirt. The skirt is cut high on the sides and falls just below her knees in the center. She is spotlighted with yellow light as she enters the room. She turns to her right (with her back to the camera), is spotlighted with white light and vanishes. The white spotlight is used here to draw attention to her as she vanishes.

The second time she appears she is wearing a tight fitting white dress. She is filmed here from the head to just above the knees (medium shot). In this scene, she walks seductively past a group of men as she plays with her hair. This sequence is filmed in black and white with high-key lighting on her and low-key lighting on the men in the background. The high key lighting illuminating her white dress along with the placement of her in the foreground make her stand out and draw attention to her action (seductive walk, playing with hair).

The third time she appears in a helicopter with singer Ricky Bell as he begins the narrative, "I went out last night, that's when I met a sexy girl." In this scene she sits beside Bell and smiles. Here sound plays a crucial role in the portrayal of the woman. Her appearance on the words "sexy girl" reinforces the use of her as a sex object.

The narrative progresses and she appears on singer Michael Bivens' balcony, distracting him from his work at his drawing board. She is wearing a tight fitting green suit, walks across the room behind Bivens and is filmed in a medium shot. At this point Bivens places his hand on her hip as he says, "she and I choosed to cruise in my love boat." The next shot of the two is filmed at a slightly high angle with her in the foreground. According to Giannetti, "A person seems harmless and insignificant photographed from above" (p. 12). Her face is not in this shot and we see Bivens behind her leg as he states he is "proving his manhood." The following shot is filmed at a high angle also, only this time it is a medium shot (head to waist). Here, she pulls him close to her and stares at him while he looks into the camera, virtually ignoring her. The pair later reappear with the woman putting on her jacket.

Ricky Bell's interlude with the woman is filmed in black and white, primarily at high oblique angles. In this sequence the couple is sharing an intimate moment in a living room near a fireplace. In the second shot of this sequence (a full shot), we get a vivid picture of what is transpiring. Bell is on top of the woman (displaying dominance) in an intimate position. Although neither Bell nor the woman are fully undressed or directly engaging in intercourse, sexual implications are still present.

The final romantic interlude takes place between singer Ronnie Devoe of BBD and the woman in an antique car. Again, we don't directly see the couple engaging in intercourse, however it may be inferred through their actions and the lyrics. This sequence is also shot in black and white with high-key lighting and is filmed at a bird's eye angle. Before we actually see the couple in the car, a slow pan of the camera (also at a bird's eye view) from the front end of the car to the front seats reinforces a phallocentric theme.

In the final scene of this video she reappears in the same white dress she wore in the first scene. She approaches the three guys, walks through them and walks away. The guys react to her in both a surprised and disgusted manner. Here, she walks into the frame with her back to the camera and is filmed waist down (the guys are in the background). As she walks toward them we get a fuller shot of her.

This video combines high camera angles, high-key lighting and the use of cool colors (green) in costume in order to portray a Black woman as a sex object. Although the video reinforces the song's lyrics, the woman is portrayed distastefully, appearing as condescending. She appears mindless at times and is dominated by males most often.

Women's Reactions

The questions the women were asked about the specific music videos pertained to the following categories: message; similarities; description of dress, portrayals, etc.; reaction; context of lyrics to video; and opinion of women/video. After the women viewed "BBD (I Thought It Was Me)" I asked them if they would like to see it again because it consisted of many quick cuts. They immediately responded somewhat furiously, "No!" While five of the women stated they never viewed the video, they were quite perceptive of the representations of Black women in it.

Most of the women saw a connection between the message the artists were trying to get across in the song and video. One woman who was not familiar with the song, Michele said:

> ...though the woman approached them individually as though she wanted a special relationship, she did this with large numbers of men. There was nothing special about them... "it was not me."

Similar to this response was the response from Gloria who also never viewed the video. "...he thought the woman's sexual reaction to him was uniquely because of who he was, but he found out that 'she's like that with all the other guys.'" Angela, who was neither familiar with the song nor the video was in agreement with Michelle and Gloria. She stated:

> The artist(s) was (were) trying to imply that he was an influence on the woman's behavior. He later found out he wasn't, that she was like that anyway; although he seemed to imply that she was somewhat indiscriminate "She's like that with all the guys.":

Other women felt that the message of the video was primarily to present the women as sex objects. Toni, who had seen the video on other occasions, stated the message was "that women are promiscuous and that sex is the only thing women are good for." Barbara, who was somewhat familiar with the video (viewed it once or twice) stated, "That he thought the girl was a 'tramp.'" Hazel felt the message to be "that women are 'play things'—objects for men's sexual fantasies." bell stated the message she received from the video as "... the girl had 'used' him." Of the eight women, only one, Patricia, who had viewed the video once or twice, "...didn't really consider that there was any specific message."

The women also touched upon the Eurocentric characteristic prevalent not only in this video, but in other music videos by Black male artists. Six of the women made mention of the physical features of the woman in this music video. Most of them stated she was either white or was passing for white. Hazel explored this characteristic in great detail:

> The woman that was mainly featured throughout the video had typical features of what Black men call "redbone,"—light skin; long, sandy brown, curly hair; thin facial features and an hourglass shape. The other women that were dancing in the background were darker brown and closer to the physical features of most Black women. But that in itself is diverse since Black feminine beauty comes in a variety of colors, shapes and features.

This same woman responded to the opinion of women question by stating the women were beautiful, "all of them."

When asked their reaction to the music video, most of the women directed their anger at the way the women were portrayed focusing primarily on physical attributes. Patricia stated, "My strongest reaction is a negative one because I feel that, predominantly, the women were portrayed as sex objects, despite the fact that they held jobs (e.g. construction.)" Equally bothered by the portrayals, Toni stated she was, "Angry, because the women are portrayed as subservient people whose only purpose was to serve and satisfy men." Hazel stated, "I don't like the way that they were portrayed. They should have accentuated more than just their physical attributes. What about intelligence and standards? One good point is that the women were not shown nude or performing strange sexual acts." bell was disturbed by the objectification of the women, "I am offended by the way women are portrayed as 'utility pieces.'" Gloria felt this video was similar to many others, "Since I don't remember the specifics, I guess my overall reaction was that these women were the usual sexual stereotypes that populate music videos." Angela reacted to the women's actions and physical appearance, "I feel they are always too skimpily dressed, also too provocative. They seem to rely on physical attributes to get ahead in life. They are often in the background, and they often seem to 'react' to men."

One of the women was also disturbed by the presentation of men in the video. Michele stated,

> Truthfully I was as equally bothered by the men (BBD) as the women. Images of young black men being enthralled and then rejected by the white and bright are not uncommon, but a bit disconcerting. However, it is disconcerting to think that intelligent, professional appearing women are depicted as lacking the capacity for commitment and loyalty in a relationship.

In general, the women disliked this music video, finding the women displayed as subservient and mere objects.

Many women expressed a desire to never again view this video. Patricia stated. "The music and lyrics are fine. But, I feel that the women could have been used in a different way to better reflect the meaning behind the song." Others saw this video as promoting the view of women as objects to be used at the discretion of men (Toni and Hazel). bell stated, "I did not like the video. As a Black woman it made me feel that the 'ideal' woman does not look like me and unlike me that woman has *no* 'depth'(e.g. thoughts, feelings, spirituality, etc.). It makes me wonder if other types of women are 'worth' singing about or worth showing in videos." Due to the immediate desire to never view the video again after the initial showing, along with the women's responses to it, it is safe to say that the portrayal of Black women as sex objects, promiscuous, submissive and mindless was a major turnoff to the participants.

"You Can't Buy My Love"

The second video the women viewed was rap group Kool Skool's "You Can't Buy My Love." This video was like the previous in the sense that it is a concept video which incorporates performance and narrative. Only in this video the women portrayed as sex objects aren't part of the narrative. The song is the story of a woman who breaks the lead singer's (rapper) heart and leaves him for another lover. However, we only see this woman twice in the entire video.

This video is set in Las Vegas. We see the woman in two scenes, first when she leaves the lead singer by driving off in a Rolls Royce. Later, when she tries to return, she no longer has the car and is barefoot as she runs back to him.

Apart from the woman in the narrative there are several women, both Black and white, who appear as Las Vegas showgirls. Their costumes are sequined and resemble bikinis. In some cases, the women wear G-strings over their stockings. These women are often filmed at extreme close-ups from the waist to mid-thigh (bikini area) as they are dancing. Although these scenes are mostly filmed in black and white, the sequins on the costume make these scenes stand out. In other instances these women are filmed from the neck to mid-thigh. The framing of the shots, in combination with the costumes, present women as sexual objects, present only for show since they have no apparent ties to the narrative.

Women's Reactions

Just as in the previous video, very few of the women were familiar with this song or video. Their unfamiliarity with the video, however, did not inhibit their response to it. Most of the women related the message of the video, not being able to be bought, to the title of the song. Michele felt the woman was attempting to make amends. "That the women portrayed would have to make a real commitment rather than being involved elsewhere and coming back to make amends with whatever (buy)." Patricia related being bought with trust. She stated,

"I guess that he couldn't be 'enticed' into giving his love; his lack of trust in the woman."

Gloria and bell respectively saw the women using glamour to "hustle what they could obtain from men." Angela stated:

> He apparently thought some woman he was interested in had "done him wrong" and was trying to get back in his good graces by buying him material things.

One woman related the message to the theme of objectification and Eurocentrism prevalent in this and the previous video. Hazel stated, "In order for a woman to be appealing to him, she had to be scantily-clothed and have those thin features." The subjects' reaction to this music video for the most part was influenced by their interpretation of the message.

The women in the study were somewhat bothered by the dress of the women in the video. Many felt their presence had nothing to do with the context of the song. Michele felt the focus should have been on interpersonal relationships. "Certainly, women involved in dancing are not unusual. But what of the transition from "Showgirl" to something else? Why a chorus line when one is focusing on interpersonal relationships." Toni, Barbara and Gloria did not see the point of the dancers being in the video. Toni wrote:

> I feel that the presence of the showgirls did nothing to explain the message of the video. Because of this, I am not sure just what the message was. I did not like the fact that the only things the women did was prance around in showgirl costumes.

Gloria stated,

> If the song were about nightclub dancers whose love was "bought" by rich men it would make sense, but since the song seems to be about a man whose love can't be bought by a woman, the images don't match.

Patricia was bothered by the camera angles. She wrote:

> Completely negative (reaction); I feel that the camera focused too much on their legs and lower torso.

Hazel had a mixed reaction:

> Neutral (reaction). Again, they were not performing strange acts and were not physically abused. They did show a lot of hip, but that was part of the costume."

The reactions to this video displayed a dislike for the value placed on the women, not only according to how they were dressed, but more so to how they were filmed.

Many of the women surveyed not only developed a feminist stance to the video, they took a realistic view to the use of the showgirls in this video.

> Three snaps down. Wouldn't buy it. Tired of the world according to young men's machismo. (Michele)

> I think the message "You can't buy my love" could have been more accurately portrayed without using the females as skimpily clad dance-hall girls. (Patricia)

> I don't think the video and the song had anything to do with each other. The group had an O.K. song and to make it sell better and get more TV time they put half-naked women in their video. (Barbara)

> What was the purpose? Who on earth did Kool Skool (Kool Fool is more like it) think wanted to buy him anything? First off, he should learn to talk—the first 30 seconds or so were unintelligible. He seemed to think he was actually desirable to someone. Then to suggest that someone was trying to buy his love!!?? Who—one of the showgirls? On whose salary—certainly not hers. (Angela)

These responses show that the women were doubly objectified. First, they were used as objects, purely for show, in the video. Also the fact that they could have possibly been used to sell the song and get more airplay, as Barbara suggests, shows they were not only used within the video, but they were inherently used by the industry to sell the video.

"Just Can't Handle It"

The final video the women viewed was Hi-Five's "Just Can't Handle It." The teenage male vocal group sings a narrative of a relationship between a 16 year old boy and a 25 year old woman. In "Just Can't Handle It," the woman is presented as a seductress who tempts a young boy from school. She is often costumed in a short black tank dress, cut mid-thigh, and black high heel pumps. There is also another scene in which she is wearing a suit which features a low-cut jacket and short skirt with no blouse) as she carries a briefcase. Although there is more performance by the group in this video than narrative, we do see the woman objectified. There are a couple of shots of her legs, first as she sensuously rubs her hand up her leg and second, as she undresses. In the final scene of the narrative, the woman is dancing seductively on one side of a fence making the boy climb the six foot fence to be with her. Like the previous two videos, the framing of the shots along with costuming, serve as primary elements in presenting Black women in a stereotypic light.

Women's Reactions

While not pleased with this presentation, the women surveyed viewed the woman in the music video as a seductress. Michele stated, "A woman can be professional, but deep down she is always a temptress." Four other women also felt the message of this video was that beautiful women were out to "spoil the innocence" of these young boys. bell wrote:

> That obviously black-looking women were seductresses and out to spoil the innocence or contribute to delinquency.

Angela had a problem with the ages and maturity of the women and boy. Her response was,

> Anger and disbelief! What 25 year old woman in her right mind would want a 16 year old boy! Just to hear him scream?!!

This stereotype of Black women being seductresses not only comes from film history, but also American history as Black women were often objectified sexually by white men during slavery.

In addition to displaying dislike for the image of the seductress, most of the women in the study equally displayed a dislike for the video.

> Bit disturbed, especially in view of the recent situation, about this older woman propositioning this kid. And we can be professional but... These things do happen, but videos just seem to

> magnify the negative stereotype of the temptress...I would not buy this one either, but it comes closer to the one I would buy than the other two. (Michele)

> Highly negative and unfavorable (reaction). I feel that women were portrayed as temptresses and seducers out to manipulate the minds of younger men...Negative; I don't think that it (video) had any redeeming qualities. And really depicted women in a negative manner. (Patricia)

> I feel that the woman was portrayed as a "hot" older woman who liked to seduce helpless, innocent young boys. I was angered by this portrayal...I did not like the video at all. It portrays women as being scheming and conniving to take advantage of innocent men. (Toni)

> I didn't like the way she gyrated and teased. She was again portrayed as a sex symbol, a plaything to be used for sex. The woman was extremely attractive and seemed to be on the ball. Why didn't she look for a more meaningful relationship with a man of her own age with similar goals and values. (Barbara)

> I was offended. I did not like the video. A lot of young boys making gyrations was a turn off and the portrayal of Black women as corrupters did not help much either. (bell)

> Shoot her! Give her a real job, if she survives!!...Totally dumb (video). Do people actually spend money to produce such garbage? I try not to watch it, if at all possible. If I see it once, I won't see it again. (Angela)

While the majority of the women disliked the video, one woman saw it as cute. Gloria had a positive reaction. "I thought it was a cute video. It was cute, light-hearted, true-to-life for a stage of growing up."

Conclusion

There were similar responses to the issues discussed in this analysis of reactions to representations of Black women in music videos. The women is this study expressed quite candidly they felt these images were problematic. Some of the women stated they were bothered by a certain image; they mentioned the women were presented in a limited range of narrow, one-dimensional roles; further, many of the women stated they never wanted to view these videos (or those like them again). Such limited portrayals which teach disrespect of and devalue Black women do absolutely nothing to further Black liberation. They are certainly not representative of Black women as a whole and makes one wonder, as bell stated, "if other types of women are 'worth' singing about or worth showing in music videos." When women in media are first used as a utility piece in a media text, then used as a commodity to sell a product, they are doubly oppressed. Bringing this to light is only the first step in actively struggling to end this form of oppression. Educating others is also important.

In some of the cases, the women surveyed felt that the women in the video could have been displayed in a different manner to get the message across. Often camera angles and framing play an instrumental role in exhibiting dominance/submissiveness, and making images appear more sensual. In order for more accurate pictures of Black women to be presented in the media, sensitized Black women are needed to paint the picture. With the advent of more Black women directors and producers in the media industry we will see a definite change in the media portrayed image of Black women.

References

Bogle, D. (1989). *Toms, coons, mulattoes, mammies and bucks: An interpretive history of blacks in American films.* New York: Continuum.

Bowser, P. (1982). Sexual imagery and the Black woman in cinema. In G.L Yearwood (Ed.), *Black cinema aesthetics: Issues in independent Black filmmaking* (pp. 42–51). Athens OH: Ohio University Center for Afro-American Studies.

Carby, H. (1987). *Reconstructing womanhood: The emergence of the Afro-American woman novelist.* New York: Oxford.

Collins, P. H. (1991). *Black feminist thought: Knowledge, consciousness and the politics of empowerment.* New York: Routledge.

Combahee River Collective. (1983). Combahee River collective statement. In B. Smith (Ed.), *Home girls: Black feminist anthology* (pp. 272–282). Albany, NY: Kitchen Table/Women of Color Press.

Craig, K. W. (1991, January) Bell Biv Devoe: The secret of their mass appeal! *Black Beat* p. 78.

Dates, J. L. and Barlow, W. (Eds). (1990). *Split image: African Americans in mass media.* Washington DC: Howard UP.

Davis, A. (1971). Reflections on the Black woman's role in the community of slaves. *The Black Scholar. 3.4*, 3–15.

Giannetti, L. (1987). *Understanding movies.* Englewood Cliffs, NJ: Prentice Hall.

hooks, b. (1989). *Talking back: Thinking feminist, thinking black. Knowledge, consciousness, and the politics of empowerment.* New York: Routledge.

Simpson, D. (1990, October 10). Interview with Michael Bivens. (L. Cole Executive Producer) *Video Soul.* Washington, DC: Black Entertainment Television.

Viera, M. (1987). The institutionalization of music video. *ONE TWO THREE FOUR: A Rock 'n' Roll Quarterly 5*, 80–93.

Vincent, R., Davis, D. K. and Boruszkowski, L. (1987). Sexism on MTV: The portrayal of women in rock videos. *Journalism Quarterly* 64.4,: 750–754.

Wallace, M. (1990). *Invisibility blues: From pop to theory.* New York: Alpine Press.

14

DISCOURSE ON DISNEY

BIBLIOGRAPHIC REFERENCES & WOMEN PLAYING IN THE LIFE OF THE LION KING

Adwoa X. Muwzea

Introduction

Disney Pictures has never made reference to Sundiata, the original Lion King, or to the dramatic human elements of his life as they set about promoting the blockbuster film *The Lion King (TLK)*. Their version of the lion king story is about cartoon animals, and curtly disguises the dynamic life of an African emperor. This chapter identifies five published accounts of the original Lion King story, and compares Disney's version to classical accounts of the story. A deconstruction of the most salient features of the film is accomplished using the literary discourse of Toni Morrison (1992), from her book *Playing in the Dark, Whiteness and the Literary Imagination.* This chapter achieves a three-fold purpose: to recount the primary legend of the Lion King, using bibliographic references, to profile and uplift the role of women in the life of Sundiata, based on classical accounts of the story, and to devise a theoretical basis for cinema discourse by testing the application of Morrison's views using selected films, including Disney's *TLK*. Through the prism of Morrison's literary discourse, this essay addresses how images and icons of blackness, including aural cues, are used as a shortcut to support a legacy of white supremacy in Disney's *TLK* and in other mainstream American films.

Discourse on Morrison

Racial unconsciousness and the use of icons and figurations of blackness as literary shortcuts to express specific phenomena are two of the primary issues Morrison pursues in her monograph, *Playing in the Dark*. Her work is a challenge for the literati to reconsider the American canon of literature, without blindly ignoring the 400 year presence and impact of Africans and African Americans, in the United States.

Morrison first insists that "Black Matters," the title of chapter one in the book. Citing the autobiographical text of French author, Marie Cardinal, Morrison is struck by the author's description of her own madness. Cardinal discloses the initial frenzy of her emotional breakdown in the context of attending a concert by Louis Armstrong. Morrison muses "what on earth was Louie playing that night?" Later in the novel Cardinal suggests that the moment she first knew she was in danger of a breakdown was when she understood that the French were to assassinate Algeria, where she was born and which she considered as her real mother. Cardinal clearly associates Algeria with the pleasures of her childhood and the budding sexuality of her youth. Symbolically Cardinal's conflicting pain over the war in Algeria translates as "moving images of matricide, of white slaughter of a black mother," Morrison surmises. "Again, an internal devastation is aligned with a socially governed relationship with race" (Morrison, p. ix). Given Cardinal's colonialist background as a child, her associations with race and color are not particularly unusual. However, Morrison's primary query is "whether the cultural association of jazz were as important to Cardinal's 'possession' as were its intellectual foundations." She goes on to say "I was interested, as I had been for a long time, in the way black people ignite critical moments of discovery or change or emphasis in literature not written by them" (p. viii).

Morrison views these descriptions from Cardinal's text, as the impetus for her discussion of how specific imagery and icons of blackness work as a catalyst for moments of discovery, in the canon of American literature. Blackness, or figurations of blackness become a marker for benevolence, wickedness, spirituality, that which is voluptuous, sinful, and deliciously sensual, accompanied by demands for purity and restraint, according to Morrison's discourse on the American canon of literature text.

Morrison references an accumulation of examples from the early works of white (American) writers. In these works metaphor, rhetorical gesture, despair and closure are dependent upon an acceptance of blackness as associated with dread and love in the English language (p. x). Examples from film raise questions about the shorthand, assumptive nature that lies in the conventional use of cinematic language, the sources of imagination from which particular images are drawn, and the effect that such images and aural cues have on the text (Morrison, p. x).

The task of determining how icons and symbols of blackness are drawn from the text of a film, to serve the film narrative, is pertinent to the criticism of modern American cinema. Film, television, animation, each has its own canon which is equivalent to the canon of American literature. Collecting instances of narrative shortcuts that use blackness or figurations of blackness in film is not an idle occupation. The consistency with which such shortcuts are used in mainstream American films is intense. This discussion is not intended to recount or list each film that displays blackness as a narrative shortcut for benevolence and wickedness, etc. A few examples adequately make the point, along with a discussion of the way Disney Pictures uses symbols of blackness as shortcuts and symbols in *The Lion King.*

The first instance collected for this study in which blackness and symbols of blackness are used as a narrative, presumptuous, shortcut, is culled from the film *Pretty Woman.* The film clearly is not about anyone of African descent, but it opens with a black man singing in the streets, cautioning New York City visitors to be wary.

There's only one other African American character in the film—the chauffeur. The primary narrative is about Julia Roberts, who plays a prostitute and Richard Gere, who plays the john. Gere, a wealthy business tycoon in the film hires Roberts, a poor, street-level, working girl, to spend the week with him as a professional escort so that he can avoid the bother of any emotional entanglements. The chauffeur is used to facilitate the change in their relationship on two separate occasions. The first change is when Gere asks Roberts to go to the opera, as a date, rather than as a hired woman. When she agrees he uses the chauffeur, to take him on the date—facilitating a turning point in the couple's romantic life. At the close of the film the chauffeur is used again to facilitate the romantic life of two people that he is otherwise, in no way connected. Instead of taking Gere to the airport at the end of the business week the chauffeur takes him to the young woman's apartment.

Imagining the chauffeur's role as one in which he would involve himself in the romance of a white hooker and a white john dregs up what Morrison calls an American Africanism—a character culled from the peculiarity of a white American imagination. From an imaginative standpoint the filmmakers could have imagined the chauffeur as any race or color, but he was imagined as an African American man. Casting the African American man in the role of a benevolent servant is an imaginative shortcut, to alleviate the filmmaker's from imagining the man's participation in the film in any other way. The device that's used to turn a hooker/john relationship into an equal relationship of male/female romance is the cultural convention of a date. The writer/director team of *Pretty Woman* imagines that the best way to change the relationship between the couple is to use the chauffeur as an intermediary. There are numerous other imaginative options for facilitating a date, including the possibility of Gere driving himself to the airport, renting a car, or taking a taxi.

Morrison's review of text from the American canon of literature cites instances in which a black man is written as a character in Edgar Allan Poe's *The Narrative of Arthur Gordon Pym*. Her discussion of Poe emphasizes that whiteness, which is emphatically described as an important presence in the canon, exists only in the imaginative presence of blackness, which is de-emphasized in the critical discourse of the American canon of literature. White is affirmed only in the context of an opposite to whiteness. White men are affirmed as strong and important and civilized, only if an Africanist character can be imagined and drawn as weak, or fearful, or unimportant, or uncivilized, in white, American narratives,.

The second example culled for this study has Tom Cruise affirmed as an important man in the film, *A Few Good Men*. An African American marine on trial for murder was tried, along with his younger, white, protégé, and found to be not guilty of murder, not guilty of conspiracy to commit murder, and guilty of misconduct and conduct unbecoming a marine. The two marines are released on time served and dishonorably discharged. The African American character stresses that as a marine, his honor was above all else. Although he is not guilty of murder, he feels defeated and humiliated. As a good marine, he obeys the orders of his commanding officer rather than question authority. He is benevolent in his role as the moral conscience of his innocent, white protege, who he ultimately leads down a path of ruin.

Tom Cruise plays the role of Lt. Caffey, the defense lawyer for the African American man. Caffey becomes what his co-star, Demi Moore, called an "incredible" attorney. He demonstrates courage in the face of danger as he pursues a line of questioning for a high ranking officer, played by Jack Nicholson. Cruise hammers away at Nicholson until the officer breaks down and testifies that he ordered a code red on the marine base at Guantanamo. The code red, executed by the two marines on trial, results in the death of a third marine—a Latino named Santiago.

So through the death of a Latino man and the recognition and discharge of an African American man, Tom Cruise is verified as a brilliant, courageous, and honorable man. This scenario provides another example that extends the concept of Morrison's thesis of the Africanist character and of racial unconsciousness, to filmic media.

Disney clearly establishes a canon for what animation in American filmmaking espouses to be; but measured in terms of the presence or absence of racially symbolic text, the construction of meaning, even in the innocuous fare of a Disney production, has to be reconfigured. The discourse on filmic media, unlike literature, is measured on multiple platforms since the development of such media includes motion and visual imagery on multiple planes, and a multiple layering of sound. Meanings are construed on every platform of motion picture text.

Disney's *The Lion King*

The film begins. Strong, deep, rich voices from an African choir rise, the deep hues of an African sunset appear on the horizon, as the lush landscape unfolds before us. The audience of Disney's *The Lion King* (*TLK*) can be assured that they're in for a rousing and dramatic story. African spirituality, music and the imagery of the African savanna have the power to move people and Disney Pictures know how to wield power. Nuances of traditional African culture in *TLK* are so compelling that it prompts outside investigation into the nature and origin of the story. Disney's press kit affirms that their producers paid a visit to Kenya in southeast Africa, before the script's completion. The narrative, however, mimics the legend of Sundiata, the Lion King of Old Mali. Although cues are in place for an epic film, a little bit of poking around will alert even a casual investigator that Disney has more or less trivialized a story that has great historical significance for women and for the African Diaspora.

Some obvious precedents are overlooked in Disney's claims of originality. Claims that the story is based on no other published story is disguised by Disney's use of animal characters. According to Disney, *TLK* story originated in their story department. However, three different accounts of Sundiata's life have been published in the United States since 1960. The legend of Sundiata has such an incredibly long, rich tradition that makes it apparent that the legend has been borrowed and reinterpreted for the Disney film. Written and oral accounts of this real life figure and his mother, Sogolon, have epic proportions.

Table 1 A LUIS Search

Search Request:	K=LION KING	WILSON PERIODICALS INDEX
Search Results:	35 Entries Found	Keyword Index
WILSON RECORD	30 of 35 Entries Found	Brief View
ARTICLE TITLE:		Sundiata (BOOK REVIEW) lion king of Mali
AUTHOR(S):		Wisniewski, David
REVIEWED BY:		Lasker, Joe
JOURNAL:		The New York Times Book Review 97:55 Nov 8, '92

Admittedly, a reference to Sundiata as the Lion King is fairly remote when conducting a search on the library information system. Nevertheless, Lasker's review of the Wisniewski text is clearly published and available in one of the most widely recognized publications in the world. Yet as Disney set about to tell "an African-based" coming-of-age story" (Disney, 1994, p. 2), their writers, publicists, producers, directors and legal crew apparently missed Lasker's 1992 review. The review of texts, authors and publishers listed in Table 2, are used to compare and contrast the historical validity of the legend of Sundiata.

The purpose of this research and criticism, is not to discredit Disney's ability to be entertaining. Rather deconstructing the images and messages that the film carries is essential, primarily because *TLK* is *so* entertaining. The film was a rousing success at the box office and has had success in video rentals too. Its artistry and narrative as a coming-of-age-story for children is commendable. However, the power to instill messages in media goes far beyond a movie's entertainment

Table 2 Bibliographic references for Sundiata, Lion King of Mali

1. ***Sundiata. An Epic of Old Mali,*** D.T. Niane, 1960. (Original version: Soundjata, ou lEpopee Mandigue, Translated by G. D. Pickett, 1965). Longman African Classic,1986; Longman African Writers, 1994. This text is considered as a classical account of the legend. Other authors refer to Niane to compare and contrast their versions of the story. Niane asserts that he is delivering the story as it was told to him by the griot, Mamadou Kouyate' (a traditional, oral historian and storyteller).
2. ***Sundiata, The Epic of the Lion King,*** Roland Bertol, Thomas Y. Crowell Co., New York,1970. This is another early version of the published story. Bertol's account of the legend of Sundiata closely resembles that of Niane's. The author asserts that he too is relating the story as it was told to him by the griot, Mamadou. The names of other characters in the story are often identical to Niane's classical version.
3. ***Sundiata, Lion King of Mali,*** David Wisniewski. Clarion Books, New York, 1992. Wisniewski has created and photographed an incredibly beautiful set of paper cutouts to illustrate the legend of Sundiata. His version is classified as a biography for children's literature. Many of the names and details of the story coincide with the earlier and classic versions of the legend. Wisniewski's text was reviewed in the New *York Times* in 1992.
4. ***Oya, In Praise of the Goddess,*** Judith Gleason, 1987. Shambhala Publications, Inc., Boston, Massachusetts. Distributed in the U.S. by Random House. Gleason focuses upon the Yoruba deity, Oya. Yourba, an ancient religion, is associated with modern day Nigeria, as the traditional religion of the Mande. Gleason's text emphasizes Sundiata's mother as the spirit of the Buffalo of Do, and his father as the spirit of a Lion, which is the ancient symbol of Mali. Here the transformative qualities of Oya, are related to the spirit of the Buffalo and Sogolon Kedjou, who is consistently identified as Sundiata's mother.
5. ***Flash of the Spirit, African & Afro-American Art & Philosophy,*** Robert Farris Thompson, 1983. Random House, Inc., Vintage Books Edition, August 1984. Thompson expounds upon the survival of Mande traditions over time. Sundiata is referenced as "a masterpiece of Mali oral literature." This story coincides with the classical version, which is referenced in Thompson's notes. Thompson mentions the *tana* of Sundiata's principal enemy, Sumaoro or Sumanguru. When Sundiata learns of *the tana* that is a threat to Sumaoro's strength—in this case the spur of a rooster—he uses it to undermine his enemy's sorcery. The *tana is* mentioned in each version of the story that discusses Sundiata's exploits as a warrior.
6. ***Walt Disney Pictures Presents The Lion,*** The Walt Disney Company, 1994. This is a part of Disney's press package for the film. The 79-page text is an outline of the basic story of Simba, the central character of the Disney feature. It lists all of the characters and voice actors, as well as, the film's principal crew, writers, artists and animators. The text mentions that the producers and the director take a trip to Kenya, but there is no mention of their visiting Mali or Sundiata.

value. A blow by blow description of the movie would facilitate a full reading of the film, but criticism of a few key aspects of the film is more expedient. Discourse on the opening scene, the presence of African symbolism, and the overall narrative of *TLK* provides insight into how Disney Pictures uses blackness and icons of blackness as a presumptuous, narrative shortcut.

The opening scene

The opening is 4 minutes long. The rich vocals of the African choir become background for the *Circle of Life* soloist, singing "From the day we arrive on the planet and blinking step into the sun, there's more to see and do than can ever be seen or done." She continues, "There's far too much to take in here, more to find than can ever be found."

The field animals pose, erect. The energy of the forest is focused entirely upon the birth of a king in the animal world. The song continues, "But the sun rolling high through the sapphire sky heats great and small on the endless ground. It's the circle of life, and it move us all, through despair and hope, through faith and love, till we find our place, on a path unwinding, in the circle, the circle of life." All is preparation for ceremony.

The narrative opens with the equivalent of a traditional African naming ceremony, but the Disney version of the story is used to name an animal rather than a person. A community of forest animals assembles to pay homage to the progeny of the king and queen, Mufasa and Serabi. Mufasa is a lion, muscular with a ruddy hue and a thick red mane. The lioness, Serabi, is distinctively beige. Her hue is fairer than her mate's. The king's brother, Scar is a scrawny, black mange lion, who chooses not to attend the ceremony; instead he's caught in the act of attacking a gray-white mouse. Mufasa's hue and countenance revives the old adage, "strong, silent type," as he chooses his words carefully. Serabi's hue reinforces a cultural taboo against mating with women who have a dark complexion, and a social preference for women who have fair complexions. Scar's black mane and his overall demeanor symbolically castigates him as the villain, an evil threat to anything small, innocent and of course white.

The opening depicts beast of land and air coming together. Birds wing their way toward the valley. One bird arrives and perches on the ledge where Mufasa stands. The bird, Zazu, a blue DoDo, bows low, wings spread, and Mufasa bestows an imperious smile and a nod of approval upon him. The baboon Rafiki's rattling gourd precedes his appearance, as it rises above a sea of animals. Rafiki appears, using the gourd-stick as support, and moves through a cloud of dust and sunrays, on a path that lies open for him to climb the mountain where Mufasa waits. Mufasa is pleased when Rafiki arrives, dark, gray-bodied with a blue and red face, framed by white whiskers. Rafiki embraces Mufasa with both arms, symbolic of the circle of life.

Rafiki anoints the cub, Simba. The animals paw the earth, rise up and bow reverently below a mountainous cliff, as the elderly baboon then lifts the tiny cub skyward, in a pose reminiscent of the slave Toby naming his daughter Kizzy, from the television mini-series, *Roots*. Meanwhile, the black faced monkeys, with white teeth shining, screech and laugh and jump up and down, insanely, representing another example of how the color black is imagined in the film.

Voice actors are essential to animation, and in *TLK* Mufasa, Serabi, and Rafiki are African American actors. Simba, who is adored, and Scar, who is evil, are both played by white actors. So the film opens with a clear message that the most significant participants in this story are white. Mufasa dies. Serabi rarely appears, and plays no compelling role in the life of her son. The benevolent Rafiki is a dark and colorful character who represents the spiritual conscious of the lion kingdom, and who facilitates the ascension of a white king in Africa. The hero nor the villain of this African-based, coming-of-age story are neither African nor African American. Morrison might ask how these characters were invented in the minds of their creators, so that this ultimately becomes a story about a guilt-ridden white boy and his jealous, green-eyed uncle.

The presence of African symbolism

The rattle and movements of Rafiki's hands during the announcement of Simba's birth, is akin to a Christian baptism. He breaks open a gourd and a liquid spews forth. He uses the liquid to anoint the cub's head. The young cub already has three perpendicular marks across his forehead. These symbols are nearly identical to the traditional scarification that appears on ancient and modern, West African, Yoruba statuary, usually associated with Nigeria. Rafiki crosses the three symbols with the liquid in a way that creates a Christian cross for each mark. Then he gathers a handful of dust from the earth and blows it into the cub's face. The symbolism of the ceremony is African. It includes liquid to make the path of life sweet and dust to make the journey prosperous. This is very similar to a traditional naming ceremony in the religious and cultural practices of the Akan, a West African ethnic group, whose roots are from Ghana.

The traditional story of Sundiata includes the father passing the heritage of kings to his son. Disney's version of the story emphasizes this gesture when the cub is taken to the edge of a cliff and shown the boundaries of the land within the king's domain. This interaction includes a moment when Simba asks his dad, "what about that shadowy place?" He's instructed never to go there. It turns out that the shadowy place is an elephant graveyard. Elephants, significantly enough, are one species over which the lion has no dominion. Simba is told that "everything the light touches" will one day be his. The lessons of heritage are quite symbolic of African royal behavior, but ownership of land is usually foreign to African culture. Rulership of land is conceptually more African than ownership. If light is akin to whiteness, Mufasa's instructions to his son is also an emphasis that what is light is good and what is dark is bad, evil, foreboding and forbidden.

As the story of Sundiata unfolds, another African symbol will emerge, that appears in *TLK* movie. Simba is exiled at some point in the story. He muses about the stars one evening after dinner, and remembers his father telling him about the significance of the stars. Simba's two friends laugh at the notion that the stars are ancient kings who watch over earthbound creatures. Simba becomes melancholy and sighs so heavily, that he stirs up a breeze. The breeze carries dust and fur and feathers across the lands until they reach Rafiki, who reads them as a seer would read an oracle of cowrie shells. The wind is Oya, a Yourba deity who brings change. Oya is goddess of the whirlwinds and wherever she is, dramatic change occurs. She is the storm, the wind, the hurricane. In the discussion of Sundiata's legend and the role of women in his life, Oya's role is clearly, prominent.

Finally, the closing credits of *TLK* film are interspersed with symbols that clearly represent some of the Adinkra symbols that identify Akan religious mysteries. Gold letters appear on a black background as credits roll, reminding viewers of Ghana's rich, gold coast. The tiny

Table 3 Signs and symbols

symbols that appear randomly, are gold markings on a black background (see Table 3, Signs and symbols). When Rafiki realizes that Simba will return to Priderock he sings, "Asante sana," mimicking a traditional Akan saying, and adding "a squashed banana."

TLK is a conglomerate of ancient, multi-cultural symbols. Ancient societies rarely draw rigid distinctions between their cultural, social and religious life, so the ancient symbols of the Yourba, the Akan, a Hawaiian war chant, and the Jewish saying "Hakuna Matata," have religious significance. *TLK* co-opts and then trivializes the cultural relevance of all the symbols used in the film. The 57-voice African choir is used as background music that supports the filmmaker's use of Africa as a landscape rather than as the habitat of indigenous peoples and cultures. The closing credits acknowledge the Los Angeles and San Diego zoos, the Miami and other wildlife centers. Although Disney's press package mentions a trip to Kenya, there is no mention of Kenya in the credits. Lobo M (from South Africa) performed the African vocals, African solos and created the improvisations. Lebo M, Andre Crouch, Mbongeni Ngema and Nick Glennie-Smith conduct and arrange the chorale. Mbongeni Ngema is also listed as the

Choirmaster. There are no other clear references that African Americans participated in the making of the film, except as actors. Disney's publicist affirmed in a phone conversation, that approximately 14 of the 65 animation department workers for the film, were African Americans.

The overall narrative of TLK

Table 4 supports textual references to Sundiata, by juxtaposing characters from the legend beside characters from Disney's version of *The Lion King*. The characters themselves tell a story of sorts. However, a comparison between the legend and the movie strongly suggests that Disney's claims of an original, in-house story, simply isn't credible. Although the linear narratives of the legend *and* the film both have the earmarking of a traditional folktale, Sundiata was a real life character. *The Lion King* movie and the legend of Sundiata share phenomenal similarities between narrative structure and the identity of characters. Mali history readily embraces the mythology that's also associated with the epic of Sundiata as the Lion King. There are many versions of the story of Sundiata. The most authentic ones are consistent with the story told by D.T. Niani. Most stories actually reference Niani, who is a griot from Guinea.

Niani is a direct descendant of Mali, and according to John Heinrik Clarke (1996), he's probably living in Senegal or Guinea today. Niani claims to have gotten the legend from Momoudou Kouyate, who was instructed by Bala Fasseke', Sundiata's griot. The body of literature about Sundiata makes a number of references to the role of women in the life of the Lion King, factors minimalized in Disney's version of the story. A part of the Lion King story that's unlikely to otherwise come to light is the multi-textured stories of the women in the life of the Lion King.

One aspect of griotology that's most significant here, is the fact that the griot's are all male. On one hand, it's been rumored that women keep the culture alive. Yet it's typical of Arab, African and western patriarchy, that men are consistently sanctioned as the most credible historians. The role of women in the life of the Lion King, is mediated by the male-centered perspective of Mali historians. The focus here is a reference to Niani's and Gleason's versions of the legend. Niani's work is classical and as a woman, Gleason adds credi-

Table 4 The legend vs. the film

Niane	Bertol	Wisniewski	Thompson	Gleason	Disney
Mamadou	Mamadou	Griot		Sekou Traore	Allers, Minkoff et.al. Rafiki
Sundiata Mari Djata The king with two names	Sundiata Mari Djata The king with two names	Sundiata	Sundiata	Sunjata	Simba
Nare-Famakan	Nare' Maghan	Maghan Kon Fatta		Nare Makah Maghan Kon Fatta	Mufasa
Niani	Bright Country	Bright Country	Mande/Mali Niani		Pridelands
Sogolon Koudouma or Kondouto Sumanguru Sorcerer King of Sosso Tana	Sogolon Kedjou Soumaoro Sorcerer King of Sosso Tana	Sogolon Kedjou Sumanguru Sorcerer King of Sosso Tana	of Do) Sumaroro Tana	(Buffalo Sogolon	Sarabi Scar (Scar)
	Niger & Sankarani Rivers		Niger & Sankarani Rivers	Africa (Kenya)	
(Sundiata's siblings)	(Sundiata's siblings)	(Sogolon's children)	Sundiata's sister		Nala Pumba Timon (friends)
Sassouma Berete (the step mother)	Sassouma Berete (the step mother)	Sassouma Berete (the step mother)			Uncle Scar (& 3 Hyenas)
Bala Fasseke (Sundiata's griot)	Bala Fasseke (Sundiata's griot)	Bala Fasseke (Sundiata's griot)			Zazu (Simba's guardian) Rafiki (as griot)

bility to the discussion's focus on the importance of women's roles in history. Gleason's text also provides the only description of the legend where women are the focus of the story, rather than at the periphery.

Specific elements of Table 4 enunciate the legend of Sundiata, the original Lion King. The first row of the table identifies the 6 authors referenced earlier. Each column, read top to bottom, references 10-primary aspects of the legend according to each author. A brief consideration of the attributes and similarities between the variety of characters presented, also represents a review of the legend itself.

Niane's version of the story is a translation of the oldest written text about the legendary emperor. It references the first character identified on the chart, Mamadou Kouyate, as a griot or oral historian. Bertol's text usually supports Niane's. The names he uses are often identical to Niane's. Gleason's version of the legend, acknowledges Sekou, a descendant of the Traore brothers, as the one who conveys the story to her. The Traores were major participants in the legend. Disney Studio producers and writers are identified as the storytellers for the film; but the character, Rafiki, plays the role of historian or griot in the film. Rafiki knows who is born, who dies, and the order and significance of all that happens in the Pridelands.

Swahili is the language of commerce in Kenya, where the Disney team conducted their research before producing the film. The film borrows the name Simba from the Swahili word for lion, but the Lion King story originated in Mali, where the Mandinka people speak Mande. Diata means lion in the Mande language. Since hunting is a primary occupation of Mali, there is also a relationship between the name Simba and simbon, the Mande word for great hunter. Soun means thief in the Mande language. According to legend, Soun was attached to the emperor's name because even by age seven, he could not walk or talk. He crawled around in the dust and stole things from the compounds in his village. The names were integrated into one name—Sundiata. However, he was also called Mari Djata, thus Gleason refers to him as Sunjata. The fortelling of a Mali king greater than Alexander included notice that the future emperor of Mali would be the king with two names. Thus the emperor is called Mari Djata and Sundiata.

Nare Famakan was Sundiata's father. He married Sogolon, Sundiata's mother, who has a legend of her own. It's not unusual for an individual to have multiple names. Some are middle names; some are an integrated version of a name, etc. Disney's version of the older king's name has been translated as Mufasa. The Lion King's father ruled lands loosely organized around the Sankarni River in West

Africa, after the fall of the Ghana Empire. The capital city of Mali is called Niani, which in Mande, roughly translates to Bright Country. Disney uses the name Pridelands for the locale of the story, but in a rite of passage in the film, Mufasa passes the heritage of Pridelands to Simba, noting that "everything the light touches will be yours."

The name and identity of Sundiata's mother, Koudouto or Koudouma roughly translates to a word that means hunchback—for Sogolon was rumored to have seven deformities, including a hunched back. Kedjou, which Bertol and Wisniewski use, may be the actual family name and part of a historical reference for Sogolon. Gleason doesn't reference a last name for Sogolon, but emphasizes her role in the legend of the Buffalo of Do. Disney's *The Lion King* translates Sogolon's name to Sarabi, a Swahili name.

Sumanguru is a larger than life figure in the legend of Sundiata. Certainly he is Sundiata's nemesis in each story that references the Lion King's prowess in battle. Sunjata's exploits as a fearless warrior-hunter, lend themselves especially well to animation or live action, as the impetus for a film. Sumanguru's exploits as a fierce and ruthless ruler also inspires cinema, particularly animation, because of the magic that's associated with the Sorcerer King of Sosso. The tana, fetish or curse that's attached to Surmanguru's character in the legend, is translated into an obvious mark on Disney's character Scar, who is Simba's uncle and his nemesis.

Trying to piece together myth and legend to determine Sundiata's family life has been difficult. The simplest construction between Niane, Bertol and Thompson would support that Sundiata's mother, Sogolon, the second wife of King Nare Famakan, had three children, of which Sundiata is the oldest. When Niane talks of the future king's exile though, Sogolon carries her son, two daughters and another child, Manding Bory, out of Mali to protect them. Manding Bory is the son of Nare Famakan's third wife, who dies while Sundiata is still a boy. One of Sundiata's sisters also plays a prominent role in protecting Sundiata and in providing him with information that prompts his emergence from exile.

Other versions of the story include references to Sundiata as the twelfth son of Nare Famakan. Obviously there are sons from the king's first marriage. Bertol alludes to a favorable relationship between the 12 brothers. He notes that Sumanguru kills all of Sundiata's brothers and pillages Mali.

When the fierce conqueror kills the eleventh brother, Sundiata is only seven; but when Sumanguru confronts the young, future king, Sundiata utters his first words, props himself up on the staff of Mali's throne, and dragging himself from the ground, begins to walk for the first time in his life. From that point on, according to the legend, Sundiata begins to assume a princely demeanor. His neighbors look upon him fondly, whereas they once ridiculed him. He is always a leader among many friends and his brother, Manding Bory.

Disney, perhaps as a matter of simplification, makes Simba an only child. Nala, a girl cub is Simba's only friend before he is exiled. Later, as in the legend, he acquires two friends, Pumba and Timon, whose ingenuity aid his climactic battle with Scar. The legend has Sundiata gathering an army during his trek from Mema, the city of his exile, to Mali, his homeland. Rafiki also appears, at this juncture in Disney's version of the story, to remind Simba of his heritage, while admonishing the adult Simba that what's in the past doesn't matter. The griot, Balla Fasseke appears in the legend to counsel the young king when Sundiata decides to return to Mali from exile. At any rate, Nala, Pumba and Timon clearly represent a plethora of colleagues for Simba, when measured against the legend of the Lion King of Mali.

The table foregrounds two other prominent characters from the legend. The first, Sassouma Berete, is Sundiata's stepmother, the first wife of Nare Famakan. One of Sassouma Berete's sons is clearly referenced in the text and is named Simba in one version of the story. Ultimately, each version of the story that references Sassouma Berete, refers to her as a stepmother who wants her own son to ascend to the throne. The first wife represents another aspect of the resistance that Sundiata faces in claiming the throne of Mali. It is because of threats from Sassouma Berete, that Sogolon decides to take her children out of Mali, a fact that foregrounds the role of Sogolon as a wise and determined, single parent. Disney's uncle Scar, on the other hand, represents the force that compels Simba to leave in the film version of the story, so he is a comparable character to Sassouma Berete.

Finally, Bala Faseke is a primary character in the legend. The king was very disappointed in Sundiata's development. Nevertheless, remembering the predictions about the child of Sogolon, the king decided to follow tradition. Every African king has a griot. The griot's duty is to keep the history, the names of battles, those who fought and those who died. So Sundiata's father conferred upon his son, the griot, Bala Fasseke. Bala Fasseke had learned the art of oral history from his father, who had served Nare Maghan Kon Fatta for many years. Shortly after Bala Fasseke came to serve Sundiata, king Nare Famakan died. Bala Fasseke later provides Sundiata with information about Sumanguru's tana, which ultimately brings about the defeat of the king of Sosso.

Women in the Life of the Lion King

Without supporting ideas of essentialism, this study focuses upon some of the deeply spiritual aspects of women in the life of Sundiata. Gleason's version of the story focuses upon Oya, one of several riverine goddesses (orishas), in the tradition of the Yourba. Even today Oya has a cult of followers among the Mande or Mandinka people of West Africa (Thompson, p. 74). Oya plays a prominent role in the life of the Lion King, by actually intervening in his conception. Her role is tied to the complex and multi-textured story of Sogolon Kedjou, Sundiata's mother.

Sundiata: Oya

According to legend, Sundiata was born of lion and buffalo. His mother is considered as the spirit (or wraith) of the Buffalo of Do, a nation neighboring Old Mali. The lion is the traditional totem of Mali. Sundiata's father, the King of Mali, is considered the spirit of lion. Lion and buffalo are natural enemies, so the heir of such a union would be a powerful heir to the throne of Mali.

The legend begins in a land called Do. When it was time for the king's daughter to assume the throne, her younger brother wrestled it from her and banished her to the countryside. Soon afterward, a wild buffalo began ravishing the countryside, terrorizing the people of Do. The buffalo was said to be the spirit of the angered sister. Two hunters from Mali, known as the Traore' brothers, Oulamba and Oulani, were able to subdue the Buffalo, by following the strict advice of Oya.

According to Niani, Oulamba, the eldest brother, tells the story to King Nare' Maghan Kon Fatta, Sundiata's father, saying:

> An amazing buffalo was ravaging the countryside of Do. The king, Do Mansa-Gnemo Diarra promised the finest rewards to the hunter who killed the buffalo. In the land of Do we saw an old woman by the side of a river, weeping and lamenting, gnawed by hunger. No passer-by had deigned to stop by her. Touched by her tears I took some pieces of dried meat from my hunter's bag. When she had eaten well she said. 'I know that you are trying your luck against the Buffalo of Do, many before you have met their death through their foolhardiness. Arrows are useless against the buffalo. I am the buffalo you are looking for, and your generosity has vanquished me. I have killed a hundred and seven hunters and wounded seventy-seven. The king, Gnemo Diarra, is at his wit's end... (Niani, p. 8).

Then the old woman instructs the two hunters in precise details, how to find the buffalo and how to subdue it. The old woman is Oya. She says,

> As for me, I have run my course and punished the king of Do, my brother, for depriving me of my part of the inheritance (Niani, p. 8).

Oya's only condition, for making herself vulnerable to the hunters, is that they must choose Sogolon when the king offers them a reward. Oya says,

> You must search the crowd and you will find a very ugly maid—uglier than you can imagine—sitting apart on an observation platform; it is her you must choose. She is called Sogolon Kedjou, or Kondouto, because she is a hunchback. You will choose her for she is my wraith She will be an extraordinary woman if you manage to possess her (Niani, p. 8).

Sundiata: Sogolon

Ultimately, Sogolon's story reminds us that women were regarded as property in the 13th century. Some say the Traore's gave her to the King of Mali as an afterthought. Niani says, "the conqueror of the buffalo had not been able to conquer the young girl" (p. 11). It is also significant to note that Sogolon was a girl when she became a wife and mother. Neither the Traore's nor the King could possess her at first, because Oya possessed her as the spirit of the buffalo. Later we learn that the King's threats render Sogolon helpless. He says,

> "The blood of a virgin . . . must be spilt . . . Forgive me, but I must accomplish my mission. Forgive the hand which is going to shed your blood."
>
> "no, no—why me?—No, I don't want to die," Sogolon cries.

He seized her by the hair with an iron grip. So great was her fear, that she fainted. When she woke up she was already a wife—essentially she was raped. That very night Sogolon conceived. So the legend of Sundiata really begins with Nare Famakan's second wife, Sogolon, and her pregnancy.

Legend establishes Sogolon as central to Mali history. Throughout the literature, Sundiata is called the son of Sogolon. Her son's role in Mali history was prophesied, in a way reminiscent of biblical prophecy of Christ's coming. Sogolon was predicted as a maiden from the land of Do, who would be the king's wife and provide the king with an heir to the throne. "The child of Sogolon will be called Maghan after his father, and Mari Djata, a name which no Mandingo prince has ever borne. Sogolon's son will be the first of this name" (Niani, p. 14). This language is a tribute to Sogolon. It was also predicted that Sogolon's son would be greater than Alexander. (In ancient times it was typical to refer and compare a great leader to the legendary feats of Alexander the Great, who conquered Egypt.) Drake says "Persian rule ended in 332 B.C. when Alexander the Great, a Macedonian Greek, captured the Delta and was greeted as a liberator" (1987, p. 257).

The role of the king's third wife is vague, but his first wife, Sassouma Berete plays a distinct role in the life of the Lion King. Sassouma greatly resented Sogolon's marriage into the family. She wanted her son to reign after the death of Nare Famakan. When Sundiata was born the first wife became even more disturbed than before. Her envy dissipated though as it became obvious that the child, Sundiata, was unable to talk, walk or even stand. Sogolon Kedjou had three children—Sundiata was the first born, then came a daughter, Sogolon Kolonkan, and another daughter named Sogolon Dja'-marou. When Sundiata was 7 years old, he stood up and walked and spoke for the first time. The Niani villagers had ridiculed Sundiata and his mother Sogolon for many years because the child was crippled and mute, but when Sundiata rose from the dust and spoke, he became a threat to the throne of Mali, which Sassouma Berete ruled through her son, Sundiata's stepbrother, Kononioko Simba.

Sogolon's role as a mother is an important part of the legend, because she deliberately empowered her son with knowledge. Her protecting, and nurturing prepared Sundiata to rule Mali in the 13th century. She taught him about plants, herbs, medicine and the divining arts, which represented one of the traditional means of survival for a hunter or Simbon. Sassouma Berete's persistent plots against Sundiata prompted Sogolon to flee the nation with four children. She feared that Sassouma Berete would try to harm the youngest of her children to discourage Sundiata from trying to take his place on the throne. The youngest child Dja'marou and a fourth child, Manding Bory, one of Sundiata's stepbrothers, had no divining powers and were vulnerable to attack by Sassouma Berete. It was especially to protect these children, that Sogolon took the family into exile.

Kolonkan, like her mother, Sogolon, knew the divining arts and was not vulnerable to Sassouma Berete's plots. She played a prominent role in Sundiata's life on several occasions. Once, when Sundiata was under attack by the evil forces of his stepmother, Kolonkan intervened, without his knowledge. Sundiata was surprised when he later discovered that his sister had been watching out for him. In exile, the young family was weary and sometimes unwelcome. Some nations they visited feared the wrath of Sassouma Berete, who many people recognized as the one who really ruled Mali, through her son Simba. Traveling from one land to another, the family finally found rest in the northern regions of the continent, in a land called Mema. The king of Mema had no son and welcomed the family. The king had known Maghan Kon Fatta as a just and wise ruler, and held Sogolon, the widow, in high regard. He welcomed Sundiata as his son, and that's where Sundiata grew into manhood, favored by the King of Mema.

During the family's exile his sister, Sogolon Kolonkan took over the marketing chores. One day Kolonkan, returned from the marketplace and told her mother about meeting travelers from Mali, whom she recognized by the traditional foods they were buying. Kolonkan brought the travelers home to meet her mother. They told Sogolon of how troubled the land was and of Sumanguru's continual threats to the well being of the kingdom. The news helped Sundiata to recognize his duty to Mali and to assume his role as the king of Mali.

It was Kolonkan's insight that led to his return from exile, and his legendary reign.

Sundiata learned many things from Sogolon and the King of Mema. The king of Mema taught Sundiata how to rule a kingdom; how to act like a prince; how to wield power; and how to win in battle. By the time Sundiata was 18 years old, he had a strong following of friends and colleagues—the princes of neighboring kingdoms sought him out for his fearlessness, strength and wisdom. He was a fine young man.

Sundiata also essentially retraced the path he had traveled during the early years of his exile. He mobilized an army along the way and his army grew. He led his army into many battles and won them as he approached Mali to face the wrath of Sumanguru, the Sorcerer King of Sosso. Sundiata had learned, through his griot, Bala Fasseke, that Sumanguru's tana, the spur of a rooster, would render the sorcerer king powerless. The fierce Sumanguru recognized that his demise was imminent, for it had been predicted that when the mountain moved, he would be defeated. Sundiata amassed an army so great, that they covered the side of a mountain and moved toward Sosso, Sumanguru's capital city. Legend has it that when Sundiata and Sumanguru finally met face to face, the Sorcerer King touched by the tana, backed into the side of a mountain to avoid a direct battle with Sundiata, It is said that the mountain swallowed Sumanguru whole. In Disney's *TLK*, Scar is backed against a cavernous wall, and the scene ends with fierce hyenas approaching him.

The Sorcerer King's unceasing threats to Mali ended. Sundiata ruled his kingdom with fairness and wisdom. Sundiata's name is known throughout Africa. His early life, exile, triumphs as a warrior, and his rule as the Lion King of Mali mingle history and myth to create the legend of Sundiata. The legend, in all of its manifestations and attributes, serves as inspiration for modern day griotology—the cinema.

Other women in the life of Sundiata

Disney's version of the Lion King story uses 3 dark, foolish, vicious hyenas, in league with Simba's nemesis, uncle Scar, to challenge his ascent to the throne. However, the legend of Sundiata foregrounds three (sometimes nine) witches who were powerful, but not evil. One of Sassouma Berete's schemes to get rid of Sundiata was to visit the witches of Mali and convince them to curse Sundiata. The witches refused, saying that the boy had done nothing to earn their disfavor.

The stepmother then hatched a plot for the witches to raid Sogolon's herb garden. She surmised that Sundiata would spurn them for stealing and thereby earn their wrath. However, when Sundiata saw the witches in his mother's garden he spoke kindly to them and encouraged them to visit the garden whenever they needed herbs. From that point on, the witches protected Sundiata and considered him as a wise and kindly child.

Marriage is seldom mentioned in stories of The Lion King. However, Van Sertima *(They Came Before Columbus*, 1976, p. 38) provides an historical account of African interest and activities in the New World, saying, "It was the year 1310, in the city of Niani, on the left bank of the Sankarini. Abubakari the Second, grandson of a daughter of Sundiata, was holding court." Niani is the traditional capital of Mali, and Van Sertima calls Abubakari "The Mariner Prince of Mali." Sundiata's father had three wives. A significant part of Mali history is tied to Islam and an ideology of multiple wives, so it would be customary for the Lion King to have at least one wife. If Sundiata had a daughter, it can be assumed that he had a wife. The actual identity of Sundiata's wife/(wives) needs investigation.

Conclusion

Research into the legend of Sundiata continues. He is referenced as Sundiata Keita in Diop's *The African Origin of Civilization, Myth or Reality* (1974: 147). John Henrik Clarke (1993) discusses the three great kingdoms of Ghana, Mali and Songhay, between 770 and 1591 A.D. He states that "Three great rulers... made Mali one of the great empires of West Africa during the thirteenth and fourteenth centuries" (p. 36). Clark cites Mansa Musa as the best *known* of Mali's rulers, but notes that Sundiata is known as one of the three *greatest* rulers of the empire. There are 9 references to Sundiata in Van Sertima's text, *They Came Before Columbus* (1976). The legend of Sundiata is not new, nor does the origin of *The Lion King* story lie within the studios of Disney Animation.

The legend of Sundiata, Lion King of Old Mali, has a potential for dramatically portraying a live action, screenplay, or adaptation of the emperor's life. When Sundiata's exploits as an action-oriented, warrior-king are considered, the story works well as an animated screenplay, with all of the magic and excitement of animation. There is no need to diminish Disney's film version of *The Lion King* story yet, it seems obvious that an animated version of Sundiata's epic could be an incredibly dynamic work of art that uses human characters for principal roles, rather than animals. The concept puts Disney's work into a much clearer perspective, in terms of both history and entertainment values.

A reading of Sundiata's mother, Sogolon as a courageous, independent woman who raised an emperor and three other children while surviving in exile, inspires a completely different type of cinematic venture. The legend describes her as an ugly hunchback, but her stamina and determination forms the image of a woman whose beauty is atypical, but phenomenal. Casting the role of Sogolon in a film version of her life, would be an imaginative fete-a-complete. Any production of the original legend would probably best be written and directed by a person whose heritage is African. The probability that icons and symbols of blackness would be stereotypically drawn and imagined in such a film would be less likely if it was developed from the perspective of someone who does not have to invent an Africanist character. A cinematic rendering of Mali's epic history would be a story where the indigenous people and their culture are central to the film's narrative, and where the landscape supports the world of the story.

References

Allers, R. (Director). (1994). *The lion king* [Film]. Burbank, CA: Walt Disney Pictures.

Clarke, J.H. (1993). *African people in world history.* Baltimore, MD: Black Classic Press.

Diop, C.A. (1974). *The African origin of civilization, myth or reality* (Trans. Mercer Cooke). Westport, CT: Lawrence Hill and Company.

Gleason, J. (1987). *Oya, in praise of the goddess.* Boston, MA: Random House.

John, E. (1994). Circle of life. *Lion king vocal score selections.* Milwaukee, WI: H. Leonard.

Kozloff, S. (1992). Narrative theory in television. In Robert C. Allen (Ed.), *Channels of discourse: reassembled.* Chapel Hill, NC: University of North Carolina Press.

Marshall, G. (Director). (1990). *Pretty woman* [Film]. Burbank, CA: Touchstone Pictures.

Morrison, T. (1992). *Playing in the dark: Whiteness in the literary imagination*. New York: Vintage Books.
Niane, D.T. (1994). *Sundiata, a epic of old Mali.* (Trans. G.D. Pickett). Essex, England: Longman African Writers.
Reiner, R. (Director). (1993). *A few good men* [Film]. Burbank, CA: Columbia Pictures.
Thompson, R.F. (1984). *Flash of the spirit, African and Afro-American art and philosophy*. New York: Vintage Books.
Van Sertima, I. (1976). *They came before Columbus.* New York: Random House.
Walt Disney Company. (1994). *Walt Disney presents The Lion King*. Burbank, CA: Disney.
Wisniewski, D. (1992). *Sundiata, lion king of Mali.* New York: Clarion Books.
Wolper, D. (Executive Producer). (1984). *Roots*. Burbank, CA: Warner Home Video.

SISTUHS WATCHING AND READING: REPRESENTATIONS IN MASS MEDIA

SECTION 2

SISTUHS READING: QUIET STRUGGLES THROUGH LITERATURE

15

"LEAD ON WITH LIGHT"

A PHENOMENOLOGY OF LEADERSHIP AS SEEN IN GLORIA NAYLOR'S *MAMA DAY*

Jeanne L. Porter

Leadership is an important cultural process which functions to make sense of reality and bring meaning to social and personal events and circumstances (Apps, 1993; Crosby & Bryson, 1993; Drath & Palus, 1994; Roswell & Berry, 1993; Smircich & Morgan, 1982). As a cultural practice, leadership as enacted in American organizations, political systems, and community institutions is constituted by the world view and belief system of Western culture and is reflected in the social arrangement of this country. The nature and function of leadership are revealed in and maintained by leadership discourse, that is, "the texts, conversations, writings, rituals, and ceremonies that socially construct our knowing and understanding of leadership" (Rusch, Gosetti, & Mohoric, 1991; p. 3). This discourse primarily has been shaped by white male ideals to the exclusion of the experiences of women, particularly Black women.

Kalwies (1988) traced the ideal of leadership in American culture to the ancient Greeks who often illustrated the concept through the stories about its heroes. Greek heroes were usually male, often of divine descent, and always endowed with great strength, ability, and courage. The notions of leadership that are deeply ingrained within Western culture include ideals of independence, physical or intellectual acumen, and suasive control. Indeed leaders, according to this view, are individuals who induce other people to act through physical or persuasive force.

As a cultural phenomena, leadership is evidenced in and reinforced by the language, images, metaphors, and assumptions of our society. Stivers (1993) traced four key images of leadership pervasive in Western organizational thought. She found the following four images of leaders in her review of the literature: (a) leader as visionary, (b) leader as decision maker, leader as symbol, and (d) leader as definer of reality (Stivers, 1993). Stivers proceeded to explore each of these images and showed how they work together to create a general image of leadership that reinforces the men who have traditionally occupied public leadership roles, and works against women, especially women of color and working class women, who traditionally have not held public leadership roles. The purpose of this article is to bring to light the tensions between the traditional conceptions and Black female conceptions of leadership, and to offer an alternative model of leadership grounded in the experience and expression of Black womanhood.

Leadership Ideology

As previously intimated, leadership functions ideologically, and is an "important cultural myth by which we make sense of and impart significance to organizational and community life" (Stivers, 1993; p. 59). The ideological functions of leadership allow a subtle perpetuation of the so-called dominant culture and may silence or treat as invisible people who don't fit the heroic image of leader. At the same time, traditional images of Black women ensure that she not fit the images of leader embossed into the cultural fabric of our society.

For instance, cultural and historical studies have identified recurrent images of black women in American society as "mammies," sexually loose "jezebels," and emasculating "matriarchs" (Collins, 1990; Weitz and Gordon, 1993). More recently, the "sapphire" (Jewell, 1993) and the "welfare queen" (Collins, 1990; Nahata, 1992) have been added to the litany of images of African-American women. Together the perpetuation of the traditional controlling stereotypes of Black women, coupled with the perpetuation of the mythical but accepted heroic image of leaders, position Black women as anti-heroines and therefore incongruent with accepted notions of leadership.

Furthermore, leadership ideology reinforces accepted organizational, communal, and societal arrangements, and tends to exclude women from the very definition of leader (Stivers, 1993; Scott, 1982). For instance, Stivers noted that research indicated that both men and women overwhelmingly expected leaders to be male, and even when women held positions of leadership, they were either not recognized as such or they were hesitant to accept the title "leader" (Andrews, 1992; Owen, 1986). Furthermore, even women who have written about influential women tended not to attribute the label leader to these women. For instance, Gilkes (1980) attributed the title "community workers" to those women "who have worked for a long time for change in the Black community," many of whom were professionals with formal executive and administrative positions in community agencies (p. 217; see also Gilkes, 1983).

Even in her classic primer on the impact of Black women in America, *When and where I enter*, Paula Giddings (1984) tended to refer to historic African-American female leaders such as Sojourner Truth, Ida B. Wells, and Mary McLeod Bethune as abolitionists, activists, and educators. These women were noted for their work in and support to the community and their actions toward race uplift, and perhaps the word leader(ship) was so embedded with masculine cultural assumptions that it did not adequately describe the collectivist orientation that these women took in their community work.

Those who have studied leadership have concentrated on the traits, behaviors, characteristics and accomplishments of great public figures to the exclusion of leadership and influence that occur in private or informal institutions such as families and community networks (Scott, 1982). Even when leadership in communities and informal networks was considered, the images of leadership from the public domain, especially business and industry, prevailed. Pettegrew (1982) argued that business models and frameworks are not appropriate for community, nonprofit or informal enterprises.

Furthermore, Collins (1991) accused the predominately social scientific approach to leadership of focusing on "public, official, visible political activity even though unofficial, private, and seemingly invisible spheres of social life and organization may be equally important" (p. 141). Her remarks give insights into the inadequacies of the social science approach in explicating the phenomenon of leadership. Consequently, what is needed is another approach to explicate the experience of leadership that more closely speaks to Black women. Gloria Naylor's *Mama Day* presents us with one source in which to explore leadership as experienced and expressed by Black women.

A Phenomenology of Leadership

According to van Manen (1990), the emphasis of phenomenological research is "always on the meaning of lived experience" (p. 62). The point of phenomenological research is to better understand the "deeper meaning or significance of an aspect of human experience" by borrowing other people's experiences and their reflections on these experience. Van Manen (1990) notes that "literature, poetry, or other story forms serve as a fountain of experiences to which the phenomenologist may turn to increase practical insights" (p. 70). According to van Manen (1990), story provides us with what is possible in human experiences, enables us to experience life situations that we would not normally experience, and allows us to broaden our horizon. Through a good novel, he argues, "we are given the chance of living through an experience that provides us with opportunity of gaining insight into certain aspects of the human condition" (p. 70). Likewise, Peterson (1992) in her phenomenology of the human will appealed to the literature of Black women as sources for themes. She used the fictional writings of Zora Neal Hurston, Toni Morrison, and Alice Walker, as well as the biographical writings of Hurston and Maya Angelou to uncover the essential themes of romantic love, motherhood, practical wisdom, friendship, faith, dreams, patience, and vision, and to provide "a clear picture of the kind of strength and courage for which Black women are known" (p. 63).

Furthermore, Bremer (1986) used literature as a basis for analyzing ethnic-minority women's leadership style. She argued, "literature is an experiential and synthesizing language act, rather than conceptual and analytic, it can give us access to knowledge that our conventional concepts cannot comprehend and our analyses often misconstrue"(p. 26). She offered leadership images as metaphors for leadership styles rooted deep within the cultures of the ethnic-minority women writers.

To that end, with *Mama Day*, Gloria Naylor presents us with an appropriate source from which to draw out understanding about leadership from the perspective of an African-American woman.

Naylor situates the story of the Black matriarch in the private domain of the home and community in a mystical island off the coasts of South Carolina and Georgia. Mama Day's leadership is situated within a network of family members and friends, is "woman-centered" (Perry, 1993, p. 226), multiperspectual (Perry, 1993, p. 232), invokes physical and metaphysical principles, and is transformative.

Mama Day

Miranda Day is one of the descendants of Sapphira Wade, an African-born "slave woman who brought a whole new meaning to both them words" (Naylor, 1989; p. 3). Sapphira was a conjure woman whose Norwegian slave master, Bascombe Wade, married her. In 1823, legend had it, Sapphira smothered Bascombe Wade and lived to tell the story a thousand days. She had married Bascombe Wade and bore him seven sons in just a thousand days and had persuaded Bascombe Wade to deed all his slaves "every inch of land in Willow Springs" (p. 3). It is through a series of dialectics that Naylor presents this community leader to us.

Mama Day—The Woman

Mama Day, whose given name is Miranda, is the "legendary" matriarch of Willow Springs (p.46). Although she owns five thousand acres of waterfront and timber land, she lives in a silver trailer across the road from her younger sister Abigail. Mama Day is a midwife, a traditional leadership role for women in the Sea Islands, yet her gift as a natural healer places her in competition with the male doctors of the region. The doctors, however, learn very quickly to work with Mama Day and not against her because her so-called folk medicine and advice is much heeded by the islanders. Her acumen in the healing arts, and not a formal title brings her respect. Mama Day is small in stature but large in strength. Barely 5 ft tall, she "could have been snapped in half with one good sized hand" (p. 176). She is "powerful" (p. 112) and as one character noted, her strength showed not in her stature but in the "set of her shoulders. . . . the dark brown skin stretched tight over those high cheekbones and fine frame glinted like it was covering steel" (p. 176). Inner strength centered this leader.

Ironically, Mama Day is birth mother to nobody. Yet, Mama Day has gifted hands that "gave to everybody but herself" (p. 280). As she explains it, she "caught babies until it was too late to have my own" (p. 89). This single, childless woman is revered mother to the entire Island. In this way, Mama Day leads the islanders in giving and nurturing.

Mama Day is sensual, yet spiritual. She has the acuteness of sight to distinguish the medicinal roots and herbs of the field. In massages, she has a touch that brings comfort and peace. Mama Day "had ancient eyes" (p. 152) and "a face broken down with the weight of knowing what is coming" (p. 258). Mama Day listens for the rustling of the trees (p. 312); she tries to listen under the wind" (p. 118) for voices from the past to protect her immediate family, the Day legend and the island family. And most of all she listens to the messages from within her soul. This leader is vigilant, tactile, aural, discerning. In other words, she is sensitive to the people and forces around her.

Through these series of dialectics we get a glimpse of Mama Day. Naylor presents us with a picture of a strong black woman rooted in her community and family. Out of her springs an essence of leadership captured by four themes. These leadership themes that coalesce in Mama Day include the preserver of the land, the sustainer of culture, community builder, and sustainer of hope.

Mama Day—Preserver of the Land

Willow Springs is a mythical Sea Island on the border of Georgia and South Carolina; it is "49 square miles, curves like a bow, stretching toward Georgia on the South End and South Carolina on the north" and "right smack in the middle where each foot of [the] bridge sits is the dividing line between them two states" (p. 5). Willow Springs is a developer's paradise and businessmen from "beyond the bridge" flood into Willow Springs to purchase the land from the islanders.

The islanders send the developers to Mama Day to handle their inquiries. She reasons with them that "there was a enough land—enough shoreline, that is—to make us all pretty comfortable. And calculating on the basis of all them fancy plans they had in mind, a million an acre wasn't asking too much" (p. 6). "The land wouldn't be worth that", the developers counter, "if they couldn't *build* on it"

(p. 6). Mama Day's frank reply is, "And they couldn't build on it unless we sell it." (p. 6).

Mama Day's concern is for the protection of the islands and what rightfully belong to the islanders. Her rationale is "we get ours now and they get theirs later" (p. 6). Recalling the plight of St. Helena Island, Dafauskie, and St. John's, Mama Day reasoned, if left to their own devices, those developers would "get theirs now and us never" (p. 6). If Mama Day could help it, Willow Springs will never be turned into a "vacation paradise" (p. 6), even if she has to come back from her grave to see to it. Consequently, the Islanders will not sell their property. They proclaim, "if Mama Day say no, everybody say no" (p. 6).

Mama Day — The Sustainer of Culture

Willow Springs is full of ritual and tradition. One particular community ritual must be noted. Every December 22, community members "take to the roads—strolling, laughing, and talking—holding some kind of light in their hands" (p. 110). This ritual has come to be known as Candle Walk night, the day in which all members of the community parade down the roads of Willow Springs.

There are various stories that have been passed down about Candle Walk. One legend has it that

> God spit the island out from his mouth, and when it fell to the ground it brought along an army of stars. He tried to reach down and scoop them back up, and found himself shaking hands with the greatest conjure woman on earth. "Leave 'em here, Lord," she said. "I ain't got nothing but these poor black hands to guide my people but I can lead on with light" (p. 110).

Mama Day, however recalls what her Daddy had told her about Candle Walk night.

> Used to be when Willow Springs was mostly cotton and farming, by the end of the year it was common knowledge who done turned a profit and who didn't. And with a whole heap of children to feed and clothe, winter could be mighty tight for some. And them being short on cash and long on pride, Candle Walk was a way of getting help without feeling obliged. Since everybody said, "come my way, Candle Walk," sort of as a season's

> greeting and expected a little something. Them that needed a little more got it quiet-like from their neighbors. And it weren't no hardship giving something back—only had to be any bit of something as long as it came from the earth and the work of your own hands. A bushel of potatoes and a cured side of meat could be exchanged for a plate of ginger cookies, or even a cup of ginger toddy. It all got accepted with the same grace, a lift of the candle and a parting whisper, "Lead on with light" (p. 110).

Mama Day sustains the cultural ritual through the oral tradition, recounting the stories passed on to her from her father and father's father. Woven deep within this tapestry of tradition is the thread that ties this time period in Willow Springs with the past and that is the tradition of coming together, with lights in hand. This tradition also signifies the importance the culture puts on leading their lives with the brightest integrity.

Mama Day—The Community Builder

While sustaining cultural tradition, Mama Day also is building community. Candle Walk is not only a cultural tradition, it serves a community building function. Candle Walk brings the community together, young and old, female and male; sanctimonious and still keeper; children and parents. What is significant is that most people on the island use Candle Walk as a time to thank Mama Day for her help throughout the year—for healing patients, delivering babies, and giving advice. They bring bushels of food, and sundry gifts to show their great appreciation to her. By doing what she does on a daily basis, helping, healing, nurturing, giving advice, cleaning house, Mama Day is building community one by one. Mama Day connects members of the community to her and then to each other. The Candle Walk night becomes a material witness of these bonds within the community.

Mama Day—The Provider of Hope

Mama Day can feel change coming and consequently helps others to prepare for change and thus provides hope to them that they can withstand changes about to face their island. Mama Day "prepares" Bernice for the difficult birth of her first and only child. Mama Day feels the incoming hurricane, drawing on her memories of the hurricane of 1920, and prepares herself for the coming storm.

When members of the community complain that the younger generation is ruining tradition, hinting that in so doing they will also destroy the community, Mama Day assures them that change is not necessarily destructive. For instance, some of the islanders express that the younger people are changing the Candle Walk ritual. When many of the young people start working "beyond the bridge" on the mainland and bringing in more money, they start buying "gadgets for candle walk and expecting gadgets in return" (p. 110). Mama Day assures these naysayers, however, that change is nothing new, that Candle walk in her young days was even different than today. She recounted:

> After going around and leaving what was needed, folks met in the main road and linked arms. They'd hum some lost and ancient song, and then there'd be a string of lights moving through the east woods out to the bluff over the ocean. They'd all raise them candles, facing east, and say "Lead on with light, Great Mother, Lead on with light." Say you'd hear talk then of a slave woman who came to Willow Springs, and when she left, she left in a ball of fire to journey back east over the ocean.

Mama Day continues,

> [My Daddy] said in his time, Candle Walk was different still. Said people kinda worshiped his grandmother, a slave woman who took her freedom in 1823. Left behind seven sons and a dead master as she walked down the main road, candle held high to light her way to the east bluff over the ocean. Folks in John-Paul's time would line the main road with candles, food, and slivers of ginger to help her spirit along (p. 111).

And Mama Day continues, asserting that her Daddy said his daddy said Candle Walk in his time was different still.

> His daddy said it wasn't about candles at all—was about a light that burned in a man's heart. And folks would go out and look up at the stars—they figured his spirit had to be there, it was the highest place they knew. And what took him that high was his belief in right, while what buried him in the ground was the lingering taste of ginger from the lips of a woman. He had freed them all but her, cause she had never been a slave.

Mama Day provides hope that the spirit of Candle Walk will prevail though the specific rite might be modified down through the years. The real light of candle walk, indeed is in the hope of freedom that had been granted or taken and must never be lost or given away. The hope that Mama Day brings is the continuity and strength of community.

Summary

Mama Day presents us with a redefined image of Black womanhood and a vibrant expression of leadership. Mama Day, the leader, is multi-faceted: sensual, spiritual, respected, and feared. She is rooted in the community yet, grounds the community. She is the heroine that makes heroes out of everyday people. Mama Day presents us with a deeper understanding and appreciation for the leadership experience of African-American women who operate in a realm ignored by dominant forms of inquiry, and who operate in a manner silenced by traditional leadership discourse.

Black women's leadership entails preserving place and space. It entails providing resistance to threats to our homelands and providing meaning around the importance of home. Black women's leadership encompasses the sustaining of cultural traditions, not as museum artifacts but in the rituals, stories and everyday practices passed on from generation to generation. Leading is indigenous to this cultural tradition: leading in character, in helping, and leading with light.

Black women's leadership is centered on building community. Through interaction and dialogue, individuals are built up and connected. Individuals are healed, nurtured, humbled and protected in the community. African-American women have lead the way in building up and edifying the community.

Black women's leadership focuses on providing hope for individuals and for the community. This hope is rooted in the past, spread in the present and points to the future. It is a hope of continuity in the midst of change. It is a hope that the community can and will withstand natural threats because of the perseverance of its members. Furthermore, it is hope that is reminiscent of the hard earned freedom of our foremothers.

This brief picture of Gloria Naylor's *Mama Day* provides us with an alternative view of African-American woman as leader. In resisting prevailing, controlling stereotypes that serve to keep African-American women invisible in the traditional leadership discourse, this brief portrait redefines leadership and presents an identity that honor an indigenous leadership tradition that is constituted by Black womanhood.

References

Apps, J.W. (1993, Summer). Leadership for the next age. *Journal of Extension*. pp. 3–5.

Bremer, S.H. (1986). Literary perspectives on ethnic-minority women's leadership styles. In W.A. Van Horne (Ed.), *Ethnicity and women*.

Christian, B. (1985). *Black feminist criticism: Perspectives on Black women writers*. New York: Pergamon Press.

Collins, P.H. (1991). *Black feminist thought: Knowledge, consciousness, and the politics of empowerment*. New York: Routledge.

Crosby, B.C., & Bryson, J.M. (1993, Spring). Leadership and the design and use of forums, arenas and courts. *National Civic Review*, pp. 108–115.

Drath, W.H., & Palus, C.J. (1994). *Making common sense: Leadership as meaning-making in a community of practice*. Greensboro, NC: Center for Creative Leadership.

Giddings, P. (1984). *When and where I enter: the impact of Black women on race and sex in America*. New York: Bantam Books.

Henderson, M.G. (1989). Speaking in tongues: Dialogics, dialectics, and the Black womanwriter's literary tradition. In C.A. Walls (Ed.), *Changing our words: Essays on criticism, theory, and writings by Black women*. New Brunswick, NJ: Rutgers University Press.

Gilkes, C.T. (1980). "Holding back the ocean with a broom:" Black women and community work. In L. F. Rodgers-Roe, (Ed.), *The Black woman* (pp. 217–231). Beverly Hills, CA: Sage Publications.

Gilkes, C.T. (1983). Going up for the oppressed: The career mobility of Black women community workers. *Journal of Social Issues, 39(3)*: 115–39.

hooks, b. (1992). *Black looks: Race and representation*. Boston: South End Press.

Jewell, K.S. (1993). *From mammy to Miss America and beyond: Cultural images & the reshaping of U.S. social policy*. New York: Routledge.

Kalwies, H.H. (1988). Ethical leadership: The foundation for organizational growth. *Howard Journal Of Communication, 1*, 113–130.

Nahata, R. (1992). Persistent media myths about welfare. *Extra!, 5*, 18–19.

Naylor, G. (1988). *Mama Day*. New York: Vintage Contemporaries.

Perry, D. (1993). *Backtalk: Women writers speak out*. New Brunswick, NJ: Rutgers University Press.

Peterson, E.A. (1992). *African American Women: A study of will and success.* Jefferson, NC: McFarland & Company.

Pettegrew, L.S. (1987). Organizational communication and the S.O.B. theory of management. *Western Journal of Speech, 46,* 1779–191.

Roswell, K. & Berry, T. (1993). Leadership, vision, values and systemic wisdom. *Leadership & Organizational Development Journal, 14,* 18–22.

Rusch, E.A., Gosetti, P.P., & Mohoric, M. (1991). *The social construction of leadership: Theory to praxis.* Paper presented at the 17th Annual Conference on Research on Women and Education, San Jose, CA.

Scott, P.B. (1982). *Some thoughts on Black women's leadership training.* Wellesley, MA: Wellesley College Center for Research on Women. (ERIC Document Reproduction Service No. ED 254–597).

Smircich, L. & Morgan, G. (1982). Leadership: The management of meaning. *The Journal of Applied Behavioral Science, 18,* 257–273.

Stivers, C. (1993). *Gender images in public administration: Legitimacy and the administrative state.* Newbury Park, CA: Sage Publications.

Van Manen (1990). *Researching lived experience: Human science for an action sensitive pedagogy.* New York: SUNY Press.

Walker, A. (1967). *In love and trouble: Stories of Black women.* New York: Harvest/HBK Book.

Washington, M.H. (1982). Teaching Black-eyed Susans: An approach to the study of Black women writers. In G.T. Hall, P.B. Scott, & B. Smith (Eds.), *But some of us are brave.* Westbury, NY: The Feminist Press.

Weitz R. and Gordon, L. (1993). Images of Black women among Anglo college students. *Sex Roles, 28,* 19–34.

16

LESSONS IN BLACK FEMINIST PEDAGOGY

ERNEST GAINES" *A LESSON BEFORE DYING* AND THE TRANSFORMATION OF PEDAGOGY

Doris Yaa Dartey

> Pedagogy appropriate for voicing and exploring the hitherto unexpressed perspectives of women must be collaborative, cooperative and interactive. It draws on a rich tradition going back to Paulo Freire, John Dewey, and even Socrates, of involving students in constructing and evaluating their own education. It assumes that each student has legitimate rights and potential contributions to the subject matter. Its goal is to enable students to draw on their personal and intellectual experiences to build a satisfying version of the subject, one that they can use productively in their own lives. Its techniques involve students in the assessment and production, as well as the absorption of the material. The teacher is a major contributor, a creator of structure and a delineator of ideals, but not the sole authority (Maher, 1985, p. 30).

This extract from Maher (1985) conveys the essence of critical pedagogy in relation to black feminism, specifically in terms of the ideology, content, and method underlying this pedagogical perspective. In the above excerpt, Mayer (1985) summarizes the key themes of various types of feminist pedagogies. She identifies the classroom as the potential site for equipping students with the techniques for critical thinking and consciousness raising, skills they will need to lead satisfying lives in later years. In critical pedagogy, the teacher's role is that of an initiator and a facilitator who constantly challenges students to re-define themselves and to re-vision their goals. The method used is a combination of collaborative, cooperative, and interactive techniques to help students empower themselves, and acquire the skills to resist stereotypes and barriers that can hinder their progress. My task in this chapter is to reflect on the significance of critical pedagogy to black feminism as an oppositional approach to teaching a disadvantaged minority group in society. Critical pedagogy is presented here as a useful approach to black feminist scholarship and practice, and for influencing the dynamics of social change and cultural transformation in underprivileged communities. Ernest J. Gaines' (1993) novel, *A Lesson Before Dying* provides a backdrop for the analysis.

The novel's story revolves around a college educated plantation school teacher in Louisiana in the 1940's and Jefferson, an illiterate black young man sentenced to die in the electric chair. He was present at a liquor store shooting where his two companions and one white store owner were murdered. At Jefferson's trial, a public defender, in his enthusiasm to free him, referred to him as a "hog," an unintelligent animal incapable of successfully executing a plan to commit a murder. The public defender also made references to Jefferson's African ancestry as an "inferior" race.

The reference to Jefferson as a hog triggered a resolve in his aunt and other black women in the story. Without denying the important role of a Christian minister to save Jefferson's soul, the women also sought to involve a school teacher in a re-education of Jefferson before his death. They noted the fact that a teacher's role in society is distinctly different from the traditional role of preachers and the church. Jefferson's aunt, an illiterate woman who was his primary care-giver from childhood spearheaded the re-definition of what it means to be a man, and of the importance of formal as well as informal, education in society. By the end of the novel, both Jefferson and his teacher undergo an emotionally draining learning experience that culminates in each helping the other to explore and find answers to the paradox of their existence: living as black males in America.

Jefferson's aunt and the teacher both described the pedagogical method used to "reach" Jefferson as "talk." At the beginning of the novel, the teacher's position on the goals and methods of pedagogy stood in sharp contrast to his position at the end. The change in perspective was a result of his intense involvement with Jefferson. His earlier opinion of the teachers' role in the education of students was simply "to teach reading, writing and arithmetic" (Gaines, 1993, p. 13), or the three R's. He acquired his perspective of a teacher's role from college where he received his training for a career in elementary school education. During his professional life thereafter, he was not inclined to depart from the three R paradigm of teaching. The transformation of his opinions occurred, ironically, only through the urging and encouragement of the black women—individuals who did not have the benefit of formal education.

"Talk," the method they suggested using to "reach" Jefferson the convict, is a discursive practice in which both the teacher and student engage each other in the subject matter under study. Talk is communication. It involves posing questions, probing further, and exploring the underlying issues of a subject matter. When talk is encouraged, inhibitions are reduced to a minimum, and give way to more open and honest inquiry. Teaching the three R's, on the contrary, entails positioning the teacher as the supreme and definitive site of knowledge. The three R's approach is the traditional method of teaching. It entails a great deal of memorization. The processes of asking questions and conducting discussions in the traditional method are pre-determined and controlled by the teacher, the site of knowledge and power in the teacher-student relationship. However, in the novel, the teacher and Jefferson, together, both learned not only the importance of reading, writing and arithmetic, but through discursive practices, extended pedagogy beyond strictly formal academic confines to moral, individual, and community development.

Before Jefferson's death in the electric chair, he satisfied his aunt's main goal: "to walk like a man." Through discourse, the teacher was able to "reach" Jefferson who began communicating with people around him particularly his family, the prison officials, and others with whom he interacted. His bitterness toward society gave way to a calm demeanor and bravery, and a demonstration of respect and love for himself and for others. Jefferson, a semi-literate young black male who before, never wrote anything down began to keep a journal in which he recorded his thoughts, questions, and opinions about issues. He also began to engage the teacher in discussions of the issues that he found both interesting and disturbing.

The intervening process underlying the main outcome of discourse, as suggested in the novel, is the ability to reach the person with whom one communicates. "Reaching" as a pedagogical concept refers to the process of establishing and sustaining connections between teachers and students. "Reaching" entails achieving success at building trust between the interactants, and as a result, opening the lines of communication between a teacher and his/her students. The purpose of ensuring that a teacher "reaches" his/her students is to encourage a free exchange of opinions and concerns in an effort to explore issues and arrive at a deeper understanding. When the goal of "reach" is realized, it becomes possible to establish alternative ways of making sense of experiences. Another implication of the need for teachers to "reach" students in the pedagogical process is to make the classroom a site for making a long-lasting and life-sustaining impact on the individual and on society. It is only when the impact of pedagogy is deep, long-lasting, and far-reaching that the goals of self-development and empowerment can be realized.

One might ask: why use a fictional piece, set in Louisiana in the 1940's to call attention to black feminism and the possibilities of pedagogy for a period in history that is on the threshold of the twenty first century? Ernest Gaines' (1993) *A Lesson Before Dying* is significant for black feminist pedagogy in several ways. The novels' story line is a celebration of the capability and potential of black women to initiate a process of re-definition and re-visioning the goals and possible outcomes of a pedagogy that might be appropriate for empowering various underprivileged groups.

It is worthy to note that the women who initiated a change in the perceptions of their community members and the potential of the classroom to bring about favorable social changes themselves lacked formal education. Their conviction was a result of their experiences and observations of society in general, and the oppression of their people in particular. In challenging the relevance of the epistemological foundations, processes, and outcomes of traditional formal education, the black women recognized that on their own, they were incapable of directly bringing about the changes they desired. Their method was to use persuasive means to challenge a career teacher, a professional with the access, skills and ability to reassess the potential of formal education as an instrument for social change.

Perhaps, what is most striking in the novel is the several pedagogical themes suggested by the black women, as well as those which emerged from the teacher and other men in the story through the urging of the women. A critical reading of the novel also uncovers revolutionary de-constructions and re-constructions of otherwise taken-for-granted phenomena of the effects of pedagogy on culture and politics.

The black women in the novel, led by Jefferson's aunt, a woman who could not read and write, defined what the ultimate outcome of formal education should be, particularly, for underprivileged people in any society. She derived strong support for her convictions from her friend and confidant, the teacher's aunt, who also lacked formal education, but who had sacrificed all she owned to pay for her nephew's college education. The women expressed their frustrations and disappointments with the past suffering of their people. They had a determination to influence the direction of the present and the future. They saw teachers as the torch bearers of this task. The significance of their re-definition of pedagogy for their community to black feminist thought is unique when viewed against the background of their simplicity and determination to influence change. Through the prompting of the women, the teacher, the preacher, Jefferson himself, and even the prison officials began to re-vision and re-define what the goals, processes, and outcomes of education should be for a minority group that is experiencing the difficulties associated with living in a racist society, and to empower them to redirect their destinies toward a positive course. Although the content and intent of the pedagogy espoused by the women may seem idealistic, it is justifiable because it is rooted in their unique lived experiences of the realities of their people.
Admittedly, contemporary theory is not likely to accept the legitimacy of "ordinary," illiterate persons as the black women in the novel as thinkers and sources of a theoretical position. The site of their knowledge, which is solely experiential, is atheoretic from the vantage point of conventional thinking. As Collins (1986) has argued, there is a long tradition of black feminist thought that can be traced to oral traditions. From the time of slavery, through the Civil Rights Movement, to the present day, ordinary black women have played key roles in homes, churches, communities, and in American society as a whole. For instance, Rosa Parks who is recognized and honored as the mother of the Civil Rights Movement was at the time she staged her

quiet defiance of authority, an ordinary black woman. Her contribution to the dynamism of the Civil Rights Movement is traced to the day when she calmly but firmly refused to give up her seat for a white person. Like the women in Gaines' (1993) *A Lesson Before Dying*, a wealth of "everyday" wisdom has been produced by ordinary black women (Collins, 1986). The women in the novel were mothers, aunts, members of the local plantation church, a school teacher, and older girls attending the local plantation public school. These women were all ordinary by conventional theoretical standards. However, it can be argued that the black woman's insider status in black communities, no matter how ordinary, enhances her likelihood of contributing to pedagogy for the upliftment of her people.

Working from within the community does not only ensure one's ability to develop good insights, but it also entails possessing a voice to address the problems of the group. Working from the inside also guarantees the visibility and influence of black women in re-directing the focus of black emancipation. On their own, illiterate black women will be unable to document their experiences and participate in academic discourses that can lead to the development of theories. However, if their lived experiences are documented and brought into academic discourse, they can contribute to the development of theories that are applicable to a vast number of people, both in ordinary and exceptional circumstances.

Any discussions of the role of black women in finding solutions to the problems of black people resonate the stereotypic images of black women as matriarchs who are strong and powerful, with a perpetual and superb ability to take care of everyone (Peterson, 1992). This image of the black woman is often criticized and perceived to be burdensome and demeaning. Consistent with this stereotypic image of black women, the black women in *A Lesson Before Dying* were described as being "like boulders, their bodies, their minds immovable" (p. 14). Although this image of black women as strong has often been perceived as negative (Collins, 1986), it does have some positive implications for black feminism and for solving the problems of black people.

When the image of black women as strong matriarchs is viewed from an externally defined framework, the stereotype becomes easily perceived as negative. Collins (1986) has argued that self-valuation and self-definition give more meaning to who black women actually are. She cautions that stereotypes publicized about black women are a means of exerting control from external sources so that women feel guilty and uncomfortable about those images, and about themselves. The motive behind popularizing stereotypes may be cynical. The stereotypes might not necessarily have any detrimental effects on the targets. Stereotypes could even have beneficial effects on the progress of a group depending on their self-valuation. With an underprivileged minority racial group whose men have been described in different disturbing ways including "endangered species" (Gibbs, 1988), having their women as an embodiment of strength who are capable of moving them on a path of progress should be welcomed. It is therefore argued here that the stereotype of black women as strong contains some hope and possibilities for the emancipation of blacks in American society and underprivileged minority groups in general. The black women in Gaines' (1993) novel demonstrated much assertiveness. Although they were outside the confines of formal education, they challenged those trained and equipped to provide formal education to the youth to re-define and re-vision the essence of pedagogy, and to incorporate this new vision into their work for the emancipation of underprivileged groups. The methods and goals espoused by the women regarding a pedagogy that is liberating are consistent with critical pedagogy and with black feminism. According to Giroux (1995), the fundamental principles that inform critical pedagogy are

> the conviction that schooling for self- and social- empowerment is ethically prior to questions of epistemology or to a mastery of technical or social skills that are primarily tied to the logic of the marketplace (p. 30).

In this passage, Giroux (1995) shifts the locus of education to the development of self and society, a development tied more to moral issues than to the mere acquisition of the skills needed for the marketplace of employment. In explaining the ultimate goals and expected outcome of pedagogy in formal education, Sullivan (1987) also contends that "a fundamental assumption of critical pedagogy is that it is a broad educational venture which self consciously challenges and seeks to transform the dominant values" in society (p. 63).

What is central in the assertions of both Giroux (1995) and Sullivan (1987) is that while not discounting the importance of learning the skills necessary for success in functioning and surviving in present day capitalist societal structures, the acquisition of skills alone during the process of obtaining formal education is inadequate. The assumption behind the contention is that the possession of mere skills reduces a person to a tool in the marketplace of a capitalist economy. Incorporating a critical pedagogic approach into formal education brings an additional ingredient to the development of the whole person. The goals of critical pedagogy are broader and more intense for both the teacher and student. Ultimately, therefore, critical pedagogy is expected to be transformative, hence its relevance for underprivileged groups in society. Critical pedagogy and black feminism are also relevant for self and social empowerment, and for the emancipation of black people and other minority groups.

Thematic Lessons from Gaines

A reading of *A Lesson Before Dying* highlights several themes that are oppositional to dominant pedagogical practices. Giroux (1995) has described the traditional view of instruction in the classroom as a typically "neutral or transparent process antiseptically removed from the concepts of power, politics, history and context" (p. 30). This assertion is in reference to both the process and outcome of formal education. For Giroux and other critical scholars including feminists, it is unethical to reduce the classroom to a mere instructional site. Critical scholars agree that an understanding of the cultural, historical, economical, social and political underpinnings of society is crucial to successful instruction. In the same way, through the eyes of the black women in Gaines' (1993) novel, questions are raised on the fundamental assumptions of dominant pedagogical practices and outcomes. The oppositional themes in the novel hold relevance to a black feminist pedagogical perspective. Some of the themes were suggested directly by the women while others were suggested by other characters in the novel through the prompting and constant prodding of the illiterate black women.

Through the urging and determination of the black women in *A Lesson Before Dying*, some parameters are provided for the content, approach, and goals of pedagogy. These themes center around the issues of strength of character and the need for role modeling by teachers, the depth and far-reaching responsibilities of the teaching profession, the nature of the relationship that should exist between teachers and their students, and the roles of educational institutions in their communities.

Heroism

The ultimate goal of pedagogy as presented in *A Lesson Before Dying* is heroism. A hero is not necessarily a person who in the eyes of the public, is economically and politically successful and who, as a result, has an arrogant image of self-importance. Rather, a hero is someone who unselfishly does things for others. A hero is different from the average person. He/she should be capable of doing things for others on a scale and in a manner that other people are not capable of attaining. Heroism calls for a strength of character, unique in its calm demeanor and its demonstration of dignity in resistance.

From the perception of the women in *A Lesson Before Dying*, this height of heroism can only be attained with a pedagogy that is capable of liberating oppressed, underprivileged people. For them, traditional pedagogy, with its focus on reading, writing, and arithmetic is not enough. A pedagogy that is critical and liberating should also instill in students life-long lessons of dignity, loving, and caring.

With an oppressed minority group in society, the goal of pedagogy should be to question the racial, ethnic and gender inferiority myths and challenge the status quo. Prevailing myths about inferiority inhibit people from taking the kinds of actions that could bring about a transformation of their lives and that of society. However, to successfully chip away at the myth of racial and gender inferiority and gain respect for a minority group, non-traditional pedagogical approaches become the only option available for successful emancipation.

Responsibility, Dignity, Pride and Liberation

Through the urging of the women in *A Lesson Before Dying*, pedagogy was redefined as a means to inculcate pride and dignity in students. Through discursive practices, teachers can challenge students to analyze and understand their history, the unique circumstances of their existence, and to explore the possibilities available to them concerning how to attain higher goals. Pedagogy is also presented as being able to impart a sense of responsibility to students. Responsibility refers to good behavior, responsibility toward one's self, others, and in all aspects of one's life. Responsibility has certain benefits. When one behaves responsibly, he/she is able to command respect from others. Responsibility, dignity and pride could culminate in the liberation of oppressed people.

Pedagogy is presented in *A Lesson Before Dying* as a holistic approach to the development of a complete person. A link is established between school and the quality and direction of one's life. Formal education only provides the building blocks for moral development and self-empowerment, key factors for a successful life. From the vantage point of the black women in the novel, formal education must also prepare students to live a full life, and at the time of death, be able to die in dignity. For them, the award of a diploma is not an adequate guarantee that successfully completing one's formal education will lead to the development of a complete person and one who will make constructive contributions to his/her community in particular, and to society in general.

Partnership Between Teacher and Student

Another theme that emerged in the novel was the issue of partnership. Pedagogy is presented as a partnership between the student and the teacher. From the women's standpoint, pedagogy should necessarily entail an involvement and a demonstrated invested interest by both the teacher and student in the process and product of formal education. Formal education is viewed as being more beneficial only when it is moved to the plane of the informal. Partnership is not achieved through the passive transmission of knowledge to students. Rather, pedagogy should be active and be characterized by a lively and dynamic discourse between students and teachers. The arguments suggested by the pedagogical themes in the novel originated from the unique lived experiences of the black women. For them, what it means to be schooled and educated is beyond the confines of conventional pedagogy.

Characteristics of the Teacher

Some themes emerge with regard to the characteristics and roles a teacher must possess in order to become a successful practitioner and an implementor of critical pedagogy. One key theme mandated by the women is the concept of commitment. A key goal of pedagogy espoused by the women is the ultimate moral upliftment of oppressed people. This goal requires a certain kind of teacher. Pedagogy is not a one-time proposition. Rather, it requires a commitment characterized by intensity and passion.

Commitment to pedagogy as presented in the novel implies feeling it, living it, behaving it, and using it to positively influence other people in order to have a far-reaching impact on their lives. To accomplish the ultimate goal of pedagogy, the teacher is untiringly obligated to helping students to realize their own self-identification. Commitment calls for certain qualities in the teacher who uses a critical pedagogical approach to learning. The teacher must be exemplary, and should demonstrate the qualities he/she teaches—responsibility, dignity, pride, heroism, and love of one's self.

A key issue raised concerning commitment is the teacher's attitude in the face of difficulties. Since the charge of the teacher from the perspective of critical pedagogy is to assist a troubled community accomplish the unusual—freedom and the strengthening of the moral fiber—the teacher has a charge to continue to work, even in difficult neighborhoods and in difficult situations in order to make a difference of any significant depth. From the women's standpoint, therefore, teaching is a calling. Teachers do not have the liberty to abandon their responsibilities in the community unless the ultimate goal is accomplished.

The roles of the teacher as espoused by the illiterate women in *A Lesson Before Dying* is to impart knowledge to students, become a community leader, a role model, and a representative of his/her people. Having formal education and being trained and equipped to become a teacher does not excuse one to leave their communities. Whenever there is a leadership vacuum in a community, by the women's definition, the teacher has a responsibility to rise and take on that leadership role. A leadership role is characterized by humility and dignity.

Knowledge is presented in the novel as a burden. The process of learning and imparting knowledge, as well as the process of acquiring knowledge is presented in the novel as challenges. The teacher's role as a reservoir of knowledge is to facilitate the process of gaining freedom for oppressed people. This implies that by virtue of one's profession as a teacher, one is bestowed with a unique responsibility from which one cannot turn away.

Questioning the Myth

Black feminist theory and scholarship is an oppositional ideology that deals with repression along gender, racial, and class lines. As Collins (1986) observed, a key recurring theme in black feminist writings is the interlocking nature of race, gender and class oppression. Explorations of black feminism do not have to be restricted to issues concerning black women. Exploring critical pedagogical approaches in black feminist thought in an effort to contribute to the emancipation of gender, racial, and class hegemony in society will help put black women on the front-line of the emancipatory and transformatory struggles in their communities and in society as a whole.

Joseph (1988) has also described black feminist theory as a "theory of change with Black feminist pedagogy being the change agent in and outside the classroom—wherever education takes place" (p. 180). She explains further that the uniqueness of black feminist pedagogy lies in its ability to

> raise the political consciousness of students by introducing a world view with an Afro-centric orientation to reality, and the inclusion of gender and patriarchy as central to an understanding of all historical phenomenon (p. 177).

Black feminist pedagogy therefore offers political, cultural, historical, and social dimensions to formal education in the classroom and to community development. The unique potential of a black feminist pedagogical perspective is the challenge it offers to examine various facets of education—the formal and informal, the secular and the spiritual, the political and the non-partisan, the classroom and the community, males and females,—in order to unearth the underlying problems and find solutions to societal problems. As Joseph contends, the usefulness of black feminist pedagogy is not restricted to only African-American education and communities, but to other underprivileged minority groups in the US and elsewhere. Black feminist pedagogy calls for the need for a re-awakening, and the development of responsibility for one's self and the community. Political, social, and cultural responsibilities are prerequisites for emancipation. Black feminist pedagogy is therefore an empowering ideological perspective that has the potential to give voice to muted and marginalized groups.

Further Implications and Conclusion

The themes that emerged from Gaines' *A Lesson Before Dying* carry further implications for black feminism and for pedagogy. An obvious call is made to teachers and schools to extend formal education beyond the strict confines of the classroom. After all, teachers and schools reflect the social, political, economic, and cultural milieu of their environments. Providing public service to both the immediate and extended communities of educational institutions helps to establish and maintain a partnership between schools and their communities. For educational institutions to continue to claim to be frontiers of knowledge, they have a responsibility to help in providing solutions to problems that face their communities and society in general. This is a far-reaching responsibility for formal education, for teachers, and for educational institutions. More immediately, the themes suggest that it is important for schools and teachers to provide services to the community if they are to make any substantial and direct impact on that community and in society as a whole. Limiting pedagogy to the classroom is therefore not enough. For a holistic approach to pedagogy, the classroom should not be the only site for education. The suggested connection between the classroom and the community at large also emphasizes the need for teachers to be conscious of the possible long-lasting impact of their teaching on students and on society.

The above suggestions have some limitations. Although they may seem idealistic, the suggestions hold deep implications for not only the curriculum and the methods of classroom teaching, but for the type and life styles of teachers as well. While these suggestions may appear idealistic on a broader level, there is no doubt that when pedagogy is extended beyond the confines of the classroom and school compounds, the usefulness of a black feminist pedagogy in problematizing and investigating the every day informal as well as the historical patterns of power will make it possible to reduce the limiting outcome of traditional pedagogical practices. If these perspectives are applied to the development of specific communities with unique sets of issues, critical black feminist pedagogy holds promise to bring to the fore the political, economic, and social facets of matters of race, gender, and class which are all underlying factors that inhibit social emancipation for certain segments of populations.

Exploring knowledge from the voices of muted groups who are traditionally without voices have its benefits. When voices that are without pens are raised, those voices can contribute toward the setting of agendas that can in turn, lead to changes desired by oppressed groups and even have an impact on the trend and direction of history. Black womanhood has its myths and realities (Mullings, 1997). It is through the exploration of the realities and the immense potential that the constructive role of black women in their communities and in society can be fully realized.

References

Collins, P. H. (1986). Learning from the outsider within: The sociological significance of Black feminist thought. *Social Problems*, *33*, (6), 14–32.

Gaines, E. J. (1993). *A lesson before dying*. New York, NY: Vintage Books.

Gibbs, J. T. (1988). Young black males in America: Endangered, embittered, and embattled. In J. T. Gibbs, A. F. Brunswick, M. E. Connor, R. Dembo, T. E. Larson, R. J. Reed, & B. Solomon (Eds.). *Young, black, and male in America: An endangered species* (pp. 1–36). Dover, MA: Auburn House Publishing Co.

Giroux, H. A. (1995). Radical pedagogy as cultural politics: Beyond the discourse of critique and anti-utopianism. In P. McLaren (Ed.). *Critical pedagogy and predatory culture: Oppositional politics in a postmodern era* (pp. 29–57). New York, NY: Routledge.

Joseph, G. I. (1988). Black feminist pedagogy and schooling in capitalist white America. In M. Cole (Ed.). *Bowles and Gintis revisited: Correspondence and contradiction in educational theory* (pp. 174–186). New York, NY: The Falmer Press.

Maher, F. (1985). Classroom pedagogy and the new scholarship on women. In M. Culley, & C. Portuges (Eds.). *Gendered subjects: The dynamics of feminist teaching* (pp. 29–48). Boston, MA: Routledge and Kegan Paul.

Mullings, L. (1997). *On our own terms: Race, class and gender in the lives of African- American women*. New York, NY: Routledge.

Peterson, E. A. (1992). *African American women: A study of will and success*. Jefferson, NC: McFarland.

17

SELF-DEFINITION AND SILENCE

BLACK FEMINIST THOUGHTS AND AUGUST WILSON

(SCATTERED THOUGHTS FOR A WORK IN PROGRESS)

by R. Goldman Vander

Settling into the final phase of a reading assignment on early black feminist writing, I am attempting to collect my thoughts and commit them to the page. Continuously I remind myself of the importance of being concise. I tell myself: "I will be succinct. Articulate the facts. Apply the theories." Having completed a short reading assignment of black feminist thought and some of the works of August Wilson, I have prepared my notecards and outlined the essay.

It is, admittedly, rather late in the evening to be theorizing about the depiction of black women in Wilson's works. I have had a long day and am, at this point, most interested in quietly settling down to reflect upon my work. The peacefulness offered by twilight calms my senses and delivers a welcomed point of departure for the writing of my essay. I am truly in my space - personally, physically and intellectually. I am alone and appreciating the quiet time I have allowed myself for the completion of this project. My thoughts slowly, teasingly begin taking shape and I am moving towards productivity.

As the opening sentences are unfolding and writing themselves, I am startled and disturbed by the sudden activity coming from upstairs. The young brother above me is having music lessons late in the evening hours. His rhythmic sounds unsettle me momentarily, yet I'm continuing my efforts to write. Two hours pass. His music continues. No longer performed within the context of lessons. Percussion instruments and a piano are played alternately, but with equal ferocity and abandonment. They induce vibrations in both my apartment and my mind.

I am unable to concentrate on my project. The young brother upstairs has stifled me. I tell myself it is an impossible task to proceed with this phase of my work. Working under these conditions is difficult to imagine. Caught up in the frustrating experience of silenced thoughts I am angrily aware of my invisibility to him. Yet even more, I am aware of black women's acknowledging this and similar occurrences. I recall that in 1977, Barbara Smith pondered the starting point for her own discussion of black feminist thought. Aware of the problem of black women's invisibility in black male and white women's writings, Smith initiated her discussion by addressing this situation. At that time she stated, "Black women's existence, experience, and culture and the brutally complex systems of oppression which shape these are in the 'real world' of white and/or male consciousness beneath consideration, invisible, unknown. This invisibility, which goes beyond anything that either Black men or white women experience and tell about in their writing is one reason it is so difficult for me to know where to start" (p. 1).

In his dramatic works, August Wilson has attempted to articulate the experiences of the black community throughout the 20th century. Chronicling these experiences throughout the decades, Wilson's material covers traditional themes of racism, racial exploitation, connection and discontinuity through history and the pursuit of the American dream. With overall strong character development, his plays exist primarily through male-centered subjects. His characters are depicted as ambitious, troubled, and struggling to attain personal dignity throughout their lived experiences. The women in contrast are not. Although the women are not depicted as confronting similar issues, they are often shown as being defined by their relationships to and experiences of others. In general, what is being illustrated is the dual minority status held by black women - that of race and gender and the inability to address specific issues within a defined community. In her article, "A Response to Inequality: Black Women, Racism, and Sexism," Diane K. Lewis asserts, "Black women, due to their membership in two subordinate groups that lack access to authority and resources in society, are in structural opposition with a dominant racial and a dominant sexual group...Historically, their interests as blacks have taken precedence over their interests as women" (p. 45). In stating this, Lewis suggests Black women's issues have been placed in subordinate position to those of race. More over, in the articulation of racial issues, these have most often been conveyed through the lens of patriarchy.

In the 1987 Pulitzer Prize drama *Fences*, Wilson tells the story of Troy Maxson and his on-going efforts to deal with black life in America. We are informed that Troy is a former Negro League baseball player who was too old for the sport when the game was integrated. He now earns his living as a sanitation worker. Dealing with lost dreams Troy has sought to make the best of his life with steady employment, a wife and family. In the introduction to the printed text, Lloyd Richards wrote, "...Troy learns that in the land of equal opportunity, chances for a black man are not always equal...He learns that he must fight and win the little victories that - given his life - must assume the proportion of major triumphs...He learns that to take a chance and grab a moment of beauty can crumble the delicate fabric of an intricate value system and leave one desolate and alone" (p. vii).

When Richards speaks of Troy grabbing a "moment of beauty" he is commenting upon Troy's extramarital activities which eventually result in a daughter. With the emphasis on Troy, very little is known of Rose, Troy's wife. The focus rests on Troy's needs for exploring and learning more about himself outside the confines of his everyday existence. According to Troy, the affair was an attempt to achieve more in his life. Feeling he had failed to realize his fullest potential in a "safe" environment, he senses a need to take chances.

Using baseball as a metaphor Troy suggests that life - his life - has been comprised of missed hits. Instead of attempting a home-run he has played it safe, bunted, and ended up on first base afraid to attempt stealing second. Attempting to explain his feeling to Rose he states, "...I done tried all my life to live decent...to live a clean... hard...useful life. I tried to be a good husband to you...When I found you and Cory and a halfway decent job...I was safe...Then when I saw that gal...she firmed up my backbone. And I got to thinking that if I tried...I just might be able to steal second. Do you understand after eighteen years I wanted to steal second" (p. 70).

The affair in Troy's thinking, was an opportunity to explore the unknown dimensions of life. It was never meant as a negative commentary on Rose or family life. It was an attempt for Troy Maxson to gain some sense of self within a different context. In *Fences*, Wilson seeks to illustrate the continuous struggle of minority life in America. And again, although the emphasis is placed on Troy's perspective, it is Rose who unknowingly bares the burden of minority status as both black and female. Troy, attentive to his plight as a black male fails to recognize the toll this life has exacted on Rose. Yet, during this same scene the exchange between Troy and Rose continues. And it is now Rose who must articulate her presence, for the first time, in terms of how life has evolved for her. She states, "You not the only one who's got wants and needs. But I held onto you, Troy. I took all my feelings, my wants and needs, my dreams... and I buried them inside you. I planted a seed and watched and prayed over it. I planted myself inside you and waited to bloom. And it didn't take me no eighteen years to find out the soil was hard and rocky and it wasn't never gonna bloom" (p. 71).

Rose's comments convey those experiences of many women sacrificing personal development and individual ambitions for the sake of maintaining family oriented agendas. Rather than pursue the possibilities of her own potential, she places her development in the hands of another and silently witnesses the collapse of her own individuality and lack of empowerment. In her collection of essays and speeches titled *Sister Outsider*, Audre Lorde addresses this issue. She suggests, "Black women who define ourselves and our goals beyond the sphere of a sexual relationship can bring to any endeavor the realized focus of completed and therefore empowered individuals. Black women and Black men who recognize that the development of particular strengths and interests does not diminish the other do not need to diffuse their energies fighting for control over each other" (p. 46).

The fight for control of black women's activities and productivity has traditionally been a project in American society. Historically, women daring to speak up and out about their plight and conditions were aggressively silenced and denied full participation in determining their own life's direction. Those who continued to pursue autonomy and independence were labeled and categorized by demeaning terms.

In Wilson's first Broadway production, *Ma Rainey's Black Bottom*, the problem of patriarchal control over black women is conveyed throughout the ongoing dialogues between various male characters. Set in a Chicago recording studio in the late 1920s, Ma Rainey illustrates the manner in which large numbers of independent black women are viewed in society. Ma Rainey is depicted as opinionated, unyielding, and at times temperamental. Ma Rainey is, in fact, simply attempting to define her presence. As they organize the studio for the upcoming recording session, the two white males executives discuss Ma Rainey in anticipation for her arrival. They exchange the following:

> Sturdyvant: Listen, Irv... you keep her in line, okay? I'm holding your responsible for her... I'm not putting up with any shenanigans... I want you to keep her in line... you're her manager... she's your responsibility.
>
> Irvin: Okay, okay... let me handle it (p. 18).

Through the above dialogue we ascertain that Ma Rainey is perceived as difficult. The exchange between the two men continues as they discuss their efforts to increase profits from Ma Rainey's recordings while simultaneously anticipating a future in a more "respectable business." In discussing Ma Rainey's last recording Sturdyvant asserts that it was garbage and that times in the industry were changing. If Ma Rainey is to continue making a profit for the studio her musical style will have to change. By contrast, Ma Rainey is not limited to viewing the blues as a commodity produced for public consumption but rather as a way of living and understanding lived experiences. To limit the importance of the blues in terms of economics is to diminish and detract from the experiences that have shaped Ma Rainey's self-definition. She expresses this sentiment:

> White folks don't understand about the blues... They don't understand that's life's way of talking. You don't sing to feel better. You sing 'cause that's a way of understanding life',... The blues help you get out of bed in the morning. You get up knowing you ain't alone. Something's been added by that song. This be an empty world without the blues. I take that emptiness and try to fill it up with something (p. 83).

When Ma Rainey discusses the blues, she discusses the continuation of an oral tradition having been reshaped in the Black community by women in the late 1920s. The blues provide an opportunity for individuals to reflect upon their experiences and share these reflections with others in the community. In her book *Black Feminist Thought*, Patricia Hill Collins discusses the significance of the blues. She writes,

> Blues has occupied a special place in Black women's music as a site of expression of Black women's self-definitions. The blues singer strives to create an atmosphere in which analysis can take place...When Black women sing the blues, we sing our own personalized, individualistic blues while simultaneously expressing the collective blues of African-American women (p. 100).

Aware of her exploitation by the industry, Ma Rainey is also aware of her earning potential for the studio. This knowledge, coupled with a refusal to be objectified without contest, is at the core of Ma Rainey's behavior. She acknowledges, "They don't care nothing about me. All they want is my voice. Well, I done learned that, and they gonna treat me like I want to be treated...If you colored and can make them some money, then you all right with them. Otherwise, you just a dog in the alley" (p. 79). Considering the function of black women in the work place Collins writes, "...Black feminist thought consists of analyzing Black women's work, especially Black women's labor market victimization as 'mules.' As dehumanized objects, mules are living machines and can be treated as part of the scenery. Fully human women are less easily exploited" (p. 43).

In considering the construction of female characters in *Fences* and *Ma Rainey's* silence and self-definition have functioned as important aspects to the development and decline of the female identity. In *Fences*, Rose has remained silent for eighteen years choosing to stand by Troy despite the demise of her promise and possibilities. She has remained beside him, silent and has chosen to define herself within the context of Troy's growth. When this fails and Troy engages in an extra-marital affair, she is forced to speak up and to articulate her failure at self-definition. As the alternative Ma Rainey has actively sought to speak up and uses her music to achieve self-definition and articulate her experiences. Aware of how others perceive her, she confronts these views by continuously challenging the recording executives and validating her right to speak. In her essay, "Talking Back" bell hooks suggests,

> For us, true speaking is not solely an expression of creative power; it is an act of resistance, a political gesture that challenges politics

> of domination that would render us nameless and voiceless. As such, it is a courageous act - as such, it represents a threat. To those who wield oppressive power, that which is threatening must necessarily be wiped out, annihilated, silenced (p. 8).

Reflecting upon black feminist thought it becomes apparent the activities of black women will focus on the continued pursuit of full participation in society by means of self-definition and the eradication of silence. Building upon legacies, black women must utilize and enhance community traditions for self-analysis and the sharing of experiences. As black women continue to address their conditions in society, their articulations will in turn contribute to the on-going discussion and promotion of black feminist thoughts.

References

Collins, P. H. (1991). *Black Feminist Thought: Knowledge, consciousness, and the politics of empowerment.* New York: Routledge.

hooks, b. (1989). *Talking Back: Thinking feminist, thinking black.* Boston: South End Press.

Lewis, D. K. (1990). A response to inequality: Black women, racism, and sexism. In M. Malson, E. Mudimbe-Boyi, J. F. O'Barr and M. Wyer (Eds.), *Black women in America: Social science perspectives* (pp. 41–64). Chicago: University of Chicago Press.

Lorde, A. (1994). *Sister outsider: Essays and speeches.* Trumansburg, NY: Crossing Press.

Smith, B. (1977). *Toward a Black feminist criticism.* Brooklyn, NY: Out and Out Books.

Wilson, A. (1986). *Fences: a play.* New York: New American Library.

Wilson, A. (1985). *Ma Rainey's black bottom: A play in two acts.* New York: New American Library.

CONTRIBUTORS

Deborah A. Austin is an adjunct instructor in the Africana Studies program at the University of South Florida where she recently received her Ph.D. in Communication. She received her B.A. and M.A. in Speech Communication from the University of North Carolina, Chapel Hill. She has served as administrator of testamentary trust funds for the City of Boston and has worked in several administrative capacities at Fayetteville (NC) State University. She was awarded a McKnight Doctoral Fellowship to pursue the Ph.D. degree in Communication at the University of South Florida (USF). While at USF, Deborah authored publications in *Studies in Symbolic Interaction*, *Women and Language*, *The Journal of the Interdenominational Theological Center*, *Perspectives on Womanist Theology*, *Text and Performance Quarterly*, *Communication Theory*, and *Composing Ethnography: Alternative Forms of Qualitative Writing*.

Katrina E. Bell is an Assistant Professor in the Department of Speech and Performing Arts at Northeastern Illinois University in Chicago, Illinois, where she teaches speech communication and media studies. She received her Ph.D. and M.A. from the School of Interpersonal Communication at Ohio University and her B.S.J. from Ohio University's E.W. Scripps School of Journalism. Her research interests fall in the areas of media studies, cultural studies, women's studies, and rhetorical studies.

Doris Yaa Dartey is an Assistant Professor and chair of the Public Relations department at Mount Mercy College in Cedar Rapids, Iowa. She obtained her doctorate from Ohio University in 1996. She is a citizen of Ghana in West Africa where she worked as a public relations consultant for the country's privatization and restructuring programs of state-owned enterprises. Her research interests are in gender and development, and issues in intercultural organizational communication.

Pamela Y. Dykes received her B.A., M.A. and Ph.D. from Ohio University. She is a Communication Consultant with Andersen Consulting. Her research interests include corporate issues in organizational communication and spirituality and word based communication.

T. Ford-Ahmed is the Director of International Studies and an Associate Professor of Communication at West Virginia State College where she teaches courses in Public Relations and Mass Communication. Additionally, she has produced numerous video documentaries under grants from the Department of Humanities, the Department of Education and the Xerox Corporation. She earned a Ph.D. from The Ohio University School of Telecommunications and an M.A. in Speech Communication from New York University. She uses phenomenology and semiotics as modes of inquiry into a variety of publics and public issues.

Janice D. Hamlet is the Founding Director of the Ethnic Studies Program at Shippensburg University. She is also an Assistant Professor in the Department of Speech and Theater Arts where she teaches courses and conduct research in African American Studies, Multiculturalism, gender and communication, public speaking and rhetorical criticism. Her research has been published in *The Journal of Black Studies, The Western Journal of Black Studies* and *The Speech Communication Teacher.* She is the author of *Afrocentric Visions: Studies in Culture and Communication.* Dr. Hamlet received her Ph.D. in Communication from Ohio State University.

Audrey Curtis Hane is a member of the Communication Department at Kansas Newman College in Wichita, KS. She received her B.A. in English and history and her M.A. and Ph.D. in organizational communication from the University of Kansas. Before joining the faculty at Newman, Dr. Hane taught at the University of Kansas and Wichita State University. Additionally, she served as a research associate for the University of Kansas Medical Center. Her areas of interest as a consultant, trainer and academician include gender and diversity issues in the workplace, leadership and communication skills for women, rhetorical studies of first ladies, new communication technology, and group/team dynamics.

Priya Kapoor is an Assistant Professor in the Department of Communication Studies at Portland State University where she teaches courses in intercultural and international communication, women's studies, media criticism, and cultural studies. She received her Ph.D. from the College of Communication at Ohio University. Her dissertation "Wisdom of Interplay: Dialogues on development and fertility among women in India," won the Distinguished Scholarship Award from the International and Intercultural Division of the National Communication Association in San Diego, 1996. Additionally, she has worked as a broadcast journalist in New Delhi, India, and as Communication Consultant with the United Nation's Children's Fund (UNICEF) in New York.

Trevy A. McDonald is an Assistant Professor of Speech and Media Studies in the Department of English at North Carolina Central University. She received her Ph.D. in Mass Communication Research from the University of North Carolina at Chapel Hill where she also obtained her M.A. in Radio, Television and Motion Pictures. Her research interests include media ethnography, audience studies, mass media socialization, and issues of race and gender. Dr. McDonald recently completed writing her first novel, *Time Will Tell.*

Adwoa X Muwzea is a writer, editor and artist who specializes in media for and about children. She has taught screenwriting, film and video production at Temple University in Philadelphia, and film animation techniques at Wayne State University in Detroit. Muwzea has produced more than 12 of her own short videos in the last ten years, including documentaries and animation. Muwzea publishes articles about art and film in local Michigan newspapers and in professional journals, nationally. She is a member of various film and animation societies and serves as Secretary for the National Council of Artists—Michigan Chapter. Muwzea is Arts and Entertainment editor for the *Michigan Citizen* newspaper in Highland Park, MI and teaches writing, animation and video production workshops through her company, **THE MUWZEA EXPERIENCE.**

Jeanne L. Porter received her Ph.D. in Organizational Communication from Ohio University in Athens, Ohio. She teaches courses in multicultural communication and leadership development. Her research focuses on leadership as communicative praxis and she uses interpretive and critical methods to explore the phenomena of leadership in a variety of contexts. Her most recent publications focus on the politics of diversity in a community leadership development process; and a case study exploring leadership development as a community building strategy. Dr. Porter works with corporate and community organizations to develop transformative leaders. She is affiliated with the African American Leadership Partnership (AALP) in Chicago, a program that develops religious and community leaders; she is an Associate Professor at North Park University in the Communication Arts Department; and she is the founder of Trans-Porter Communications, an organizational and communication consulting company.

Vanessa Wynder Quainoo is an Assistant Profesor in the Department of Communication Studies at the University of Rhode Island. She received her Ph.D. in rhetoric and African American Communication from the University of Massachusetts, Amherst and her M.A. in Communication Studies from Western Illinois University. She teaches in the areas of African American communication and oral performance. Her research is in the area of African American rhetorical theory with special emphasis on the aesthetics of Maya Angelou.

Sonya Ramsey is a Ph.D. candidate in United States History at the University of North Carolina at Chapel Hill. She specializes in the study of African-American Women's and Educational History. Under the direction of Dr. Jacquelyn Hall, Ms. Ramsey is writing her dissertation entitled *More Than the Three R's: African-American Women School Teachers and Desegregation in Nashville, Tennessee, 1942–1983*. A 1996 recipient of a Spencer Foundation Dissertation Fellowship, she is currently a lecturer in the Department of General Studies at the University of Texas at Dallas.

Brigette Rouson holds a Master of Arts from the Annenberg School for Communication, where she is engaged in Ph.D. studies. She began focusing on studies of traditional African spirituality while studying at Temple University in African-American studies and communication. Previously, she worked professionally in communications and law as a graduate of Howard University and Georgetown University. She dedicates her chapter, *Journeys in African American Womanhood:...* to her mother, Vivian Reissland Rouson.

Karen Strother-Jordan is an Assistant Professor of Public Discourse at Santa Clara University in California. Born and raised in the San Francisco Bay Area has been the most influential factor which has led to her interests in issues of "difference" and "otherness" in the area of bi-ethnicity. The diverse ethnic, racial and cultural differences of California creates an environment that seeks not only understanding about those who come from diverse experiences, but an interest in how people through their diversity can communicate, interact, and live amongst each other. Strother-Jordan's Ph.D. is in Rhetoric and Public Address with an emphasis in Philosophy from Ohio University.

R. Goldman Vander is a doctoral student in the Curriculum of Comparative Literature at the University of North Carolina at Chapel Hill. She is also an instructor in the Department of African and Afro-American Studies.

INDEX